Vise and Shadow

For Doris

with love

april 2015

Vise and Shadow

Essays on the Lyric Imagination,
Poetry, Art, and Culture

PETER BALAKIAN

The University of Chicago Press
Chicago and London

PETER BALAKIAN is the Donald M. and Constance H. Rebar Professor in Humanities and professor of English at Colgate University. He is the author of seven books of poems, most recently *Ziggurat* and *June-tree: New and Selected Poems, 1974–2000*. He is also the author of *The Burning Tigris: The Armenian Genocide and America's Response*, a *New York Times* best seller, and *Black Dog of Fate*, a memoir. A new collection of poetry, *Ozone Journal*, is also available from the University of Chicago Press.

The University of Chicago Press, Chicago 60637
The University of Chicago Press, Ltd., London
© 2015 by The University of Chicago
All rights reserved. Published 2015.
Printed in the United States of America

Chapter 8 was originally published in *Art in America* (February 1996), 58-67. Courtesy BMP Media Holdings, LLC.

"Sarajevo" by Peter Balakian from *Ziggurat* © 2010 by The University of Chicago. All rights reserved.

24 23 22 21 20 19 18 17 16 15   1 2 3 4 5

ISBN-13: 978-0-226-25416-6 (cloth)
ISBN-13: 978-0-226-25433-3 (paper)
ISBN-13: 978-0-226-25447-0 (e-book)

DOI: 10.7208/chicago/9780226254470.001.0001

Library of Congress Cataloging-in-Publication Data

Balakian, Peter, 1951– author.
     Vise and shadow : essays on the lyric imagination, poetry, art, and culture / Peter Balakian.
         pages cm
     Includes bibliographical references.
     ISBN 978-0-226-25416-6 (cloth : alk. paper) — ISBN 978-0-226-25433-3 (pbk. : alk. paper) — ISBN 978-0-226-25447-0 (e-book)   1. Poetry—History and criticism.
2. Lyric poetry—History and criticism.   I. Title.
PN1136.B25 2015
809.1—dc23

                                        2014038951

for Robert Jay Lifton

Contents

List of Illustrations *ix*

Preface *xi*

1 Poetry as Civilization: Primo Levi and Dante
at Auschwitz *1*

2 The Poem as History *14*

3 Ingesting Violence: The Poetry of Witness Problem *32*

4 Theodore Roethke's Lost Son and the Confessional Era *54*

5 Hart Crane's Broken Tower *74*

6 Poet from Kars: Yeghishe Charents and Armenia's
Modern Age *94*

7 Collage and Its Discontents *120*

8 Arshile Gorky: From the Armenian Genocide to the
Avant-Garde *146*

9 The Anatolian Embrace: Greeks and Armenians in Elia Kazan's
America, America 177

10 Siamanto's Bloody News *202*

11   Bob Dylan in Suburbia *216*

12   Writing Horizontal: Notes Toward the Poem as Space *251*

       Acknowledgments 271

       Notes 273

Illustrations

Plates (following page 100)

1   Robert Rauschenberg, *Monk* (1955)

2   Robert Rauschenberg, *Black Market* (1961)

3   Arshile Gorky, *The Artist and His Mother* (ca. 1926–1936)

4   Arshile Gorky, *The Artist and His Mother* (ca. 1929–1942)

5   Arshile Gorky, *Image in Khorkom* (ca. 1934–1936)

6   Arshile Gorky, *How My Mother's Embroidered Apron Unfolds in My Life* (1944)

Figures

1   Elia Kazan, still from *America, America* (1963) *186*

2   Elia Kazan, still from *America, America* (1963) *187*

Preface

I think of *vise* and *shadow* as two dimensions of the lyric (literary and visual) imagination. *Vise* (noun): as in grabbing and holding with pressure; as in seizing firmly; as in grasping and having a grip on something; as in having a tight grasp on something, to hold the interest and attention of an audience; to have a firm grasp of and on that which is sought to be understood. *Vise* as in something that creates something under pressure, as carbon might be put under pressure to create a diamond. The pressure of the vise-grip of the imagination can yield a unique kind of clarity and knowledge. The vise-grip of lyric language, for example, gives the poem or visual work or song a value and a legacy as a deep mine of knowledge and culture in which human thought and emotion, language, and insight intersect and mingle, and come together as distinctive, memorable aesthetic form.

And *shadow* (noun): the shaded or darker portion of the picture or view or perspective, as partial illumination and partial darkness. *Shadow* as reflected image, but one that is partially opaque. *Shadow* as verb: to trail secretly as an inseparable companion, as secret sharer, to play with Conrad's trope; to shadow as a force that follows something with fidelity; to cast a dark light on something—a person, an event, an object, a form in nature. Poetry as aesthetic imagination shadows history, shadows human experience, casts its own kind of illumination, often un-romantic, sober, and shadow-like in its truths. Imagination as shadow captures the aftermath of history, and when its shadow-light expands as a shadow expands on the ground in late day, the light lessens but the insight deepens. In the shadow-imagination, the poem can embody, among other realities, trauma. Various forms and kinds of aesthetic memory can also witness the event or its aftermath the same way the shadow of the historical event brings to light—among other things—the relationship between language and history, lyric imagination and memory, whether it be personal memory, inherited memory or intellectual memory.

This gathering of essays written between 1988 and 2012 explores, among other things, some of the vise and shadow of poetry, painting, film, collage, memoir, and song lyrics. Some of the essays began as public lectures, talks, or papers, and others were first published in magazines and journals. All the published essays have been slightly revised and expanded, and those that began as lectures or papers also have been revised and expanded. The map of my interests in these essays brings together poets, writers, and artists from disparate cultural zones that move from the Armenian Caucasus to the Ottoman Empire and Anatolia, to Europe, and to the United States. I hope that the reader will find the vise and shadow connections and contiguities between figures as seemingly disparate as W. B. Yeats, Yeghishe Charents, Hart Crane, Adrienne Rich, Primo Levi, Joan Didion, Theodore Roethke, Elia Kazan, Robert Rauschenberg, Arshile Gorky, and Bob Dylan.

Poetry as Civilization: Primo Levi and Dante at Auschwitz

At a certain moment near the end of his time in the Lager in *Survival in Auschwitz*, Primo Levi recovers, in memory, part of Canto 26 of Dante's *Inferno*.[1] It is a moment that first comes as a surprise, as he is talking with the Alsatian student Jean, the Pikolo (messenger-clerk) of their Kommando. The Kommando has just finished cleaning an underground petrol tank, and Levi recalls that "the powder of the rust burnt under our eyelids and coated our throats and mouths with a taste almost like blood." Levi has become friendly with the Pikolo, with whom he shares an interest in books and language. Jean is an "exceptional Pikolo," Levi tells us—shrewd, physically strong, and also humane, never neglecting the less privileged comrades of the Lager.

Jean also has an interest in things Italian and would like to learn the language, and now the two of them find themselves in a rare moment. It is a clear, warm June day, and Jean has helped to arrange for Levi to accompany him, to be the assistant to the "Essenholen," the one who gets and transports the daily ration. Although this means carrying a pot of more than a hundred pounds on two poles, it is nevertheless a bit of a luxury amid the other grueling chores of the Lager, and, most crucially, the two will have time together, and because Jean has found a longish detour for them, they will have a whole hour together. The prospect of this small journey opens up Levi's spirit in what is perhaps his most exuberant moment in his time at Auschwitz: "One could see the Carpathians covered in snow. I breathed the fresh air, I felt unusually light-hearted."

The hour is both a small reprieve and yet a moment under pressure. They begin talking about their homes in Strasbourg and Turin, about books they've read, about the similarities of their mothers. An SS man passes on a bicycle and orders them: "Halt," "Attention," "Take off your beret!" Surely they can't fully escape the reality of the Lager, but as they walk on, aware of how precious their time is, Canto 26 rises up in Levi's mind; it just comes. The ellipses splice us there—where the poetry has risen to the surface of consciousness after how many nights of pain and mind-numbing brutality, after how much saturation in death. There it is. "Who knows how or why," Levi remarks, but there is no time to speculate.

Why *The Comedy*, the *Inferno*? The relationship between one hell and another is an obvious trope, but Levi takes on that challenge. He is also an educated Italian, a scientist by training, and he knows his nation's literature. Like any schoolboy, he knows his Dante the way a British schoolboy would know his Chaucer or Milton or Wordsworth. Levi reminds the reader, inadvertently, that this passage of this poem has been in the basement of his head for a long time, and the meanings of this short moment in the *Inferno* are many. Who can say how carefully planned or manipulated this chapter is, as all memoir must be, but it seems beside the point as the authenticity of this hour in the Lager bears the mark of experience.

Levi notices how attentive Jean is, and so Levi begins, as he puts it, slowly and "accurately." To engage poetry while trying to stay alive at Auschwitz—Primo Levi never puts it that way, and of course he doesn't need to as the moment will speak for itself. But still poetry rises to the surface in this strange and horrible situation, and this young chemist—an Italian Jew deported from

Turin—allows us to see how a man can be helped in his effort to stay alive by immersing himself, for just a short time, in a passage from Dante.

Although Canto 26 also deals with the evil counselors of Florence, who abused their talents for immoral purposes with their glib tongues (hence they are burning on fiery tongues of flame), the part of the canto that comes back to Levi is the story of Ulysses and the Greek hero's last voyage. In a moment, Levi becomes the teacher, explaining the anatomy of the inferno and its punishments and something about the poem's structure—how Virgil is reason, and Beatrice, theology. He is the hopeful teacher on the first day of class—certain that Jean is intelligent and "will understand." And like any good teacher about to convey knowledge of something he or she loves, Levi feels "a curious sensation of novelty." As a force of vitality returns to Levi, who has barely been allowed to be a man, he tells us now that he feels "capable of so much."

After months of deprivation, of near starvation, of living on a crust of bread, lukewarm liquid called soup, of cold, of half-sleep nights, of watching others die of disease or plain murder ("today in our times, hell must be like this," he says in an early chapter), here is Dante's language in his head, coming off his tongue. Not only has it come back, but he is teaching this bit of poetry to his friend Jean. It's the moment in which Virgil speaks to Ulysses (Dante's way of bringing Virgil and Homer together). As Levi recites the words, Jean is focused on him:

> Then of that age-old fire the loftier horn
> Began to mutter and move, as a wavering flame
> Wrestles against the wind and is over-worn;
>
> And like a speaking tongue vibrant to frame
> Language, the tip of it flickering to and fro
> Threw out a voice and answered: "When I came. . . ."

In the syntax and rhythm, in the drama of images, all of a sudden, here at Auschwitz, there is a bit of joy. A tongue coming out of the flame: What could be more resonant? Surely the allegory has many echoes for Levi, a Jew at Auschwitz. But even more, it seems, it's the fondling of the nuances of Dante's language that stops time for him. And it's not only recall and recitation, but translating, which is another challenge; "poor Dante, and poor French," Levi remarks, but Jean is with him fully, and he likes the "bizarre" simile of flame as tongue and even suggests the word for "age-old," as he too becomes a kind of collaborator in the translating process. The moment here reminds us that the act of translating is a deeper kind of reading, for in translating there is a reliving of the poem, a kind of rebirth of the text through the translator that involves a radical identification between translator and poet.

As they continue walking, Levi struggles to come up with the lines, and frustration prods him on. He remembers "When I came" and then is lost: "nothing, a hole in my memory." And then another line comes: "When Aeneas gave it that name." And then another hole, and another line: "nor piety to my old father, not the wedded love that should have comforted Penelope. . . ." A marvelous catch for Levi, this next tercet, but he doubts himself. "Is it correct?" he asks himself, and then slides forward a couple of lines to something he is sure of: "so on the open sea I set forth." It's a line that excites him, he likes his translation of it, and his imagination starts to churn. It's not "je me mis," he tells Jean, it's more dramatic and risky, "more audacious," he says, like "throwing oneself to the other side of a barrier." Levi is teaching and translating at once, as the process begins to rejuvenate his whole being.

The image of the sea now prods him in a Proustian way. The "open sea" is something Jean, too, knows from personal experience—he, too, has been there. Levi luxuriates for a moment in his own sense-memory as he considers how to explain this image to his Alsatian friend. "It is when the horizon closes in on itself, free, straight ahead and simple and there is nothing but the smell of the sea; sweet things, ferociously far away." As powerful as the poetry is, Levi's reverie takes him further. Here at Auschwitz, what freedom to think of the open sea, "nothing but the smell of the sea; sweet things, ferociously far away." Were it said in any other way, it might seem sentimental, but this moment of release for Ulysses in the canto becomes a moment of unexpected revitalization and a momentary emancipation of spirit for the prisoner at Auschwitz.

But then the world of the Lager breaks in, all of a sudden it seems, for they have arrived at Kraftwerk, where a Kommando is laying cable. He recognizes the Kommando engineer, also named Levi, and as he sees the man's head just jutting up above the trench: "he waves to me, he is a brave man, I have never seen his morale low, he never speaks of eating." But Levi pushes away from this jarring image of reality and returns to the poem, to the phrase "open sea." "Open sea, open sea"—it's the rhyme he's looking for—the third line of the tercet. And, as rhyme always performs that dialectical magic—pulling us forward in the poem with a new word while simultaneously throwing us back to the word with which it rhymes—Levi comes up with it: "and that small band of comrades that had never left me."

And then frustration again—as memory fails him, and he is forced to paraphrase as he explains to Jean about Ulysses's "foolhardy journey beyond the Pillars of Hercules." A "sacrilege," he calls it, "to have to tell it in prose," but at least he has rescued two lines from the scene, and "they are worth stopping for." Looking at the cable-laying Kommando, with the stench of death of the Lager in his nose, Levi rescues two more lines:

> that none should prove so hardy
> To venture the uncharted distances.

As some strange feeling of self-affirmation overtakes him, he says to himself, "To venture" is the same as "I set forth," the words he had translated just a moment ago. The nuance of phrase engages him, and he confesses: "I had to come to the Lager to realize that it is the same expression as before: 'I set forth.'" He says nothing to Jean of this small revelation, and then sees the sun and realizes it's almost midday and that his hour is running out.

But his memory darts ahead a few lines, and he continues

being the passionate teacher, teaching his last student at the end of the world. "Open your ears and your mind," he implores Jean, "you have to understand, for my sake."

> Think of your breed: for brutish ignorance
> Your mettle was not made; you were made men,
> To follow after knowledge and excellence.

"For my sake"; the phrase is haunting. At Auschwitz such meaning is almost too much. Behind barbed wire, in a world that undermines the basis of civilization, Levi holds on to lines of poetry, to a sense of "knowledge and excellence." "As if I also was hearing it for the first time," Levi exclaims, "like the blast of a trumpet, like the voice of God. For a moment I forget who I am and where I am." What more might one say about the transforming power of poetry? After six months at Auschwitz, such a moment as this is possible.

There is something singular about this moment, something different, perhaps, from other revelatory moments I can think of in the history of literature. It is a moment of poetic epiphany in which aesthetic and moral insight are fused in an instance of deep reading in a situation of great duress. It is a moment that almost takes us to a place "anterior to language" (the phrase is Elaine Scarry's), a place verging on the inexpressible, on overwhelming insight.

The exchange of energy grows in a kind of Buberian way between student and teacher, because the now faithful student is more deeply aware of his teacher's passion, even if he doesn't fully understand it, and the good and decent Jean begs his teacher to repeat the lines, because, as Levi puts it, "he is aware that it is doing me good." For a moment, Levi suggests that this little tercet is able to sum up their lives, despite what he calls his "wan translation and pedestrian commentary." He hopes that Jean, too, feels the passage "has to do with him, that it has to do with all men who toil, and with us in particular; and that it has to do with us two, who dare to reason of these things with the poles for the soup on our shoulders."

With the poles for the soup (that tepid broth of watery something that is sickening but essential for survival) on his shoulders, Levi is engrossed in the moment Ulysses speaks. "My little speech made everyone so keen," and he tells us that he tries in vain to explain to Jean the nuances of "keen," how many meanings it has; and certainly the idea that Ulysses's words affected, gave strength, inspired his men speaks to the force of language here, too, at noon in the Lager. Though Levi can't remember another four tercets, in his frustration he seamlessly folds in a bit of the cosmopolitan life of language in the Lager: *keine Ahnung*, Levi says, and Jean replies, *Ça ne fait rien, vas-y tout de meme*—and then back to Dante as Levi comes up with the powerful stanza about the sea.

> . . . When at last hove up a mountain, grey
> With distance, and so lofty and so steep
> I never had seen the like on any day.

Once again, a small reverie overcomes Levi, and the seduction of association now pulls him back to recollections of his home in northern Italy. Those mountainous waves evoke real mountains. "Oh Pikolo, Pikolo, say something, do not let me think of my mountains, which used to show up against the dusk of evening as I returned by train from Milan to Turin!" An image of the beautiful verging on the sublime, as the mountains show themselves in the distance in the light of dusk. An image of home, an exclamation mark after Turin; until now in his account of life at Auschwitz, there has been no such memory of home—a memory naturally fraught with pain so that Levi exclaims, "enough, one must go on, these are things that one thinks but does not say." In the soup line, the struggle of literary memory goes on, and we can, having come this far in *Survival in Auschwitz*, appreciate what it means for Levi to say "I would give today's soup to know how to connect 'than any I had seen' to the last lines. I try to reconstruct it through the rhymes." To give up a day's soup at Auschwitz for a rhyme—what more could one say about the pneumonic power of rhyme, about how sound and repetition shoots through the mind to make connections? In frustration "I close my eyes, I bite my fingers . . . other verses dance in my head," he exclaims, and then, as they arrive at the kitchen, with an acute sense that time is running out, he realizes it's only a tercet that he's missed, and at last he comes up with that last stanza.

> And three times round she went in roaring smother
> With all the waters, at the fourth the poop
> Rose, and the prow went down, as pleased Another.

Almost frantic, he holds Jean back in the soup line because "it is necessary and urgent that he listen, that he understand this 'as it pleased another' before it is too late; tomorrow he or I might be dead." Then he spills into a moment of uncharacteristic emotion, as his sense of ultimate meaning has been sprung by the poem: "I must explain to him about the Middle Ages, about the so human and so necessary and yet unexpected anachronism, but still more, something gigantic that I myself have only just seen, in a flash of intuition, perhaps the reasons for our fate, for our being here today. . . ."

What is Levi driving at? The Middle Ages? The human, the necessary? Something gigantic, a flash of intuition? The reason for our fate, for being at Auschwitz? Notwithstanding the power of Canto 26, it is Dante rediscovered in this context that has brought Levi to such a place of heightened feeling about art and life. For Dante, the idea of divine power resides in the notion of "pleased Another." Has the tragic ending of the greatest of classical heroes brought Levi to understand Dante's idea of God, of human fate, of suffering? And, one is prodded to ask, given this odd circumstance of Primo Levi and Dante at Auschwitz: Could even Dante have imagined the Holocaust, the idea of genocide in the modern era? Perhaps this is an implicit meaning of the vision of human behavior in the *Inferno*. Surely Levi believes this, and this is why the *Inferno* is liberating for him in more ways than one.

With his inimitable sense of irony, Levi cuts from the depth of his consciousness to the soup line, among "the sordid, ragged, crowd of soup carriers from other Kommandos." As they are pushed together in line to get their ration, the announcement is made "*Kraut und Ruben*": cabbages and turnips. He hears it in three languages: "*Choux et navets. Kaposzia es repak.*" He's back to reality, and the paragraph ends.

But not the chapter. There is just one more line, the last line of Canto 26: "and over our heads the hollow seas closed up." From cabbages and turnips to the death of Ulysses; perhaps it is not so disjunctive; perhaps it brings everything together. An image of death, and the death of the greatest classical hero, punished for his deceit and hubris. A chilling image; death by water, and a death that Dante invented for Ulysses, in a Christological revision of Homer. Dante's invention of such a death for Ulysses, his placing him in such a low circle of Hell, is punishment for Ulysses's deceit and hubris and perhaps for his perverse use of reason, the very cunning that for Homer was a virtue. But the image of drowning has special meaning at Auschwitz. As Levi makes clear in another chapter, "The Drowned and the Saved," in which he explores the psychology of survival, those who lack the necessary survival skills are doomed, in his essential metaphor, to *drown*.

In an earlier chapter, having had a brief moment of respite in which he smelled the hay, felt the warm sun, and kissed the earth, before he was jolted back to work by the Kapo, Levi notes: "Alas for the dreamer the moment of consciousness that accompanies the awakening is the acutest of sufferings. But it does not often happen to us, and they are not long dreams. We are only tired beasts." So it is here—Levi's painful awakening is a drowning back into the life of cruelty, and if one can allow for the vastly different context, a kind of Prufrockian drowning as well—the drowning back into the world of our daily existence ("till human voices wake us and we drown")—in which the soul enlightened by poetry in this noon hour excursion drowns back into the awful time of Auschwitz. The end of the canto has come. The soup line presses in on him.

>>><<<

The place of *The Divine Comedy* in Italian culture is as deep as the place of any poem in any national history. Levi was educated with the poem, and Dante was part of his intellectual coming of age. From the time of the Risorgimento, Dante has been an "emblem of national unity," an archetype of Italian identity, "la Bibbia di nostre gente." Having grown up in Mussolini's Italy, Levi was educated as Dante was being appropriated by the Fascists as national icon. Mussolini's plan to erect the famous Danteum—a complex that was to have been built in Rome in the 1930s—was part of that cultural landscape.[2] And some lines of Canto 26 are so beloved of Italians that they were recited at the lighting of the torch at the 2006 winter Olympics in Levi's home city of Turin: "You were not made to live like brutes / But to follow virtue and knowledge." Any culture would be grateful for what such a poem would bring to its people and its civilization. Surely, the United States would be a richer culture if "Song of Myself," or "Paterson," or "The Bridge" were part of its popular collective consciousness.

While Levi's encounter with poetry at Auschwitz owes a good deal to the place of *The Divine Comedy* in Italian culture, what happens to Levi at Auschwitz shows us implicitly how the poem travels from its place in culture to its place in human consciousness, where it becomes a force of imagination and language, and in this particular moment, a force that helps the battered self survive. Beyond the poem as cultural icon, Levi finds meaning, sensual joy, and some kind of spiritual rejuvenation in his recovery of poetic language: image and allegory, rhetorical eloquence, the rhyme and music of terza rima. The poem comes to him as surprise and revelation, and the revelation ignites a moment of clarity amid barbaric conditions.

Albert Camus, who had come face-to-face with Nazism in his own way, working in the French resistance movement, wrote in the aftermath of the war: "The world itself, whose single meaning I do not understand, is but a vast irrational. If one could say just once: 'This is clear,' all would be saved."³ Like millions of others, Levi lived in the "vast irrational" of Nazism, and in one unsuspecting circumstance inside Auschwitz, poetry came to him. That visitation, with all its fragmentary frustrations, compelled him to teach, translate, and interpret Canto 26 in a way that brought a moment of clarity, simple and complex—a moment that provided a counterforce to that vast irrational.

›››‹‹‹

Looking back four decades later, Levi reflected on his experience with Dante at Auschwitz for that half hour, that morning at noon, in the Lager, with his friend Jean. If the reader of *Survival at Auschwitz* left that scene wondering whether poetry could have had such meaning then and there, whether Levi had exaggerated or romanticized that moment, Levi has one more thing to say, in his most probing book, *The Drowned and the Saved*:

> After forty years I am reading in *Survival in Auschwitz* the chapter entitled "The Canto of Ulysses." It is one of the few episodes whose authenticity I have been able to verify (it is a reassuring operation: after a span of time, as I said in the first chapter, one can doubt one's memory) because my interlocutor of that time, Jean Samuel, is one the book's few surviving characters. We remained friends, we met several times, and his memories jibe with mine. . . . At that time Dante did not interest him, I interested him by my naïve and presumptuous effort to transmit Dante to him, by my language and my confused scholastic reminiscences in the space of half an hour with the soup poles on our shoulders. Well, where I wrote: "I would give today's soup to know how to join, I had 'none whatever,' to the ending," I had neither lied nor exaggerated. I really would have given bread or soup, that is blood, to save from nothingness, those memories, which today with the support of printed paper I can refresh whenever I wish and gratis, and which therefore seem of little value.⁴

To give blood at Auschwitz strikes me as a triple negative. The moment "save[d] from nothingness those memories." For Levi, then, in the face of death—and a particular kind of annihilation in which self is destroyed in a larger context of nihilism of a kind the Nazis invented—remembering the poem and trying to teach it in a compressed period of time ignited a deep part of his being and reconnected him to life before the catastrophe. The experience with Dante's canto saved his past "from oblivion," "reinforcing my identity," he notes, and reminding him that his mind still functioned: "elevating me in my own eyes and those of my interlocutor." The encounter was "liberating," as Levi put it, which at Auschwitz seemed to be a gymnastic paradox of seeming impossibility.

The moment of poetry at Auschwitz enabled Levi a self-reclamation amid brutally protracted, dehumanizing circumstances, in which the poem and the process it engendered embodied a recovered connection to culture. And this meant for Levi not only self-individuation but a reconnection with the larger archive of learning, and so Dante's canto became a synecdoche for the book. "Anyone who has read or seen Ray Bradbury's *Fahrenheit 451*," Levi continues in his reflection, "can see what it would mean to be compelled to live in a world without books and what value the memory of books would assume in this world."[5] Here, at Auschwitz, it is imagination's clamp in the force of memory and poetry, which allows for a recovered solidity of truth.

But Levi is not a romantic about culture or poetry, just as he is not a romantic about the psychology of human survival. He notes with his own skeptical sense that culture is "not for everyone, everywhere," but sometimes on that right occasion it is "precious as a precious stone" and it can make one feel "almost lifted up from the ground." And, though he says that poetry and the larger domain of culture could not help one navigate the daily trials and disasters in Auschwitz, he affirms what it *can* do, what it *can* ignite and restore—in this case, in circumstances of torture and mass killing.

In the modern annals of the great tracts on and defenses of poetry by Sydney, Coleridge, Wordsworth, Shelley, Emerson,

Whitman, Rimbaud, and on into the twentieth century, Levi's moment of reprieve at Auschwitz has its place. It reminds us of poetry's potential power in the reclamation of the life-force, of its embodiment as a primary ligature in the continuity of culture. Here, that force and continuity were propelled by the vise-grip of memory—memory that is alive in a self that can find its center in bare lines of words, images, symbolic forms, and music-making syntax that connects the rhythms of language with the rhythms of the body and mind.

The Poem as History

The typhoon which desires to be called history
« RAPHAEL LEMKIN »

Labyrinthine mouths of history
« HART CRANE »

The lyric poem occupies a strange space in the wider nexus of early-twenty-first-century culture. To many, the poem is invisible, to some simply marginal, to others intimidating and indecipherable. For those within the small culture who live by poetry, the poem is the deep reality, the most engaging inroad to self, other, culture, history. It is the coalescing of language as force and play in the mind's working out and working through complex issues. But that is, indeed, a small audience, and the gap between those in poetry's small culture and even the broader literature-reading public is wide. Yet when we enter poems, especially poems that engage dimensions of history, we find forms of knowledge, pleasure, and complexity that are found nowhere else.

The poem can inhabit an idea of history through which one can wrestle with forces of violent human events that shape the self as well as a larger culture and a kind of community that bridges cultures. This kind of poem can have an omnivorous appetite, eccentric, eclectic, never pretending to anything but a fragment or an immersion in a corner of a larger history, but an immersion that can yield different insights than long discursive texts—scholarly, journalistic, fictional—though all of those forms are important. The poem offers us various webs of signification, insights to the inner life of social chaos, seen deeply in poetic imagination.

"The past can be seized only as an image which flashes up at the instant that it can be recognized and is never seen again." "To articulate the past historically . . . means to seize hold of a memory at the moment it flashes up at a moment of danger."[1] Although Walter Benjamin is writing about dialectical materialism in his essay "Philosophy of History," he has caught something about poetry and history, about the poet's ability to catch an event as it "flashes up," and "to seize" the event and work it into something previously un-thought of, stinging or arresting, with a strange insight that keeps the event alive, that gives ballast to the event in the aftermath so that history leaves its imprint on human thinking and imagination. In the poem, we can live in time past and present through a dialectic of the imagination that can also create out of history, among other things, a broader human community.

Czesław Miłosz argues that "the language of every historical period receives its definite shape through poetry," and, even if this sounds a bit expansive in the film and digital age, Miłosz also suggests that poetry "engenders movement and change."[2] This is crucial to the poem's ability to have an impact on our understanding of history in which the self is able to imagine the other, so that the poem's ability to create a sense of otherness is a process of making a bridge and nexus and in a nonpolemical way—an ethical space. Thus, when the historical moment or event has passed, the poem, to use Pound's phrase, has made news that has stayed news.

If language receives its shape through poetry, so, too, do historical events receive their shape in the personal and collective memory through poetry. As we engage the poem in a social space and in a dialectical relationship between the self in the present and the event in the past, we can see the poem as an aesthetic force that allows us engagement with the past as well as detachment and perspective, which in turn allows us a complex and humane way of understanding the self (and ourselves as readers) in history in an expansive way that affords us a relationship to otherness.

Because the poem is capable of holding passion and irony in balance, and is informed by a tension between immersion and detachment, the poem can excavate the "typhoon" that is "history," to use Raphael Lemkin's words. In creating a tension between passion and irony, the poet notices objects, puts down dates, gives numbers validity. As Hemingway once said through his character Frederic Henry in *A Farewell to Arms*, "Abstract words such as glory, honor, courage, or hallow were obscene beside the concrete names of rivers, the numbers of regiments and the dates."[3] He was also noting a certain kind of sensibility that circulates through the poem. Poetry can name and embody the past with its peculiar and idiosyncratic language, a kind of language that gives the poem one of its inimitable natures. In doing so, the poet can locate a place, freeze a filament of *the event*, seize an image of the past, see into some of the textures that comprise *the event*. Out of poetry's idiosyncratic seeing—a seeing of both past and present that generates fresh observation—the poem embodies kinds of clarities that are otherwise not possible in the imagination's efforts to locate that fragment of the past that yields the event in arresting ways.

In the premodernist era, poets who engaged historical events did so, for the most part, in monolithic blocks or focused meditations and sustained conceits. The event was reflected on in one fell swoop, and it most often yielded a moral idea or an insight to the event. Milton's "On the Late Massacre in Piedmont," Marvell's "An Horatian Ode upon Cromwell's Return from Ireland," Wordsworth's celebration of the French Revolution in parts of the "Prelude," Shelley's "England in 1819," or Tennyson's "Charge of the Light Brigade," for example, locate a historical moment or event and vise it hard in a focused way and deliver moral opinions or lessons. Perhaps the reason the premodernist historical poem is less visible in anthologies is because the historical orientations of these poems are less complex than the poetics of historical imagination of modernist and postmodernist poetry. Milton's outrage at the Catholic slaughter of the reformist Christians of the Piedmont is more than clear: "Avenge, O Lord, thy slaughtered saints whose bones / Lie scattered on the Alpine mountains cold." And, Shelley's view of the British Crown is a bald diatribe:

An old, mad, blind, despised, and dying king,—
Princes, the dregs of their dull race, who flow
Through public scorn,—mud from a muddy spring,—
Rulers who neither see, nor feel, nor know. . . .

Perhaps the dearth of historically located poems in the pretwentieth-century Anglo-American canon suggests something about their one-dimensionality and their inclination to didacticism. And one might say that the abundance of dynamic and complex poems that deal with history in the modernist and postmodernist eras reveal a shift in the poetry's various approaches to language, to lyric form, and to history.

This shift is perhaps most fully anticipated by Walt Whitman's fragmented, sequential, lyrical form (in "Song of Myself" or "When Lilacs Last in the Dooryard Bloom'd") and his immersion in the grueling realities of the American Civil War (in "The Wound Dresser" or "Vigil Strange I Kept on the Field One Night"). The event of history in the modernist poem often comes to us in pieces, in fragments of poetic architecture, dredged up from the poet's immersion in a historical moment. In the post-Whitman era, the poem is often a filter for filaments of experience, memory, or history, "an alembic," as Emerson put it, through which the imagination can sift pieces of evidence in order to make a vision of the event in ways that the linearity of fiction or nonfiction might not. The truncations of time are melded and molded into a vision of the moment, past or present.

An image can ring like Yeats's musical phrase in "Easter, 1916," when what is "terrible" about the "beauty" that has been "born" is inseparable from the names, dates, and eighteenth-century houses that convey Yeats's lyric reflection on paradoxes of political devotion and pitfalls of the cause. Or the poem can mark a historical moment and be an affirmative rejection of alienation and a bridge between self and other, as in Auden's "September 1, 1939." And the self, the poet's persona of various sorts, often is situated in the mix of the event or is mixed into the event from her or his present perspective. Or the event is part of a shifting set of planes of perspective orchestrated by a self in its own time, and time past and time present continue to mix and shift as the poem unfolds.

The poet's ability to create rhetorical gestures, metaphoric entanglements, conceits, and layered renderings allows the self by implication or direct engagement to be situated in relation to the event. The historical is alive in the nerve-ends of rhythm and syntax and the associative leaps of language that define the poem's terrain. History comes to us in the poem's voice that both appropriates and emerges from what I would call the poet's thick description of the event.

Some of the most ambitious and far-reaching poems—poems that grapple with history and deal with the collisions of past and present, poems that pitch a voice that is at once both public and private—find their shape and force by inhabiting a historical moment or location. In doing so, they create continual movements, sometimes odd and unexpected, that give the poem its engaging view of the event as a fragment of history.

There is often a wily dance between metaphor and event in poems that take on history. The past is not static, and neither is the poem with its reach and its play. In some poems that reach into a historical event, the poet creates strategies that entangle us in a process of departure, shift, and even evasion that helps the poem to go farther, to penetrate the event more fully.

In one of W. B. Yeats's most ambitious poems—a layered, symbolistic hydra of a poem titled "Nineteen Hundred and

Nineteen"—we find the event by navigating fragments and the meanderings of Yeats's meditations on imagination, art, and history. The poem is located in a political moment—the Irish war of independence from Great Britain—and images of terror and terrorism, guerilla warfare, citizens killed in the streets inflect everything. There is no ambiguity about the location of the poem, although critics have too often ignored that location to discuss solely its aesthetics. However, those dimensions mean little without the poem's ballast in the events of 1919.

Yeats enters that political landscape through a circuitous meditation on loss and ruin, which take him into a longer view of history. As he moves into the event, he circles it, clarifying its complexity as he entangles the moment with his own particular kind of riffing, or sideways meditations. Civilization is fragile: "things fall apart," as he wrote in "The Second Coming" (material things, nations, civilizations), as "Nineteen Hundred and Nineteen" opens:

> Many ingenious lovely things are gone
> That seemed sheer miracle to the multitude
> Protected from the circle of the moon
> That pitches common things about. There stood
> Amid the ornamental bronze and stone
> An ancient image made of olive wood—
> And gone are Phidias' famous ivories
> And all the golden grasshoppers and bees.

The golden age of Phidias's sculpture and Athenian pins and combs of "grasshoppers and bees" are now but images in the mind, if they are that. Yeats's belief in art and beauty also seems lost in an old innocence: "O what fine thoughts we had because we thought / That the worst rogues and rascals had died out."

The poem darts and moves, slides off the violence of the guerilla war between Sinn Fein and the British forces: "a drunken soldiery / Can leave the mother, murdered at her door / To crawl in her own blood, and go scot-free." The chaos of violence in the daily life scissors back and forth between Yeats's private reflections on art and philosophy, his own intellectual life, and Ireland's predicament. High rhetoric collides with ancient Greek art, contemporary dance, medieval demonology.

The poem is a kind of labyrinth that keeps returning to its source—the violence of 1919—and the bloody events in the streets send Yeats into meditations on art and philosophy, and quarrels with the self in which he reexamines his intellectual values and ideals. At the poem's center, Yeats pits his artistic self against the violent, self-consuming world and asks some metaphysical questions. The poem moves with disruptive leaps between those "monuments of magnificence" that embody civilization and the blood-soaked present. Thanatos informs the poem's apocalyptic vision: "Man is in love and loves what vanishes," and civilization is marked by the "incendiary or bigot," who burns "that stump on the Acropolis, / Or break in bits the famous ivories / Of traffic in the grasshoppers or bees."

The image of Loie Fuller, the avant-garde dancer and choreographer who brought American dance to Europe, jolts the poem into one of those Yeatsian configurations that surprise and bewilder. What is she doing here in this poem about political violence? In hammering iambics that dramatize the dance, Fuller's Chinese dancers assert the human form and imagination as a counterforce to violence; they are a "shining web, a floating ribbon of cloth," until that transient beauty morphs in Yeats's view into the male dance of violence: "All men are dancers and their tread / Goes to the barbarous clangor of a gong."

The human death instinct challenges Yeats's aesthetic ideals: "O but we dreamed to mend / Whatever mischief seemed / To afflict mankind, but now / That winds of winter blow / Learn that we were crack-pated when we dreamed." In the furious, anaphoric lines of the stanzas of section four built around the refrain "Come let us mock," Yeats rages at the possible futility of all human endeavor—or what Robert Jay Lifton has called the annihilation of symbolic immortality. The accumulation of violence of World War I and the ensuing Civil War have led, in part at least, to Yeats's rant: "Come let us mock at the great / That had such burdens on the mind / And toiled so hard and late / To leave some monument behind, / Nor thought of the leveling wind." The stuccoed density of the final sixteen-line stanza brings the poem to a wild crescendo, as the conflicts in the poet and his confrontation with the world collide. The wind of violence, myth, and history bang into each other, as the stanza opens with, "Violence upon the roads; violence of horses": "All break and vanish / and evil gathers head," and then the big rhetoric gives way to the image of "Herodias' daughters [who] have returned again," inseparable from that gesture of recurrent wind: the "leveling wind" and that "labyrinth of wind" that embodies both the poet's rage and the world's violence. The wind, which is also a trope of movement, gusts into the final image out of Yeats's weird bag of occult imagination. Herodias's daughters are biblical characters associated with violence in the story of Salome's seductive dance, which led to the beheading of John the Baptist. In medieval lore, which Yeats knew well, Herodias and her daughters were symbols of dangerous female sexuality, and Herodias was a leader of witches. From Herodias, Yeats takes us to a strange, sinuous closing image of a face that "lurches past," "under the shadow of stupid straw-pale locks / That insolent fiend Robert Artisson." A propos of Yeats's own idiosyncratic mythic method, we discover that Artisson is an obscure medieval demon who was supposed to have had sex with Lady Kyteler, a fourteenth-century noble who was accused of witchcraft in Ireland. A demonic face closes a poem of meditation on ruin against the loss of ideal beauty. With the obscure, apocalyptic image of Artisson, Yeats leaves us with his haunted mind, reminding us, as well, that the poem can take us anywhere and that the most private obsessions can mingle with the most public events.

Robert Lowell's "For the Union Dead" goes after history in a less symbolistic way, but also insists on creating intersecting angles of perception, so the poem's landscape becomes layered and driven by shifts that open the horizon of meaning. He spends five stanzas looking at a spot on the old Boston Common where a parking garage is now being built and the old aquarium is just a childhood memory. Nostalgia for lost innocence and an old Boston are all that are left.

The old South Boston Aquarium stands
in a Sahara of snow now. Its broken windows are boarded.
The bronze weathervane cod has lost half its scales.
The airy tanks are dry.

Once my nose crawled like a snail on the glass;
my hand tingled
to burst the bubbles
drifting from the noses of the cowed, compliant fish.

My hand draws back. I often sigh still
for the dark downward and vegetating kingdom
of the fish and reptile. One morning last March,
I pressed against the new barbed and galvanized

fence on the Boston Common. Behind their cage,
yellow dinosaur steam shovels were grunting
as they cropped up tons of mush and grass
to gouge their underworld garage.

In remembering being transfixed by the tanks of fish at the aquarium, the new age of construction brings Lowell to a present that he'll castigate before the poem is over, but for now the five stanzas create a context for the deeper history the poem is driving toward. Lowell's encounter with the Civil War is mediated by his reflection on a celebrated frieze—a Civil War relief of Robert Gould Shaw's Negro infantry done by Augustus St. Gaudens—and that reflection prompts Lowell into a reflection on the legacy of racial tensions in the late 1950s, when the poem was written.

The presence of the Shaw sculpture opens up the past, and Lowell gives us a history of the statue as William James, the eminent Harvard philosopher, appears in Lowell's depiction of the 1897 dedication.

Parking spaces luxuriate like civic
sandpiles in the heart of Boston.

A girdle of orange, Puritan-pumpkin colored girders
braces the tingling Statehouse,

shaking over the excavations, as it faces Colonel Shaw
and his bell-cheeked Negro infantry
on St. Gaudens' shaking Civil War relief,
propped by a plank splint against the garage's earthquake.
Two months after marching through Boston,
half the regiment was dead;
at the dedication,
William James could almost hear the bronze Negroes breathe.

The poem moves into the event—the Civil War—through the image of abolitionist Colonel Shaw and his regiment of black soldiers, the first in the Civil War. As he meditates on Shaw's moral heroism and his sacrifices for the "Grand Army of the Republic" made for the pursuit of justice and liberty, the ironies of history spill out, and the idealistic past is undermined by an apocalyptic present with Lowell's effective use of a trope of "burial," which here is "the ditch" (not a monument) that Colonel Shaw's father wanted for his son.

The "ditch" is a swing image to the last section, in which the past slides into the moral ambiguities of the present—the uncomfortable present where the Hiroshima ending of World War II strikes Lowell as morally problematic. The image of an advertisement that shows "Hiroshima boiling over a Mosler Safe" is as absurd a postscript to the age of atomic weapons as is the failure of racial equality in American democracy.

Lowell leaves us with a TV image in which "the drained faces of Negro school-children rise like balloons." From visual text to visual text, the poem brings us images of school integration violence, evoking Little Rock, Arkansas, 1957, the national event that would lead the way to many others like it in the ensuing years. The ironic meaning of Colonel Shaw comes into focus fully now, and the poem returns to its opening elemental image of the aquarium and those reptilian-like cars of the late 1950s, so that "the poem's movement" engages "history's movement" in shifting planes of image-scene-perspectives.

In Czesław Miłosz's "A Poor Christian Looks at the Ghetto," the poem opens with a discerning eye on the unexpected, not with a gaze on the suffering Jews in the Warsaw ghetto in 1943. The uncomfortable opening image is a strangely disembodied one of decomposing flesh, before a shift to a wider panorama with the simple, rhetorical refrain: "it has begun." But the catalog of images, the bald depiction of things is upending—its movements are unexpected, and images of the materials of civilization evoke broad swaths of human endeavor from "trumpets" to "silk" to "gypsum" and "balls." The images evoke the destruction of a culture of commerce and a society of civilized materials; it's the inversion of civilization, or what Elaine Scarry has called "the un-making of the world."

> Bees build around red liver,
> Ants build around black bone.
> It has begun: the tearing, the trampling on silks,
> It has begun: the breaking of glass, wood, copper, nickel, silver, foam
> Of gypsum, iron sheets, violin strings, trumpets, leaves, balls,
>   crystals
> Poof! Phosphorescent fire from yellow walls
> Engulfs animal and human hair.

The poem returns to the dialectic between the destruction of the materials of civilization and the decomposing of flesh and body parts. The poet's eye focuses on the unexpected: Miłosz refers to the man inspecting the remains of bodies as "the guardian mole," a Kafka-like figure who is a new variation on the old guardian angel. He is the rodent on earth, the observer, the excrescence of the angel in a time of diabolical history, a witness to the human enterprise of cruelty. And it is to the mole the poet appeals in closing:

> What will I tell him, I, a Jew of the New Testament.
> Waiting two thousand years for the second coming of Jesus?
> My broken body will deliver me to his sight
> And he will count me among the helpers of death:
> The uncircumcised.

Again, the inventiveness of irony allows for a different approach to conscience: the idea of "a Jew of the New Testament" is a new perspective (after all, it's not the second century) through which the poet sees his own culpability in the killing of the Jews by European Christians: Is our witness culpable? Is just looking on complicity? The body is witness to itself: "broken" and "uncircumcised." The poem bears a kind of witness but gives no easy answers. Its insights emanate from the dialectic between seeing things in fresh ways and an engagement with the scene that is unsettling—and finally is mole-like. The self is splayed by its encounter with history—here, in one moment in the Warsaw ghetto in a larger event of genocide.

In "Night, Death, Mississippi," Robert Hayden takes on the challenge of getting inside the head of an aging Ku Klux Klansman in the Jim Crow American South sometime before the civil rights era. The dramatic monologue can be a vein into the past, into otherness, into the voice made of compressed monologue language that embeds the time and place. Its spareness is essential to its insight.

> A quavering cry. Screech-owl?
> Or one of them?
> The old man in his reek
> and gauntness laughs—
>
> One of them, I bet—
> and turns out the kitchen lamp,
> limping to the porch to listen
> in the windowless night.
>
> Be there with Boy and the rest
> if I was well again.
> Time was. Time was.
> White robes like moonlight
>
> In the sweetgum dark.
> Unbucked that one then
> and him squealing bloody Jesus
> as we cut it off.

Time was. A cry?
A cry all right.
He hawks and spits
fevered as by groinfire.

Hayden clearly felt truer to himself staying in his own more formal idiom rather than trying for a full vernacular voice, though there are touches of it, and so the poem moves between "robes like moonlight," and "Be there with Boy and the rest / if I was well again." As the old redneck remembers with nostalgia his days of lynching and castrating Negroes, he laments his inability to be a hunter, though he can still celebrate the "Boy" who is keeping the tradition going.

In the second section of the poem, a one-line italicized stanza floats into the poem following a four-line stanza. *O Jesus burning on the lily cross; O night, rawhead and bloodybones night; O night betrayed by darkness not its own.* The lines function as a lyric choral voice—embodying an omniscient conscience, a bit didactic at moments, but without any self overlay; the impersonality of the voice allows the lines to scissor the poem and create the layers of movement that convey the compacted perspective of an African American poet envisioning a white southern Klansman. Each italicized stanza ensues the Klansman's voice: "Christ, it was better / than hunting bear / which don't know why / you want him dead." Hayden plays the racist voice off the lyric choral voice to create irony, and although he is balancing on the tightrope of sentimentality at times, I don't think he falls off.

Hayden's formal impersonality allows the perspectives to collide and make their own music out of a culture and a historical context, one that still resonates to the psychology of violence and racist cultism. The final line encodes a bit of deconstructive symbology with unselfconscious grace. The image of "black" in Western cultural tradition is associated with evil, but here Hayden takes that assumption and inverts it through two negatives. "Night betrayed by darkness" suggests that traditional evil symbology is upended by "darkness not its own," meaning not of natural but of human making: double darkness, then, is white and white-made, and such a Melvillian ending leaves us with the knotted symbol to be untied as the poem closes into its opening.

History can be navigated, drilled for, or even sky-scanned, as Adrienne Rich does in "Planetarium," in which her search for an understanding of the relationship between intellectual work, cultural memory, gender, and power takes her into a meditation on constellations and astronomers. In this collage-like poem with its open field force, which is controlled by Rich's intellectual girding, the poet moves in associational ways between the constellation on the ceiling of the planetarium and a woman astronomer, Caroline Herschel, to whom the poem is dedicated. Herschel was the sister of the German-born British astronomer William Herschel, a distinguished and knighted scientist who worked in the eighteenth and early nineteenth centuries. Caroline, who worked by his side for much of their shared careers, lived to be ninety-seven and worked into the nineteenth century. Although the two worked together—and she was an acknowledged astronomer of the era—she worked in her brother's shadow.

Rich moves from the idea of constellations invented by men to the life of a woman astronomer as the cosmos on the planetarium ceiling jogs her imagination:

A woman in the shape of a monster
a monster in the shape of a woman
the skies are full of them

a woman "in the snow
among the Clocks and instruments
or measuring the ground with poles."

in her 98 years to discover
8 comets

Light, the poem's primary conceit, emanates from the poet's meditation on the sky. "Encountering the NOVA / every impulse of light exploding / from the core / as life flies out of us," opens the self to the science of nature and sets up the personal engagement of the closing. But here in the flow of her mind, planetarium and night sky embody an encoded history of women. Rich keeps the associative flow moving with the indented stanza that includes the voice of Tycho Brahe, the sixteenth-century Danish astronomer who paved the way for modern astronomy and Kepler's discoveries. Brahe developed telescopic instruments through which he observed a supernova and with which he mapped the moon, Mars, and other celestial bodies. His voice, "Tycho whispering at last / 'Let me not seem to have died in vain,'" keeps us in the flow of the poet's planetarium consciousness as she positions herself in the path of a pulsating star or pulsar.

It's worth noting that the phenomenon of the pulsar—a highly magnetized neutron star (remnant of a supernova that emits a beam of electromagnetic radiation)—was discovered in 1967, a year before Rich wrote the poem. The power of the pulsation of light from the star continues the idea of light for Rich so the self can become a transformed receiver: "Heartbeat of the pulsar / heart sweating through my body / The radio impulse / pouring in from Taurus." As the self receives the electromagnetic waves of light—what I would call a scientific transmutation of the old spiritual idea of light—Rich has also embedded in the notion of the pulsar discovery an interesting history of gender and the issues surrounding intellectual achievement and property.

The pulsar was discovered by the British astronomer Anthony Hewish and his young female graduate student Jocelyn Bell. Bell was the first to discover the pulsar, and when Hewish received the Nobel Prize for Physics in 1974 for the discovery, it became controversial because some scientists felt it was unfair not to have included Bell as a corecipient of the prize. It's a bit of context that lies outside the poem, but it's relevant to Rich's meditation on intellectual achievement, cultural property, and the history of women working in the shadow of men.

"Planetarium" closes with a long box-like stanza with space

gaps in certain lines to suggest an idea of the mind staggered by the bombardment of light pulsation and activity of radio signals. In this bombardment, the self configures a new consciousness as body and mind become instruments through which the poet, "translate[s] pulsations / into images." Even if the closing lines overreach into the didactic, Rich has made out of her collage of intellectual history and night-sky cosmos meditation an unusual way of aligning an idea of the past with a contemporary personal and political dilemma.

The poem is not a camera, but it has image-freezing properties that can catch that flash-up of a historical moment, which the poet "seizes," to use Benjamin's notion. In Philip Larkin's "MCMXIV," the Roman numerals suggest the date as classic and monumental—a year that many historians regard as one that launched one notion of modernity. World War I brought the West mechanized killing, biological warfare, unprecedented death tolls (10 to 13 million), nationalisms yoked to war machines, and genocide in its modern form.

The first three of the four eight-line stanzas freeze-frame the past with images of deceptive postcard-like clarity. Larkin's camera eye pans and zooms in on scenes of English life on the eve of disaster.

> Those long uneven lines
> Standing as patiently
> As if they were stretched outside
> The Oval or Villa Park,
> The crowns of hats, the sun
> On moustached archaic faces
> Grinning as if it were all
> An August Bank Holiday lark;
>
> And the shut shops, the bleached
> Established names on the sunblinds,
> The farthings and sovereigns,
> And dark-clothed children at play
> Called after kings and queens,

The tin advertisements
For cocoa and twist, and the pubs
Wide open all day;

And the countryside not caring;
The place-names all hazed over
With flowering grasses, and fields
Shadowing Domesday lines

The image—of the men lining up for military service "patiently,"
as if for a cricket or football match at the Oval or Villa Park—is
stinging. Through the light of perspective, "the sun," in stanza
one, those Edwardian hats and mustaches accentuate the innocence that preceded the great fall, or what Paul Fussell called
"the satire of circumstance," which defined the ghoulish psychology of what awaited the boys who had been raised on heroic notions of war, romantic ideas of combat, often with the medieval-
like rhetoric of Robert Bridges, Tennyson, and Rudyard Kipling.
Larkin picks up the idea of war as a heroic game or sport in the
images of the Oval and Villa Park.

The world, a culture, a focused moment, the summer of 1914
before it happened. Material culture and time frozen in lyric
image: "farthings and sovereigns," the children named after
"kings and queens," those premodern tin advertisements for "cocoa and twist." Nostalgia recapitulated through historical irony
is more crushing. The pubs are open, the countryside somno-
lent, town signs washed in summer haze, the half-tame English
countryside, only interrupted by that ghost image of "Shadowing Domesday lines," while the Edwardian world order with its
"differently-dressed servants / With tiny rooms in huge houses"
freeze the historical moment.

And then, the raw, rhetorical moment, carefully set up by the
pristine detachment of the first four stanzas.

Never such innocence,
Never before or since,

As changed itself to past
Without a word—the men
Leaving the gardens tidy,
The thousands of marriages
Lasting a little while longer:
Never such innocence again.

The repetition of "never" three times in eight lines is, for Larkin, hyperbolic; the reader will decide if the last line is too much, but Larkin's insistence on the word as historiographic rhetoric, the interpretive seeing of the poem, has to be ballasted by the whole poem. The conceptual notion of innocence is transformed in silence, as the marriages and emblematic gardens are left, and "MCMXIV" leaves the idea of the fall from innocence in a field of absence that is the poem's implicit energy.

>>><<<

Poems that tackle history with these strategies also have an uncanny and intrinsic way of resisting totalisms. In resisting being didactic, they are not co-opted by the events in which they immerse themselves. Such poems yield insight and inventive connections, which is to say metaphoric and metonymic figurations; and they create a compressed language-music that embodies frequencies of meaning as well as a longer range perspective of the event. It is in that necessary distance that we learn something— not just a depiction, an emotion, a sensory jolt, but a deeper kind of knowledge, a deeper way to know history. And in this immersion in the event, the poem maintains the free play of imagination, as a counterforce to the totalizing realities that are often at the core of the violence that is being witnessed.

For poets who take on the historical, the event can generate an accretion of meaning that history comes to embody in the grip of the poetic imagination as it cools into memory, postmemory, and perspective. Literature, whether edgy realism or transcendent idealism, is always a symbolic act—always pushing

toward the inner life of its subject or its objective correlative—
and so when a poem makes a reach for an event in the political or
social world, it can transform facts of history in ways that drive
the real and the symbolic into a symbiotic relationship. Here the
poem has its greatest energy, its reach, its expansive possibilities.

Ingesting Violence: The Poetry of Witness Problem

When Carolyn Forché's anthology *Against Forgetting: Twentieth-Century Poetry of Witness* was published in 1993, it was controversial and elicited hostility from some corners of the American poetry scene. One attack of the anthology came from the poet Chard deNiord, who asserted in a review that the anthology had degraded poetry and betrayed the higher ideals of the art. It was a response that seemed to be symptomatic of one perspective at the time, a view that I would hear among some poets in various forums. I responded to deNiord's attack of *Against Forgetting*, but I want to revisit the "poetry of witness" issue here, because I think there is misunderstanding and confusion surrounding the concept, idea, and rhetoric of what "witness" might mean, and what poets have achieved with their various lyric forms and language strategies in the realm of representing certain kinds of violent experiences.

I want to start with a summary of the exchange between de-Niord and me in 1993 as a way into my continued thinking about poetry of witness that seems still to elicit controversial reactions. In revisiting that exchange, in no way do I mean to cast aspersions on deNiord, who is a serious poet with earnest views, but the exchange remains a context for my continued thinking about this issue in poetics and poetry, which has come to have an increasingly significant impact on literary history and on how we think about poetry in the beginning of the twenty-first century. In "The High Place of American Poetry: The Problem with Witness" (*AGNI* 39), deNiord presents Forché's anthology *Against Forgetting: Twentieth-Century Poetry of Witness* as a negative problem against which he wishes to demonstrate what he calls poetry's "truer qualities." At the outset, let me say that my relationship to *Against Forgetting* is not a distant one, for two of my collaborative translations appear in "The Armenian Genocide" section of the anthology, and I was involved in the shaping of that section.

A summary of my response to deNiord in 1993 goes like this. I find it difficult to understand why deNiord has attempted to define poetry's "higher" and "truer" qualities in negative contrast to Forché's anthology, because notions of "higher" and "truer" aesthetic performances seem hardly relevant to Forché's anthology. This is a collection of international poems by many major poets and other poets of formidable gifts, including, for example, Zbigniew Herbert, W. H. Auden, Yannis Ritsos, Mahmoud Darwish, Wisława Szymborska, and Claribel Alegria.

DeNiord finds Forché's idea of poetry of witness a wrong idea and claims that the anthology represents a view of poetry that is simplistic, ideological, narrow, polemical, and generally ill suited to the "true" idea of poetry. Furthermore, he attacks Forché for exploiting poetry written by poets from countries that have endured political oppression and violence. He asks: "shouldn't this inclusive sounding term be prompting provocative discussions about the nature of poetry in general, and its inherent perspicacity specifically, as opposed simply to standing for a kind of poetry that so-called poets of witness, such as those included in *Against Forgetting*, would adamantly avoid themselves as a term to describe their work?" Just thumbing through the anthology one would note that Forché *is indeed* generating meaningful discussion about the nature of poetry.

DeNiord complains that poetry of witness is a "poetry of moral accounting," which only "politicizes" poetry, and can reduce poetry to "a two dimensional academicism" (whatever that might mean); he accuses Forché of not appreciating "poetry as an intrinsically diverse genre." "Strong poetry," he claims, resists such labels, and then he goes on to show us what strong poetry is. I must say I had hoped that by 1993 oedipal notions about "strong poetry" had given way to more nuanced notions of aesthetic performance and cultural context. However, deNiord's notions about "strong poetry" seem based on generic and romantic notions about poetic discovery, the imagination, and spiritual truth, and he often couches them in a rhetoric of clichés like "enduring poetry," "memorable truths," and "ageless answers." His glosses of poems by James Wright and Gerald Stern and Ellen Bryant Voigt's as counterforces have little to do with the issues raised by Forché and *Against Forgetting* and suggest something about his refusal to engage the various notions of poetry that the anthology embodies. To claim that "real witnessing" shows us that poetry "is based on the quality of writing," or that "good writing makes experience meaningful whereas experience does not a poem make," or that "true witnessing in poetry occurs whenever true writing occurs" is a non sequitur in relation to the poems in *Against Forgetting*; and such notions are so general to the craft and art of poetry that surely writers and literate readers need not be reminded that they are important. Forché, like any gifted poet, would agree that good writing (sustained, sophisticated, and successful transformations of language in the lyric form) is an assumption for poems that engage violence as well as for poems that engage personal love, nature, or God. Surely Guillaume Apollinaire, Eugenio Montale, Ezra Pound, W. H. Auden, Czesław Miłosz, Giorgos Seferis, and the dozens of other poets in her anthology would agree as well.

Forché's introduction, whatever its limitations, discloses a poet who has thought seriously and passionately about a relationship between poetry and history—a relationship that has led her to define or call attention to an orientation of twentieth-century poetry that is marked by or engaged with events of political extremity and catastrophe, and mass killing. In reading the introduction, I don't find anything that suggests rigid, didactic, academic, or one-dimensional notions of poetry. Explicitly and implicitly, Forché rejects rigidities; any anthology that includes poets and poems as diverse as Vahan Tekeyan's "Country of Dust," Apollinaire's "The Little Car," Georg Trakl's "A Romance to Night," Boris Pasternak's "Hamlet," Anna Akhmatova's "Requiem," Natalya Gorbanevskaya's "Sukhanovo," Miguel Hernandez's "Lullaby of the Onion," Jacques Prevert's "Barbara," Nelly Sachs's "But Look," Pound's "Pisan Canto LXXIV," Zbigniew Herbert's "Report from a Beseiged City," Nicanor Parra's "Letters from the Poet Who Sleeps in a Chair," Galway Kinnell's "Vapor Trail Reflected in the Frog Pond," Yusef Komunyakaa's "After the Fall of Saigon," and Bei Dao's "The Answer"—to mention a few of the several hundred poems—could hardly be accused of presenting poetry that is didactic, polemical, or schematic.

Quite the opposite, Forché explores the range and variousness of poetry that has been defined by what she calls "political extremity." In doing so, she offers a list of poetic features by which these poems of witness appear to be defined. The poets sometimes create epistolary modes; use religious language; resort to irony, paradox, and surrealism (a complex aesthetic that she does not define); and employ the poetic fragment. Although these notions are all common to the many strategies of poetry as well as being interpretive tools for poets and critics, I don't think that Forché makes a well-defined case for their belonging to poems of witness solely. What she *does* demonstrate, deeply, is that there is a relationship between a poet's life and the forces of history in which that life is lived, and which also can affect the nature of the poet's art. Forché's anthology demonstrates how poets whose lives have been in some way changed by what she calls political catastrophe force us to consider how those events may surface in the imagination and in the poem. And the relationship between those events and the imagination may be lyrically confrontational, as in Primo Levi's "Shema," or discursive and oblique, as in Pound's "Pisan Canto LXXIV." Or, she suggests, the facts of a life may be as politically and viscerally defined as the gruesome death of Hungarian poet Miklos Radnóti (Radnóti was executed by the Germans in 1944, and his wife had him exhumed from a mass grave after the war; she found in the back pocket of his trousers a small notebook "soaked in the fluids of the body and blackened by wet earth," in which his last ten poems were written). Such an extraordinary death would force any serious reader to ask certain kinds of questions about those last ten poems, and then, surely, about the poet's larger body of work.

Poets defined by the "impress of extremity" (the phrase is from Terrence Des Pres's *Praises and Dispraises*), Forché argues, have made interesting use of various formal conventions, including fragmentary and epistolary strategies, which enable poets to embody crisis and allow us to see as well, perhaps, how modernist techniques were informed by political disaster—and, hence, how political disaster informed poets who wrote in that context. Forché points us to poets as different as Paul Celan, Ariel Dorfman, and Zbigniew Herbert. Furthermore, she notes how crucial the language of spiritual and religious experience has been to many poets who have been impacted by political violence. Poets who wrote as differently as Akhmatova, Wilfred Owen, and Edmond Jabès disclose the pull of religious sentiment. Jabès, for example, opens himself to the "paradox of God's existence in the face of His apparent disappearance"—an idea that Forché reminds us has its origins in Kabbalah.

Quite opposite to diNord's claims, Forché's introduction reveals that the catholicity of her perspectives is also defined by her willingness to see how both New Critical concepts of paradox and irony, for example, and Frankfurt School cultural criticism inform our understanding of poems of witness. Quoting Theodor Adorno in *Minima Moralia*, she notes something about the terrain of harsh complexities with which the reader of the anthology will be forced to wrestle: "There is no longer beauty or consolation except in the gaze falling on horror, withstanding it, and in unalleviated consciousness of negativity holding fast to the possibility of what is better."[1]

Any fruitful dialogue with *Against Forgetting* should begin with an understanding of the basic premise of the anthology, which is a literary-historical one, with a geopolitical layer that Forché has added. In the geohistorical grouping of poets in the anthology, Forché asks the reader to engage in a relationship between poetry and culture-specific histories of political events, to which she refers as "extremity": genocide, war, torture, political exile, and so on. Thus, the anthology does not proceed to present poets by a chronology of birth dates and or literary-aesthetic movements (romanticism, modernism, postmodernism, etc.) as most anthologies do, but rather by culture, geopolitical situation, and history. The anthology opens with the following sections: "The Armenian Genocide," "World War I," "Revolution and Repression in the Soviet Union," "World War II," "The Holocaust," and on through various historically defined epochs, events, and periods down through "Repression in Africa," and "The Struggle for Democracy in China."

For traditional literary historical thinking about poetry, this comes as a strange and, I think, somewhat edgy idea, perhaps more so in the early 1990s than today. Forché urges the reader to think about the poem and the poet as having emerged from historical contexts and political events. In looking at her table of contents, the reader sees works of sophisticated imagination as more than just works evolving along a chronology of birth dates and brief biographies or literary and aesthetic movements (though these are, of course, vital to understanding the poet and her or his work). Forché asks her readers to take it a little further. She suggests that, at the end of a century in which about 150 million lives were lost in war, genocide, and human rights atrocities, it might be worth our while to conceptualize literary history in an augmented way. However, in this augmented literary-cultural view, the *relationship* between poetry and extremity, she makes clear, is fluid, open-ended, and multifarious. But she insists that if we refuse to historicize poetry in this more expansive way, we lose some of its essential significance, and we ignore some of what is most profound about some of the most compelling and large-visioned poetry of our time or any time.

When deNiord asserts that "whether the effects of contemporary poets endure as both topical and ageless answers is the mystery of legacy and not the poet's business," he seems to be suggesting that literary history is not made by human minds. Surely this anthology—and most anthologies, for that matter—reminds us that literary history and its legacy is made by editors, writers, and anthologists who live and write *in historical time*. There is no mystery about it, only choices made in accord, most often, within a complex cultural value system. In this case, the anthology is a presentation of poets whose lives have been shaped by political events and geographical locations that are significant enough to articulate as an important context for poems that are rich and complex.

Finally, I would add that the sheer cosmopolitanism of *Against Forgetting*—its global and international breadth—allows the reader in English to gain some insight into how similar episodes of mass violence and disaster have been absorbed by poets in cultures as different as Pakistan and China, Vietnam and South Africa, Poland and Great Britain. The cosmopolitanism of *Against Forgetting* is as impressive as anything I know in print today, and I suspect the anthology may offer us more translations of high quality in more languages than any anthology now in print. It seems true, as well, that *Against Forgetting* has brought together in an unusual way various kinds of anthologies that we have seen in the past two decades: the *Faber Book of Political Verse*, the numerous anthologies of the poetry of national literatures in translation (Armenian, Hungarian, Korean, Mexican, Polish, Russian, etc.), and certain anthologies defined by catastrophic events, such as John Stallworthy's *Oxford Book of War Poetry*, or Catherine Reilly's *Chaos of the Night: Women's Poetry and Verse of the Second World War*. Of the 144 poets in the anthology, many—like Auden, Pound, Miłosz, Mandelstam, and Yeats, for example—are major figures, while many others are less well known, and still others virtual discoveries for the reader in the United States. In this sense, it is broad reaching and seems to me to be a groundbreaking book, and certainly one that is never simply topical. Throughout,

Forché brings us poems of complex, rich, accomplished transformations, but she is never totalizing in her aesthetic choices.
Conceptual, open-ended, abrasive, antipoetic, traditional, formal,
sensual, lyrical, private, civic, graphic, abstract—are all aspects of
form and sensibility that define the poetry of *Against Forgetting*.

So why the attack? I'm forced to wonder if Forché's anthology has become a scapegoat for some American poets who feel
a growing anxiety about their place in the current landscape of
contemporary poetry. Is the idea of poetry grounded in cultural
locale and perhaps at times in events of political mass violence
or human rights disasters offensive to a certain American sensibility? Is there still an academically driven genteel sensibility
that demands that poetry be only attentive to the self's inner
life, to the freshness of the natural world, the domestic space, or
to a metaphysical sublime? These are all important dimensions
of human experience, and they are always part of poetry's reach.
But surely not the *only* part of poetry's reach. I wonder if the
impulse to eschew poetry's relationship to history and to mass
and historical violence is a lingering vestige of American intellectual life of the early twentieth century, a late Victorianism in
which American anxiety about cultural sophistication led poets
and their critics to embrace the sublime, the self-consciously aesthetic, and the romantically personal—what David Perkins once
called "an earnest pursuit of culture and a quasi-religious pursuit
of spiritual idealism."[2] In many nations, societies, and cultures,
the political and the aesthetic are at home with one another;
the engagement with collective violence and an immersion in
personal love or domestic life exist in balance. Avant-garde aesthetic performance is enmeshed with political turmoil; inventive
language and social facts create each other. Why is American
poetry culture different? Or is it different?

I also wonder if Forché's attentiveness to poets of foreign
cultures who have emerged with sometimes epic insights into
life on the planet, and often with rich and powerful and urgent
language, is threatening to some American poets. Is there some
xenophobic resentment toward poets from embattled cultures,

often poor and many miles from the United States? When de-Niord asserts that American poets should sit at home and envision their audiences as Whitman and Dickinson once did, with "a kind of mystical presence in the quiet of [their] work place," I'm wondering which Whitman and Dickinson he's thinking about. Among dozens of Whitman's poems, "The Wound Dresser," for one, reminds us of how brilliantly Whitman engaged the impact of war, the gruesome and the real, with an unflinching language that demanded the poem ingest the harsh world in an age when the vapid rhetoric of Tennyson's "Charge of the Light Brigade" was the more popular response to war and mass killing. And, Whitman like most of the poets in this anthology also wrote about love, death, and intimate and domestic experience.

>>><<<

In thinking about *Against Forgetting* and Forché's notion of poetry of witness over the years, I want to revisit the term or rubric—*poetry of witness*—and ask how useful it is. It has become a phrase or term that suggests a certain orientation of the poem and the poet, but perhaps it's both too narrow *and* too general to encompass the claims that are made in its name. It's worth noting that *witness* in its biblical etymology points to the idea of truth telling; hence, to bear false witness is to belie the truth, to lie, to not witness honestly. The ninth commandment in *Exodus* reminds us that "bearing false witness" is an ethical violation; false reports are bad. Witness suggests the importance of what is being told, the importance of the facts, the event, the circumstance that the one witnessing conveys. The poet who can be said to witness an event of historic violence is not a historian or journalist, but his or her poem does aspire to convey something of truth about the event, something that is urgent and perhaps with ethical implications. One can be a witness to a wedding, a baptism, a funeral; intimate love with another; one can witness spiritual truth in God, transcendent feeling, divine truth; and one can witness a violent event or a civic or collective catastrophic event—war, genocide, the terrorism of totalitarian regimes. If one means that *to witness* is to signify the telling of something truthful about collective, historical events of violence, then the witnessing of such human experience needs more exploration, consideration, and, finally, a clarification that might allow us to see what poetry's relationship to violent, collective-historical events might be.

Poems that engage a notion of witness are most often tied to an event that is defined by mass violence (war, genocide, massacre, state torture, etc.), and it is an event that happens to more than an individual because it happens to a culture group, nation, or community. Thus, the event accrues the breadth of a collective history and experience, and the memory of the event can accrue a collective sense of identity. But the notion of *witness*, while useful, is, I think, too general. The idea of such a poetic orientation becomes clearer and deeper if we see the poem as lyric language that is capable of ingesting violence and registering, somewhere in its complex and layered structure, some tremors of trauma or manifestations of traumatic memory.

Even if Elaine Scarry, in her groundbreaking book *The Body in Pain*, has suggested that pain and torture undo language and that torture is "anterior to language" and "speech,"[3] I would argue that the poem is able to ingest in inventive ways some dimensions of pain, no matter how transmuted and metamade or metaphorized. The poem is able to embody both the pain of the body and the pain of the mind and soul in relation to an encounter with or a memory of collective violence. But here some awareness of trauma is necessary to make sense of poetry's ambitious reach in the realm of witness.

For some poets who have engaged violence and who are tied to the event by visceral experience, the poem of witness can take on what Lawrence Langer calls "deep memory," "anguished memory," or "humiliated memory"—three layers in the cambium of the mind's groping after threads and shreds and filaments of the event. Of this kind of traumatic memory, Langer notes: "If *anguished memory* may be seen as discontent in search of a form, *humiliated memory* recalls an utter distress that shatters all molds designed to contain a unified and irreproachable image of the self."⁴ Poems of witness are often shaped by this kind of interior movement; they are propelled by a restless search for adequate or inadequate ways of *shattering the mold* in seeking ways to embody the trace of the event, and this can happen in more formal poems or in self-consciously open forms. Paul Celan's open-formed modernism in "Death Fugue," for example, is no more of an authentic trauma witness mode than Primo Levi's plain-style homily "Shema."

"Because the event is not assimilated or experienced fully at the time," writes Cathy Caruth, "but only belatedly, only in aftermath in its repeated possession of the one who experiences it . . . to be traumatized is to be possessed by an image or event."⁵ The poet possessed by some dimension of trauma is also oriented to thinking in images and thus being possessed by them. Caruth continues by noting that post-traumatic stress disorder "is not so much a symptom of the unconscious as it is a symptom of history," and I think this idea intersects with the reach of poetry. "The traumatized," Caruth continues, "carry an impossible history within them, or they become themselves the symptom of a history that they cannot entirely possess."⁶ Whether this is true for all traumatized people I can't say, but for the poet it seems more fully to the point that imagination is a manifestation of both history and the unconscious, and, of course, the conscious manipulation of language under pressure in either formal or more open forms.

Caruth and others have noted that traumatic memory returns in images, dreams, hallucinations, and fragmentary moments, and this, too, is, of course, organic to poetic imagination, although I don't want to make any simplistic correlations between the traumatized individual and the poet at work in his or her strange web of linguistic inventions. Nevertheless, the point is: The poem that witnesses, the poem that ingests violence can move along the frequencies of traumatized memory in the skin of its own craft and make new and/or arresting waves of language—bald, graphic, plain, clear, encoded, elliptical, symbolic, and so on. There are no formulaic, co-opting forms or strategies for ingesting violence or witnessing collective traumatic events. Thus, any effort to make sense of something like "the poem of witness"—or, better, I think, the poem that ingests an event of collective violence—needs to engage some notion of trauma and traumatic memory. With this perspective, we can understand the poem's aesthetic transformations, in part at least, in relation to the traumatic dimensions of memory.

There are no formulas for traumatic memory in poetry; the poem can open itself to violence in various ways and forms—in part, the poet's willingness to contemplate the event defines the poem's relationship to witnessing and traumatic memory. And while there is the memory of the poet who lived through the event, there is also a witnessing and memory of the poet who has come along after the event, and this is, as Marianne Hirsch has called it, "post memory"—a remembering and imagining that emanates from a writer who may be born *after* the event but is compelled to be connected *to* the event.[7] Perhaps Homer and the Trojan War, and Shakespeare and the history of English kings from the late thirteenth century to the early sixteenth century are the most celebrated literary records of postmemory. Clearly, the willingness simply to take on the event does not mean the poem will be greeted with critical interest, nor is there is any aesthetic virtue in the poet's taking on the event. The poet's ability to transform the experience with her or his form and language, the poem's ability to render something fresh, arresting, sustained, is as necessary for this kind of poem as for any kind of poem.

There is a broad range of poetry in *Against Forgetting*, sometimes so broad that many of the poems are responses—sometimes too general, broad, personal—to events of collective violence, mostly to war and to regimes of political repression whether in the former Soviet Union, China, or South Africa. Not all of these poems are defined by traumatic memory or intrusions of violence, but in the most traumatized and aesthetically successful imaginations among the poets in *Against Forgetting* one finds remarkable transformations and language force—in short, poems of unusual depth and significance.

I want to look at a few poems from among the several hundred in the anthology as a way to suggest the range of lyric and imaginative strategies and sensibilities of poets who have written about mass violence and historical disruption, trauma and traumatic memory. Czesław Miłosz's "Dedication" is a meditation on aftermath, and the coda, "Warsaw, 1945," situates us in time and place—at the end of World War II; after enormous ruin, Miłosz wrestles with what poetry might be or mean. The poem moves in its sober, calm syntax as an address to the dead. Miłosz does what few poets can: He makes ideas, often complex ones, into lyrical language, with elegant rhythms; and here he engages history's paradoxes: "What strengthened me, for you was lethal. / You mixed up farewell to an epoch with the beginning of a new one." In the ruins of aftermath, traumatic memory is like a clear aerial-like view over a landscape: "Here is a valley of shallow Polish rivers. And an immense bridge / Going into white fog. Here is a broken city; / And the wind throws the screams of gulls on your grave." Having built his context, he raises the issue of poetry:

> What is poetry which does not save
> Nations or people?
> A connivance with official lies,
> A song of drunkards whose throats will be cut in a moment,
> Readings for sophomore girls.
> That I wanted good poetry without knowing it,
> That I discovered, late, its salutary aim,
> In this and only this I find salvation.

For Miłosz, the possibility of "good poetry" is salvational, and in the face of great violence—after Nazi and Soviet invasion and occupation, war, and genocide—he situates poetry as a force of aesthetic and moral significance, at least for himself. As for his big, rhetorical question about "Nations or people?" he claims that poetry can, at least, demand that language have integrity and not be a "connivance with official lies." And from that premise, the poem addresses destructive power and mass violence.

From another perspective, the French poet Robert Desnos,

who worked in a surrealist mode with its freer associations and more ribald, grotesque language creates his "Ars Poetica" as, in part, a response to a world dominated by violence and torture. While the poem was part of Desnos's final book, completed just before his arrest by the Nazis in 1944, it seems prescient. He spent time in several concentration camps before he ended up in Terezin, where he died of dysentery two days after the liberation in 1945. For all the assertions that critics have made about this poem's surrealist automatism and unconscious manifestations, it's also a poem of radical inclusivity, one that takes Whitman, Pound, and Neruda to a place of contemporary witness. As the poem witnesses the self making its art, it also insists on ingesting the awful world, and it makes an insignia for poetic imagination in a new era of mass violence.

> Across the snout
>
> Picked up in the mud and slime
> Spit out, vomited, rejected—
> I am the verse witness of my master's breath—
> Left over, cast off, garbage
> Like the diamond, the flame, and the blue of sky
> Not pure, not virgin, but fucked to the core
> Fucked, pricked, sucked, ass fucked, raped
> I am the verse witness of my master's breath.

For the poem to ingest the violence and domination of "master," Desnos has created an *ars poetica* that rejects any notion of the genteel imagination. It's a Dada poem in its subversion of convention and its appeal to an antiaesthetic, an anticonvention in its drive for a new language to take on an age of brutality. If death is a "master from Germany" in Celan's "Death Fugue," "death in life" is Desnos's witness, the poet's "master's breath." Desnos's *ars poetica* is an appeal for a new age in which the language of poetry must ingest the full range of the real—with its violence and the abuses of power. In the avalanche of images and associations that make up the one long stanza of the poem, "Ars Poetica" is another version of a breathless encounter with extremity. Like Celan's "Death Fugue," Desnos's "Ars Poetica" expands the poem's reach so that the master's breath of the self witnesses extreme realities in which violence and beauty are not separable: "Good muddy earth where I set my foot," he says,

> I ride the wind, the great wind and the sea
> I am the verse witness of my master's breath
> That cracks farts sings snores
> Great storm-wind heart of the world
> there is no longer a foul weather
> I love all the weather I love the time
> I love the high wind

Desnos's poem wants to swallow the whole, big, bloody mess: "Let it break your teeth and make your gums bleed."

Georg Trakl's poems of trench war experience are transmuted by a German expressionist sensibility that finds in nature a correlative for the emotional. In his "In the East," nature is an evocative source of pathos and irony, landscapes of war are rendered with painterly emotion, and death infuses the world, as the violence-shaded world hunts down the innocent: "From bloody doorsteps the moon / hunts terrified women."

> The dark wrath of people
> Is the wild organ music of a winter storm,
> A purple wave of battled,
> Leafless stars.
>
> With broken eyebrows and silver arms,
> The night beckons to dying soldiers.
> Ghosts of those killed moan
> In the shade of the autumn ash tree.
>
> A thorny wilderness surrounds the city.
> From bloody doorsteps the moon
> Hunts terrified women.
> Wild wolves have broken through the gates.

In a similar way, Russian futurism inflects Velimir Khlebnikov's "It has the unassuming face of a burnt-out candle." Khlebnikov fought both for the Bolshevik and czar's army during the Russian Revolution, and his ingestion of violence is rendered in a viscid and sensual language as it embodies the political and natural landscape, in lines and images that fuse and infuse violence with the natural world. The wild intersection of visceral images creates a sense of dynamism, not of Filippo Tommaso Marinetti's excited modernity, but of the apocalyptic and the devouring of the war-infused landscape. Khlebnikov gives us big swaths with painterly brushstrokes:

> It has the unassuming face of a burnt-out candle
> Fire-eye, lacking its lashes
> of downpour and rain.
> It burned our fields, our land,
> whole populations of stalks and grain
> shaken like straw.
> The fields grew smokey and the grain turned
> yellow as death and fell.
> The grain shriveled and mice ate it.
> Is the sky sick? Does the sky hurt?
> Where are its watery lashes?

Of the many poems that ingest the violence of Nazi concentration camps, Edith Bruck's "Father" and Primo Levi's "Shema" offer modalities and strategies that are austere in rhythm and rhetoric. Levi turns the idea of a homily into severe, plain-style (as New England Puritans of the seventeenth century might have put it) language in which the harshness of the image intersects with a moral voice that finds a tenor of outrage in its skillful rhetorical appeal to an uninitiated audience. For a poem that emerges through traumatic memory, Levi appeals to memory as a necessary response to cruelty that, even for a secularist like Levi, is tantamount to evil. In "Shema," the austere voice, while preaching, manages to situate images of traumatic memory with a rhetoric of urgency that makes its ironic play off its title (Shema is the Hebrew prayer of invocation). In the new Shema, the post-Auschwitz Shema, the poet's traumatic memory is a will to posterity, a new dictum for the meaning of memory.

You who live secure
In your warm houses,
Who return at evening to find
Hot food and friendly faces:
Consider whether this is a man,
Who labors in the mud
Who knows no peace
Who fights for a crust of bread
Who dies at a yes or a no.
Consider whether this is a woman,
Without hair or name
With no more strength to remember
Eyes empty and womb cold.
As a frog in winter.

Levi's appeal to historical memory is a command that purports to appropriate the central Hebrew prayer—in which God and Israel are inseparable—with a prayer for the memory of the Shoah.

Consider that this has been:
I commend these words to you.
Engrave them on your hearts
When you are in your house, when you walk on your way,
When you go to bed, when you rise.
Repeat them to your children.
Or may your house crumble,
Disease render you powerless,
Your offspring avert their faces from you.

Other poems ingest violence through more oblique strategies, such as Dylan Thomas's lyrically turgid "A Refusal to Mourn the Death, by Fire, of a Child in London." Thomas wrote the poem from some distance in Wales in 1945, reflecting on having been a fire watchman during the Nazi firebombings of London. His approach to the killing of civilians, especially children, emanates from intensified rhythmic formations and a mythic language. In opening the poem, Thomas invokes a version of a cosmic creation myth that is biblical in its metaphoric girth, and in two stanzas he attempts to sacralize the death of the child and to praise the holiness of life; the death of the child must be savored so both "majesty" and "burning" are synonymous with the "child's death."

Thomas presents us with an anti-elegy in an effort to approach the mass killing of innocence, that same crime that ended Ivan Karamazov's belief in God in Dostoyevsky's novel. The poem tests the responsibility of language to resist cliché in the wake of enormous violence. The traumatic is embodied in the tumultuous rhythms of the lines, the rage embodied in the energized colliding mythic images, and the outraged stance of the poet's cosmic prayer:

> Never until the mankind making
> Bird beast and flower
> Fathering and all humbling darkness
> Tells with silence the last light breaking
> And the still hour
> Is come of the sea tumbling in harness
>
> And I must enter again the round
> Zion of the water bead
> And the synagogue of the ear of corn
> Shall I let pray the shadow of a sound
> Or sow my salt seed
> In the least valley of sackcloth to mourn
> The majesty and burning of the child's death.

The poem's final flourish, the assertion that "After the first death, there is no other," suggests Thomas's conviction that the one death is the embodiment of all the murdered, and in his prayer for the one, he prays for all the others. It's a synecdochal vision and one poet's way of offering a blessing that allows us to feel how an inventive lyricism can ingest the outrage of the poet witnessing the event.

In another zone of conflict in *Against Forgetting*, we find Mahmoud Darwish's "Psalm 2," and encounter an aesthetic that is freer with spoken rhetoric, a more open civic voice, an address to the Palestinian condition of repression and violence.

The poem is defined by a strong sense of an exiled self as part of Darwish's country's predicament and loss. Country and self merge, and psychology and history merge. Self ingests history in a personal way, a mode of rhetoric that no doubt has Arabic sources, but also comes out of a post-Whitman idiom of expansive personal voice entangled with a historical moment.

Country, turning up in songs and massacres,
Why do I smuggle you from airport to airport
Like opium,
Invisible ink,
A radio transmitter?

I want to draw your shape,
You, scattered in files and surprises.
I want to draw your shape,
You, flying on shrapnel and birds' wings.
I want to draw your shape
But heaven snatches my hand.
I want to draw your shape
You, trapped between the dagger and the wind.
I want to draw your shape
To find my shape in yours
And get blamed for being abstract,
For forging documents and photos,
You, trapped between the dagger and the wind.

Darwish internalizes his grief about his lost country and turns his exile into a lens through which to imagine the lost place; self and imagined nation dovetail in an inventive catalog of images that allows us to experience a lost country through metaphor in which the surreal and real hold a balance—"dagger" and "wind," "shrapnel and birds' wings." The idea of exile is embodied in images of trauma rendered in a moment of being smuggled "from airport to airport": "opium," "invisible ink," "a radio transmitter." And the phrase "country turning up in songs and massacres" is the refrain, though it risks large rhetoric that anchors the poet's consciousness, brings the big meaning into the orchestrations of flying images. Thus, self is enmeshed in the violence of history so that the leaps in metaphor have an anchor, and the trauma of exile is wrapped in rhetorical questions.

In one of those zones of history we seldom encounter in modern poetry, Teresa de Jesu's "Proverbs, Chile, 1973 On," we encounter a gnomic list of violent images spliced by gestures that evoke state-sponsored terror.

1) It's altogether something else with shrapnel
2) In closed mouth no bullets enter
3) In the house of the worker: knife & bullet
4) See not, hear not, speak not
5) The mummy, though dressed as a worker, is a mummy still
6) When a mummy sounds off, the shit carries
7) One hand betrays the other & both betray the face
8) One alone shuts up well, but two shut up better
9) The undercover agent who falls asleep gets carried off to Tres Alamos
10) Better one airplane on the ground than a hundred flying
11) Breed soldiers and they'll kill your sons
12) When one cell is shut, two hundred open up
13) By your mouth you die
14) Don't look a gift Mercedes in the teeth

The lines move between aphoristic witticisms and evocations of brutality. The numbered list compresses the poet's sense of traumatic moment in a minimalist way as to suggest life under pressure, the covert act of testifying to what is happening in her nation. The accretion of the list sustains a particular tension so that one comes to feel that even in times of state-sponsored violence—torture, arbitrary imprisonments, mass killing—oracular truths allow us a deeper understanding about arbitrary political power and terror. In their pithy images, de Jesu's lines ingest violence in their terse phrases, and the images upend the unexpected. The poet's approach to the traumatic slides along an axis of aphoristic assertions, but it is the absence of self, the egolessness of the poem that allows the ubiquity of the violence to be felt, the state of the state to assume its presence in that proverb list.

>>><<<

In taking in violent events and traumatic aftermaths, poetry offers no answers, but it does offer meaning and insight—and that can be redemptive or, even as Miłosz suggests, salvational. A poem allows clarity and imaginative depth in the face of forces that have sought to destroy natural and human order and, perhaps, what one might call the guideposts or ethics of civilized social order.

After Auschwitz, Adorno sensed that there should be a new kind of poetry, as the violence of Auschwitz would have to prompt the human imagination to reconsider and reflect more deeply on human experience and the meaning of history, to change its relationship to the world. I believe that the kind of poems that ingest violence, as these poems do, can have their sacramental meanings. No matter how horrible the realities they embody, these poems give us an aftermath of consciousness that allows us to understand something—personal, intimate, social, collective—about the impact episodes of mass violence leave on the landscapes we inhabit.

In this way, the poem that ingests violence also provides us with a form for memory that captures something of the traumatic event that has passed. Poetry's appeal to chant and prayer, song and psalm, whether in traumatic memory or postmemory, whether oblique and symbolistic or plain and homily-like, continues to return us to the ancient, primary human voice that poems embody. And the poem, of course, catches the event of violence in its own music, in its peculiar qualities of rhythm, in the web of language-sound that syntax creates, so that a peculiar kind of language might get stuck in the ear as it gets spun in the brain. In the lyric memory that poetry can provide, the speech-tongue-voice of the poem leaves its imprint on a historical aftermath, and it becomes one of our truest records of history, as well as an enduring embodiment of knowledge.

Theodore Roethke's Lost Son and the Confessional Era

Almost a half century after his death, it seems fair to say that the meandering shape of Theodore Roethke's career has obscured some of his best and most important work. His modest first book of 1930s formalist poems, *Open House* (1941), owed something to both W. H. Auden and the academic style of a certain strain of American poetry that in many ways was antithetical to modernism. Immediately after in the early 1940s, he dove into modernist techniques claiming William Carlos Williams as an American-grain inspiration, and using Joyce and Faulkner as poetic wellsprings. But by the early 1950s, Roethke would leave his modernist experimental phase for a passionate embrace of a kind of Yeatsian formalism in which his poems were characterized by strung iambic rhythms across pentametric lines as he performed spiritual and erotic quests. The poems were met with critical praise and earned him a Pulitzer Prize and a National Book Award.

But by the end of the 1950s he had exhausted that idiom and veered back to something more fully and sensually American in taking up a long Whitman line for his beautiful late poems "The North American Sequence." Then there was one last blast of spiritual quest in the formalist poems of "Sequence, Sometimes

Metaphysical." Then he was suddenly gone. One Sunday morning at a friend's house on Bainbridge Island near Seattle, where he was teaching at the University of Washington, after having mixed a batch of cocktails for a brunch, he dove into the swimming pool and died of a heart attack upon hitting the water. He was fifty-five.

Looking at the course of Roethke's work, one might say that he was jumping from the American ship to the Anglo-Irish ship and back, in ways that energized him; he seemed compelled to be a part of two literary cultures, to perform for two traditions and audiences. The mentorship of Auden and Williams, the forefathering of Yeats and Whitman seem to embody the double arcs of Roethke's sensibility. Whether this best served his career in the canon-making order of things will always be something for scholars to argue over.

But reading and assessing Roethke in the twenty-first century, and looking back at the evolution of poetry after the modernist experiments of the first part of the twentieth century and the evolution of a more intimate, personal, confessional voice of the post–World War II era (an orientation that still defines a large sensibility of contemporary American poetry), Roethke appears as an innovative bridge between modernism and the poetry written since World War II. As a nexus between the two literary eras, Roethke's most important achievements are his greenhouse and lost-son poems of the 1940s and early 1950s. In those poems, he found ways of forging a new kind of intimate voice—private and physiological with mythic sources and a numinous sense of nature.

It is the Roethke of the mid-1940s who found his way to a new language in a time, for him, that was marked by a new linguistic freedom and discovery; he had found his own source, or the myth of his life, the "legend of youth," as he put it, in his childhood landscape of Saginaw, Michigan, where his father and uncle owned several hundred acres of greenhouses and nurseries. In this odd, unlikely place of ordinary family business and exotic botanical profusions, Roethke found something unique and rich that he would probe and mine for all he could for the rest of his life. From this grounding and location, he created the compressed, lyric, and sometimes vestigially formalist greenhouse poems, and the longer, more protean, open-form lost son cycle of thirteen poems, which he completed with the final poem "O Thou Opening, O," which appeared in *The Waking* (1953).

›››‹‹‹

Various scholars have noted a shift in American poetry that became apparent by the mid-1950s and marked an end to what can be seen as a final phase of modernism that was ossifying into something academic, formalistic, and overly mythy.[1] Allen Ginsberg's *Howl* (1956) and Robert Lowell's *Life Studies* (1959) were important for their rejection of a kind of autotelic, symbolistic poetry that came out of late modernism. Ginsberg and Lowell, later Sylvia Plath and Adrienne Rich, then John Berryman and many others would find release and invention in breaking down the barriers between the idea of the poem—the text-artifice—and the idea of the life: the lived experience, the traumatically worn psyche, the painful or joyous manifestation of the real. American poems of the later 1950s and 1960s were a departure from the passion for mythic structures and Eliotic notions of impersonality ("the poem Eliot insisted should be a 'flight from the self'") that dominated modernism.

That Ginsberg, Lowell, and Plath could now utter lines like "who were fucked in the ass by saintly motorcyclists," or "my mind's not right," or "Daddy, Daddy, you bastard, I'm through" would have baffled or revolted Eliot, Stevens, or H.D.; they would have found such language outside of the realm of the poem as they understood it. The new confessional orientation was embodied in a poetics that appropriated a more intimate and transparent sense of autobiography; it was created out of a personal mask that was forged from an idea of intimacy, and, correspondingly, the poems were made of a language that was more demotic, more colloquial, more inflected by pop culture. Frank O'Hara, John Ashbery, and others associated with the New York School also made a poetics of this.

This new aesthetic orientation was grounded in experience that was located in the personal realm, a realm that went beyond interior consciousness (after all, Mallarmé was a kind of poet of the interior) but defined itself with a bold and visceral idea of a self located in the daily life and domestic space of stress and trauma, and often in a domain in which the dynamics of family became a location for self, history, and culture. Such an aesthetic orientation informed not only the Eastern establishment poets, like Lowell, Berryman, and Plath, but also the Beat and Projectivist poets, the new feminists, and the Black Arts poets. In the way that classical myth and Western intellectual history were essential to the modernist poet, the domestic, the personal, and the family-historical—or some variant of personally inherited history—became central to a post–World War II poetic orientation.

I would attribute some of this to the impact of World War II, the genocide of the Jews of Europe, and the inauguration of the nuclear age. Such catastrophe and cataclysm created some new assumptions about history, human identity, and, correspondingly, aesthetic orientations. Perhaps Norman Mailer's sense of the significance of the new mass violence gets at some of the impact of Word War II on consciousness and culture. "We will never be able to determine the psychic havoc of the concentration camps and the atom bomb upon the unconscious mind of almost everyone alive in these years. For the first time in all of history, we have been forced to live with the suppressed knowledge . . . that we might still be doomed to . . . a death by deus ex machina in a gas chamber or a radioactive city."[2] Some of the modernist impulses concerning the meaning and viability of a shared idea of Western civilization and its mythic structures and history had been shaken and challenged. The kinds of big myth structures and texts that girded *The Waste Land, The Cantos, Trilogy,* or *The Bridge* became less meaningful, or less usable, or less urgent for the poets of the post–World War II era. It seems to me that Western mythic structures got transmuted into historical sensibilities that were more personal, familial, and intimate. There was no loss of historical value, only now a cultural past was subsumed in a familial story or legend or myth, and so poems like Roethke's "The Lost Son," Ginsberg's "Kaddish," and Lowell's sequence in *Life Studies* became a new way of appropriating and encoding history, a new mode of inscripting the self in time and place, or locating the intimate self in a nexus of cultural crisis. Such poems can be called seminal family cycles of the new confessional era, and they were revolutionary. Roethke, Lowell, Ginsberg, and later Plath, Berryman, Anne Sexton, and others transformed autobiographical and familial sources to shape myth out of a historical context and their particular family pasts.

Lowell appropriated his family's aristocratic Protestant New England past as the source for his self-definition. Ginsberg cataloged and probed his mother's Russian Jewish socialist childhood and her émigré experience. Roethke used the seemingly mundane events and landscapes of his German émigré family in central Michigan and their greenhouse and horticultural business. In each case, the idea of a familial historical configuration became context for a self shaped by an intimate voice. It was a dramatic veering away from mythic and cultural modernism.

In various ways, the poets of the post–World War II era absorbed, in conscious ways, traumatic dimensions of personal and familial experience as well as the historical earthquakes that they inherited in the postwar aftermath. If, as Cathy Caruth has noted, "to be traumatized is precisely to be possessed by an image or an event,"[3] then the poets of the postwar era found image in event and event in image in poems that encompassed a new relationship between the personal and the historical. Poems like "Heart's Needle," "Kaddish," "For the Union Dead," "Daddy," "Cut," and many of Berryman's *Dream Songs*, such as "The Lay of Ike," "Vietnam," and others, made inventive relationships between history (the Korean War, the Holocaust, the civil rights movement in Little Rock, Arkansas, the Cold War) and trauma. And trauma as a psycho-poetics became also a Freudian encounter with Oedipal and Electra complexes and confrontations. Again, Roethke, Ginsberg, Plath, Lowell, Sexton, Berryman, and many others took on issues that dealt with painful family and parental crises. Trauma, then, for the confessional mode was simultaneously historical, political, and personal.

By the 1960s, the new orientation toward the personal-familial, confessional-intimate, vernacular, taboo-breaking voices were dominant, including Amiri Baraka, James Dickey, James Wright, Robert Bly, Richard Hugo, Ashbery, James Schulyer, O'Hara, and Denise Levertov. Lowell put it well when he noted of his own career swerve of the 1950s that his early poems written under the influence of Eliotic modernism now seemed to him "stiff, humorless, impenetrable . . . prehistoric monsters dragged down into the bog and death by their own ponderous armor."[4] He felt his poems had become "purely a craft," and there "needed to be some breakthrough back into life." However, this sense of breakthrough into life (however complex and layered that notion might be) that was defining the new confessionalism had already gurgled up in Roethke's book *The Lost Son and Other Poems*, published in 1948 before "confessionalism" had been branded as an aesthetic orientation for a new era.

In his groundbreaking book, Roethke's particular brew of Freudian and Jungian forces was essential to the shape of both the greenhouse poems and the longer five-section poem "The Lost Son," the first of thirteen poems that would make up the long poem cycle *Praise to the End.* The poems were grounded in a personal, confessing voice that owned up to a kind of psychic pain, a repressed neurosis that Roethke had already embraced in the pathological tropes in his early poem "Open House," in which he exclaimed:

My secrets cry aloud.
I have no need for tongue.
My heart keeps open house,
My doors are widely swung.
An epic of the eyes
My love, with no disguise.

My truths are all foreknown,
This anguish self-revealed.
I'm naked to the bone,
With nakedness my shield.

Myself is what I wear:
I keep the spirit spare.

The anger will endure,
The deed will speak the truth
In language strict and pure.
I stop the lying mouth:
Rage warps my clearest cry
To witless agony.

It's a bald, blueprint of a poem about poetry as an art for the confessing self and its pent-up anguish. That early, Roethke was declaring his need to be personal and psychological in a way that would be a kind of motto for what would define a good bit of the postwar confessional idiom.

Roethke's intimate voice in *The Lost Son and Other Poems* grew out of traumatic, painful experience. Unlike his modernist predecessors, he didn't impersonally sublimate his psychic pain, but disclosed it in the voice-utterance of the poem. If emotional trauma and psychic pain underlie poems like "Prufrock," "The Broken Tower," or "Sunday Morning," the reader can't locate Eliot's, or Crane's, or Stevens's personal sources of suffering or grievance—there's no personal identity standing up for it. The new Roethkean mode would push off in a different direction, transforming impersonality into a psychological self that bore the imprint of personal vulnerability and intimacy.

>>><<<

The poems were written between 1943 and 1947, when Roethke was on leave from teaching at Penn State and a writer-in-residence at Bennington College in southeastern Vermont, where he was teaching and mostly writing in a community of artists and writers. The community included several writers who would later become influential: Stanley Kunitz, Bernard Malamud, Stanley Edgar Hyman, and Kenneth Burke among them. It was during this "genesis-interlude of great change," as his friend and colleague Jim Jackson put it, that Roethke found his new sources.[5] Living alone there (except for when Kenneth

Burke joined him on semiweekly stays), on campus in a small house called Shingle Cottage, Roethke taught each semester, played as much tennis as possible, read deeply in psychology and mysticism, and "talked endlessly of the long poem" (the lost son sequence), Jackson remembered. Jackson also recalls that when Roethke wasn't teaching, he was writing at the cottage, drinking too much, often to medicate his manic states, and wandering around the cottage naked several times a day in the privacy of his yard. Jackson called these "complex birthday suit rituals" and saw them as rituals of self-birthing and "casting one's skin like a snake and then donning the skin again." Jackson insists there was no exhibitionism in it; "no one saw, it was all a kind of magic."[6] Whether anyone saw, and apparently Jackson did, there was self-dramatization in these performances, and there was a cultivation of self and persona, even if private, that was essential to Roethke's breakthrough into his new thing.

In the midst of working on the lost son cycle near the end of 1945, Roethke entered a phase of manic behavior that was certainly bound up in the excitement and exhaustion of the work on the poems. Just after Christmas, he was taken by his friends Jim Jackson and Mary Garrett across the state border to Albany General Hospital, where he was given electroshock treatment and spent weeks recuperating before he returned to the family house in Saginaw to regain his health. Using phenobarbital (supplied by Jackson) to continue to calm his manic behavior, he worked on all four of the long poems ("The Lost Son," "A Field of Light," "The Long Alley," and "The Shape of the Fire") for the next few months on the grounds of the old greenhouses. By May, Roethke was far enough along to send a copy of a manuscript of the book to William Carlos Williams, who had been one of his new, staunch supporters.

>>><<<

Roethke's childhood in his father's greenhouse, his father's death when Roethke was thirteen, and his history of mental breakdowns are the central autobiographical events informing the greenhouse world of the lost son poems. His father's twenty-five

acres of greenhouses in the Saginaw Valley and the hothouse
world of peat moss, plant cuttings, carnations, roses, cyclamen,
and compost organisms was a loamy place out of which Roethke
would find language, shape his mind, and delve into his psychic and familial past. The greenhouse chores that Roethke performed for his father—weeding, moss gathering, planting, and
transplanting—became locations of psychological exploration in
the poems. He defined the greenhouse terrain of his childhood
in his essay "An American Poet Introduces Himself":

> They were to me I realize now, both heaven and hell, a kind of
> tropics created in the savage climate of Michigan, where austere
> German-Americans turned their love to order and their terrifying
> efficiency into something truly beautiful. It was a universe, several
> worlds, which, even as a child, one worried about, and struggled to
> keep alive.[7]

The greenhouse was to Roethke "my symbol for the whole of
life, a womb, a heaven on earth"[8]—that universe of plants under glass was his objective correlative for self-evolution. Because
Roethke also lived much of his adult life with what was then
called manic-depression, for which he was periodically hospital-
ized and on occasion given electroshock treatments, his battle
with mental illness was also a passageway for him into some dimensions of the mind—its breakdowns and highs.

Appropriating these domains of his personal life—his tap-
able autobiography, his particular blend of Freudian and Jungian orientations—allowed Roethke to avoid self-indulgence
for something, as Jung would have it, more universal or archetypal. There was a tension in that blend that was aesthetically
effective and psychologically energizing. Probings of anguished,
neurotic Freudian self and explorations of the archetypal, unconscious Jungian self could overlap and subsume one another,
make a playful or painful dance. Roethke reiterated that "to go
forward [as spiritual man] it is necessary first to go back," and
he claimed that these poems "came from the tapping of an older
memory, something that dribbled out of the unconscious, the

racial memory of whatever it's called."[9] There is something very self-conscious about this raid on the unconscious, but the deeper matter remains that Roethke's immersion in Jungian psychology and his intuitive sense of approaches to the mind or, as he put it, "the psyche under great stress," was an elemental zone for him and gave rise to a new language.

Roethke's innovative psychological brew was inseparable also from his approach to and appropriation of nature. Nature was the stuff and matter through which he could forge a personal voice. For Roethke, nature was botanical and spiritual, the source of childhood and family, and an embodiment of human consciousness. His nature was more Wordsworthian and Emersonian than Frostian, and the kind of correlative for human experience that would be true later for W. S. Merwin and Gary Snyder, or Derek Walcott and Seamus Heaney in their respective organic ontologies. Roethke not only called his greenhouse a "womb, a heaven-on-earth," "a man-made Avalon," but he also mythicized the raw Michigan landscape of his childhood as a primordial place—"the marsh, the mire, the Void is always there, immediate and terrifying"; he called it "a splendid place for schooling the spirit."[10]

To create psychic landscapes, he strove for a more gnomic shorthand, a way to telescope image and symbol, and by telescopic he meant seeing up close, seeing into, and seeing with compression as a way to probe the unconscious. When he wrote in a notebook, "I wanted to write a poem the shape of the psyche under great stress," he was writing an epithet for a poet struggling with bipolar disorder, who understood syntactical compression and image encoding as a mode of probing certain zones of mental life. As he put it:

> I believe that, in this kind of poem, the poet, in order to be true to what is most universal in himself, should not rely on allusion, should not comment or employ many judgment words; should not mediate (or maunder). He must scorn being "mysterious" or loosely oracular, but be willing to face up to the genuine mystery. His language must be compelling and immediate: he must create an actuality. He must be able to telescope image and symbol, if necessary, without relying

on the obvious connectives: to speak in a kind of psychic shorthand when his protagonist is under great stress. He must be able to shift his rhythms rapidly, the "tension."[11]

Roethke's notions of "psychic shorthand" and telescoping allowed him to create a topography of the traumatized mind in motion, and Delmore Schwartz hit on something when he noted: "The reader who supposed that Roethke is really a primitive lyric poet loses or misses a great deal. Perhaps," says Schwartz, "the best way to describe what is under the surface is to quote Valery's remark that the nervous system is the greatest of all poems."[12]

Roethke was enamored of a kind of dramatic rhythm, and the aural kinetics of language was always at the heart of his poems. To Williams he wrote while he was at work on "The Lost Son" that he had written the poem "for the ear and not the eye . . . with the mood or the action on the page, not talked about, not the meditative, T. S. Eliot kind of thing."[13] And he noted influences that were oral and aural, accentuating the intuitive and kinetic: "German and English folk literature, particularly Mother Goose, Elizabethan and Jacobean drama, especially the songs and rants."[14]

>>><<<

As Roethke's new idea of self was inseparable from his remembered primordial, childhood landscape, Norman O. Brown's notion that "mother is mold, modern, matter; Mutter is mud,"[15] became for Roethke—psychologically and aesthetically—a kind of truth. The greenhouse as earth, womb, and nurturer had a rich meaning for a boy whose family made its living growing and selling plants. In a group of poems made of (deceptively) simple, vivid, compulsive, visceral images, Roethke charted a process of growth that began in earth-genesis-time amid the near microscopic life with a telescopic eye.

In those first poems of the greenhouse cycle, over which he labored for several years in the mid-1940s—"Cuttings" and "Cuttings (later)"—botanical growth evokes both sexual and biological processes and preconscious life; the language is made of hard, concrete, alliterative, monosyllabic sounds:

> Sticks-in-a-drowse droop over sugary loam,
> Their intricate stem-fur dries;
> But still the delicate slips keep coaxing up water;
> The small cells bulge.
> One nub of growth
> Nudges a sand-crumb loose,
> Pokes through a musty sheath
> Its pale tendrilous horn.

In "Cuttings (later)," the boy merges the personal voice with a plant cutting in which a vaginal-like birth process and the earth are one:

> I can hear, underground, that sucking and sobbing,
> In my veins, in my bones I feel it,—
> The small waters seeping upward,
> The tight grains parting at last.
> When sprouts break out,
> Slippery as fish,
> I quail, lean to beginnings, sheath-wet.

In the ensuing poems "Root Cellar," "Forcing House," and "Weed Puller," the persona—the lost son—takes shape and evolves through a mysterious and dark world of plant growth and germination. In Roethke's loamy underground world, the unconscious and the ego are undifferentiated; it's a place of rot and decay from which life emerges. Roethke is brilliant at teasing sexual nuance out of his perception of plants and suggesting libidinal forces that belong to a primordial kind of slime, dirt, and compost found in the root cellar, where forces of death and life and, by implication, creativity mingle: "Shoots dangled and drooped, / Lolling obscenely from mildewed crates, / Hung down long yellow evil necks, like tropical snakes."

In "Weed Puller," the boy's growth evolves as he pulls weeds in the greenhouse (a regular chore Roethke performed for his father) and finds a procreative power in the maw of primordial nature with its sexual evocations: the phallic "black hairy roots" and "lewd monkey-tails" growing out of the sensuous, even vaginal-like "fern-shapes, / Coiled green and thick, like dripping smilax." A surprising confessional voice emerges out of the boy's recognition that above him the world is blooming in beauty with "lilies" and "roses" and "whole fields," while he is still on all fours gestating in the primal slime: "The indignity of it!" he exclaims. "Me down in that fetor of weeds, / Crawling on all fours, / Alive, in a slippery grave."

Then, in the more expansive "Moss-Gathering," the lost son remembers himself as an adolescent gathering moss out in the fields for his father (a harvest that was especially important for supplying flowers for funerals and moss for lining funeral baskets). He recalls the sensuality of it, but also feels some guilt about desecrating nature, and so a moment of adolescent self-consciousness defines his sense of alienation between the human world and nature—or what we might now call our ecosphere—and this opens the lost son's voice into a startling confession:

> But something always went out of me when I dug loose those carpets
> Of green, or plunged to my elbows in the spongy yellowish moss of the marshes.
> And afterwards I always felt mean, jogging back over the logging road. . . .
> Disturbed some rhythm, old and of vast importance,
> By pulling off flesh from the living planet;
> As if I had committed, against the whole scheme of life, a desecration.

In "Big Wind," the culmination of the greenhouse sequence, Roethke pares back his line to a kind of free verse trimeter, in which the boy remembers joining the adults during a storm to save the greenhouse from ruin. Since the glass house is the source of the family livelihood, saving it takes on a small epic dimension. The sensuality of memory, the details of greenhouse technology, and the seamless movement from the human struggle against violent nature all allow Roethke to bring together familial past, personal voice, and his kind of Jungian universality.

So we drained the manure-machine
For the steam plant.
Pumping the stale mixture
Into the rusty boilers,
Watching the pressure gauge
Waver over to red,
As the seams hissed
And the live steam
Drove to the far
End of the rose-house,
Where the worst wind was

As the greenhouse survives, Roethke turns it into a ship "sailing until the calm morning, / Carrying her full cargo of roses," and childhood memory glides into a sort of Jungian ark of a metamorphosed greenhouse—an effective fusion of the personal, the traumatic, the familial, and the mythic.

In the greenhouse world, Roethke opened up a confessing voice in tight, precise, sensual poems, but in the cycle of the lost son poems, he took the voice into a complex psychological terrain, unique in various ways to modern poetry. The cycle of poems, which opens with "Where Knock Is Open Wide," an ecstatic phrase taken from Christopher Smart's "A Song to David," suggests a child's journey out of an elemental world of innocence and into a Blakean world of experience: death, grief, loss, alienation. The cycle begins in what Kenneth Burke called the "liquescent realm," a world of infantile consciousness in which Roethke creates an intuitive, nonrational sensibility that moves toward what Burke called a more a purified language in the tradition of Dante, Wordsworth, and Blake.[16]

The poems are anchored in a terra firma of sensory experience that have a dimension of the "polymorphously perverse," to use Norman Brown's phrase, where intuitive knowledge can be erotic and suprarational at once, and the body is open to a multiplicity of erotic and bodily sensations. "Where Knock Is Open Wide," is defined by a child's consciousness that Roethke creates out of a rhythmically compressed, associative language and images that bear Roethke's telescopic notion of image compression and deep seeing:

> A kitten can
> Bite with his feet;
> Papa and Mamma
> Have more teeth.
>
> Sit and play
> Under the rocker
> Until the cows
> All have puppies

Associative, nonlinear perception defines the boy's mind: "I know her noise / Her neck has kittens," or "I know it's an owl / he's making it darker." Even slightly eschatological questions emerge out of naïve language: "Who keeps me last," or "God give me a near," where punning and word play—"near" and "ear"—slide into multiple meanings characteristic of so much of the play of language in these poems.

In the wake of the death of the boy's father, the poem is driven by childhood memory, shaped by the trauma of loss and search for meaning:

> He watered the roses.
> His thumb had a rainbow.
> The stems said, Thank you.
> Dark came early.

Insomnia, restlessness, dreamlike estrangements emerge in pared-down, intuitive, minimalist, telescopically compressed language in the next poem, "I Need, I Need":

> A sneeze can't sleep.
> Diddle we care
> Couldly.

Went down cellar,
Talked to a faucet;
The drippy water
Had nothing to say.

A kind of jumprope, nursery rhyme embodies the lost son's private pain in an encoded language. "It's the spring and rush of the child I'm after," Roethke once said. "Even Steven all is less / I haven't time for sugar / put your finger in your face / and there will be a buger." Or the boy's sexual energy merges with nature.

The green grasses,—would they?
The green grasses?—
She asked her skin
To let me in:
The far leaves were for it.

As the lost son moves with pains and exultations into self-discovery, he slips and slides in primordial landscapes that are both organic and psychological, and sexual: "Touch and arouse / Suck and sob. / Curse and morn," as Roethke's telescopic language dredges up primal urges. In that world of minimal nature and watery landscapes, often swampy, stagnant places, Roethke created his essential emblems of the unconscious, playful and resonant images that strike me as new tropes for modern poetry; as he put it, "that dark pond, the unconscious." His metaphors for the unconscious are always tied to water and primordial nature, as the lost son navigates a world of marshes, ponds, plants, and mud in his labyrinthine journey as these moments suggest: "It's a cold scrape in a low place," "follow me further back / Into that minnowy world of weeds and ditches," "the soft pond of repose," "return the gaze of a pond," "The deep stream remembers: / Once I was a pond," "I've crawled from the mire, alert as a saint or a dog."

Simple syntax, crabbed, cryptic images; sexualized nature, often autoerotic and masturbatory, define the inventiveness of the boy's voice here: "I've left my nose out / I could melt down a stone." Seductive, subliminal desire: "Believe me, knot of gristle, I bleed like a tree." Swashbuckling with wet nature: "I could love a duck," "I've played with the fishes / Among unwrinkling ferns," or in "Praise to the End":

> It's dark in this wood, soft mocker,
> For whom have I swelled like a seed?
> What a bone-ache I have.
> Father of tensions, I'm down to my skin at last.

The anatomy of self here is at once Freudian-ontological-personal in its neurosis and pain and Jungian-phylogenetic-archetypal in the evocations of a broader, more transpersonal notion of self. This kind of compacted confessing voice keeps the self and other (natural world) in healthy tension.

In the masterpiece of the cycle, "The Lost Son," Roethke finds a form to create what he called "the shape of psyche under great stress," a pithy trope for much of his work. Here the traumatized mind implodes the organic world in a way that gives form to what I would call a psychic landscape, in which the lost son ventures into the traumatic mind through the lens of private grief. The poem proceeds from the father's death and the young boy's journey into that grief. The primordial landscapes are cold, wet, dark: "A slow drip over stones, / Toads brooding wells." The landscape is both mythic and sterile: "Fished in an old wound, / The soft pond of repose; / Nothing nibbled my line, / Not even the minnows came." Roethke's abruptly shifting rhythms and frantic movements embody the sense of loss and confusion, and the stagnant, rank, swamplike landscape is so tactile you feel the oozing. A reversion to infantile syntax now takes the form of riddles—that opaque and oracular rhetorical language that pushes the child-initiate, be it a Job or an Oedipus, to confront ultimate questions. The lost son's journey into experience demands a decoding, or a wrestle with this torqued language:

> Where do the roots go?
> Look down under the leaves.

Who put the moss there?
These stones have been here too long.
Who stunned the dirt into noise?
Ask the mole, he knows.

In the next section, "The Gibber," with Roethke riffing on the idea of meaning-encoded gibberish, the lost son is cast out and in Roethke's expressionistic, somewhat biomorphic vision of nature (comparisons with the paintings of Gorky, Stamos, de Kooning, and Frankenthaler are worth noting) becomes hellish, evoking suicidal suggestions: "The weeds whined, / The snakes cried, / The cows and briars / Said to me: Die." Then, in a hallucinatory, nervous-breakdown scene that encodes and alludes to Roethke's own breakdown, hospitalization, and electroshock therapy in late 1946, the poem evokes an institutional scene in which the traumatized self awakes from medication. The lost son recalls "the mouths of jugs / Perched on many shelves" as his "own tongue kissed / My lips awake." From there, the mind bursts into a prose poem-like stanza as syntax, diction, and image are jolting and swirling in one of the more inventive probings of a manic mind in modern poetry.

Let the gestures freeze; our doom is already decided.
All the windows are burning! What's left of my life?
I want the old rage, the lash of primordial milk!
Goodbye, goodbye, old stones, the time-order is going,
I have married my hands to perpetual agitation,
I run, I run to the whistle of money.

Money money money
Water water water

Here the mind searches for meaning in the throes of confusion and primal urges, in the blur of a coherent incoherency. And then, in an arresting minimalist couplet, the dichotomy and tension between "money" (the material/superego/avarice) and "water" (the generative life force of the unconscious), the lost son bangs into fundamental tensions of human experience.

In section four, the way back from near death is through

the greenhouse—through deep, Freudian memory to the earth womb. As Roethke noted, "there is a perpetual slipping back, then a going-forward."[17] Now he remembers a night when as a boy he fell asleep there: "The roses kept breathing in the dark. / . . . There was always a single light / Swinging by the fire-pit." When the father appears in the morning light, his Prussian-ness is evoked as the boy recalls the German word *ordnung* [all's right, all's in order]!: "Ordnung! ordnung Papa is coming!" There's a calm that issues from the father's presence into the final section, "It was beginning winter," in which the unconscious— the primary force of the poem until now—gives way to reason and the ordering mind. The landscape changes from its rank muck to a clear, beautiful place. The lost son now has sight that yields insight—the natural unfolding into something meditative. Out of such seeing comes one of the most beautiful landscapes in modern poetry:

It was beginning winter,
An in-between time,
The landscape still partly brown:
The bones of the weeds kept swinging in the wind,
Above the blue snow.

It was beginning winter,
The light moved slowly over the frozen field,
Over the dry seed-crowns,
The beautiful surviving bones
Swinging in the wind.

Light traveled over the wide field;
Stayed.
The weeds stopped swinging.
The mind moved, not alone,
Through the clear air, in the silence.

Was it light?
Was it light within?
Was it light within light?
Stillness becoming alive,
Yet still?

A lively understandable spirit
Once entertained you.
It will come again.
Be still.
Wait.

Roethke strove throughout his life to find tropes and images for mystical experience. He was vain about his spirituality, calling Eliot "a fraud as a mystic." (Do the enlightened pull rank like that?) But here, Roethke found one of his most moving linguistic configurations for probing the spiritual life: "light" (nature); "light within" (spirit within, or inner light as the Quakers call it); "light within light" (transcendent knowing). Out of trauma, grief, pain, and near disintegration, the lost son comes to a momentary island of clarity and insight. The poem's closing, it might be said, consummates the dialectic and overlay between the unconscious and the rational.

In these compulsively written poems, written during a time of personal crisis and psychological breakthrough in which Roethke enacted an "envagination as home-coming," as Burke put it, Roethke created a new kind of voice—one that is always wrapped in a layer of impersonal forces and myth—while simultaneously accruing a personal voice and a tone of intimate experience. In that nexus between ontogenetic and phylogenetic, Roethke created inventive biomorphic and natural landscapes in which self and nature are correspondingly psychologized and sexualized; in doing so, he managed to keep the confessing voice from self-indulgence or cliché. The best confessors in the decades that followed *The Lost Son and Other Poems* pursued Roethke's approach to the self, even if they often took it to a more personally bald and blunt place.

Hart Crane's Broken Tower

It's difficult to think of a poet in modern American literature who lived as chaotic, excessive, tumultuous, and messy a life as Hart Crane (and there is some good competition). His rough and volatile personal dramas have some analogue in his poems with their aesthetic ambitions, relentless fusions of sensory and metaphysical domains, their synesthesias and impossible goals, which left some of his best poems in linguistic predicaments and uncanny places. I don't mean to suggest any easy correlations between life and art; poems have their overlappings with lived experience, but the poem is always an invention and an imaginative transformation of whatever filaments of experience underlie it.

Hart Crane has been mythologized and romanticized as a Jazz Age extravagant; the drunken, bohemian poet of New York in the 1920s; a post Shelleyian modernist whose impossible conflicts seem to have led to his suicide by jumping off the back of an ocean liner north of Havana around noon on an April day in 1932. He was gay in a time when being gay was still an underground identity; his hookups with sailors and men he met at bars and on the wharfs often led to brawls and fights that left him bloodied and humiliated. And his one heterosexual relationship was a short-lived romance with Peggy Cowley, who was in the process of divorcing her husband Malcolm, and the drama of the relationship was tangled up in Crane's death.

There was nothing romantic about Hart Crane. He was a tortured man who couldn't hold a job, a man whose mental state rocketed between manic and depressive phases and whose emotional impulses and needs consumed him. His poetry bore some imprint of his excesses: a love of extremes, a sensual gluttony, attempts to yoke extremes. When he hit his notes well, the phrase, the line, or the stanza was exquisite; when he missed, his language caved in on itself—clotted, self-indulgent, opaque without payoff. Yet still I find the failed Crane more exciting, challenging, and interesting than most poetry of the era, and his best work a distinctive achievement in modern literature.

Crane's alcoholism often left him penniless, and his nightlife cruising for sailors (and the fights that ensued) sometimes left him in jail. Unable to hold a steady job throughout his twenties, his compulsive traveling in search of sensation and excitement and some hoped-for community led him to France, Spain, the Caribbean, and Mexico. His quests for intensified experience were defined by manic-depressive cycles in which great highs were followed by lows, paranoia, disenchantment, and suicidal threats.

By the age of twenty-nine, his face was ruddy and blistered from alcohol and pugilistic encounters with men at bars or on the wharfs; his hair was prematurely white, his eyes large and intense—all of which were disarming on his otherwise boyish face. For a man in his twenties who had grown up in Garrettsville, Ohio, and had spurned the possibility of going to Columbia University, he had assimilated a vast range of literature, culture, and history, and he was a collector of art who had instinctive anthropological interests in indigenous cultures. He lived by handouts from his friends Waldo Frank and Otto Kahn, and his generous father C. A. (Clarence Arthur) Crane. By the time Crane was at work on the epic poem *The Bridge*, he was living in Manhattan and Brooklyn in the middle of the first modern countercultural decade. His benefactors did their best to keep him housed and fed while he was at work on what they believed would be a groundbreaking epic poem about America, and a poem that would confirm the genius of a rising star.

In the time following the publication of *The Bridge*, Crane's life continued to slide into chaos. Living between bootleggers, speakeasies, and waterfront dives, he was always in debt, so when he received a Guggenheim Fellowship in the spring of 1931, he was eager to leave the country. At first he thought he would go to France again, where he had lived in 1929, much of the time in Paris in a reckless haze of partying, often as a guest of his friends Harry and Caresse Crosby. Harry, the young Bostonian millionaire poet and publisher, had pulled Crane into his circle of drinking, partying, and high living and was so excited about Crane's new epic poem that he contracted to publish *The Bridge* with his then new Black Sun Press in Paris. Looking back at his time in Paris with Harry, Crane recalled "he drank plenty of Cutty Sark and did very little writing." Before Harry could bring out *The Bridge*, he would die in a suicide pact with his lover Josephine Rotch in a Detroit hotel room in December 1929, and Crosby's widow Caresse would publish *The Bridge* the following January 1930.

Crane was planning on returning to France again until he heard from his friend Malcolm Cowley (then best known as a poet), who had just returned from Mexico. Cowley was so taken by the people, the landscape, and the culture that he urged his friend to consider going to Mexico for his Guggenheim year. Convinced by Cowley's passion and bolstered by reading D. H. Lawrence's *The Plumed Serpent*—that vivid sensual story about Lawrence's journey into native Mexican culture—Crane quickly changed his mind, exclaiming: "No, Europe isn't my cure, after all!"[1]

In the time between the publication of *The Bridge* in 1930 and his last poem, "The Broken Tower," in 1932, Crane had been unable to write, and for a poet whose mature writing life was only about a decade, this was a considerable stretch. "The Broken Tower" is one of Crane's most admired poems, and I would call it a signature poem for the realization of his aesthetic aspirations and its transformed sensibility and vision. It's a poem that emerged from a personal moment so dramatic that one might see in it an embodiment of Crane's inner struggles and conflicts as well as his aesthetic aspirations—all of which seem inseparable from his suicide. The situation surrounding Crane's last great poem is so rich with personal drama and cultural context that it's worth recalling the events of his Mexican Guggenheim year as a way into the poem and its expansive vision and language.

The relationship between text and context is always layered and opaque. A poem is never autobiographical in any simple sense; it festers and grows out of personal feeling and possibly a personal moment or situation reassimilated and made through memory and literary invention. The relationship between the text and its configured context can be at times visceral, even empirical; or obscure, oblique, barely discernible. In "The Broken Tower," there is, I believe, an amalgamation of the visceral and the oblique, the personal moment and the poetics of transformation.

His time in Mexico, mostly in Mixcoac (a suburb of Mexico City) and in Taxco (the Tepotzlan sites of Aztec antiquity), were the settings for his last blast of imaginative renewal. It was a moment, for him, of cultural excitement, extravagance, and momentary self-purgation, all of which in various ways intersected with his first sexual relationship with a woman and which led him to feel for the moment that he was no longer an outsider. The poem is in various ways inseparable from Crane's experience of the rituals and dramas of the Christmas and New Year celebrations of 1932 in Mexico—the fusion of Indian and Catholic rituals and performances that exhilarated and transfixed him.

As soon as he arrived in Mexico he began drinking heavily and was even jailed for not paying bar tabs and taxi drivers. Among the American writers in Mexico City at the time, Katherine Ann Porter recalled how Crane, who was staying at her house for two weeks at the start, behaved in erratic ways: He was charming in the morning and loud, self-indulgent, disheveled, and drunk in the evening. His troubles with the law for not paying his bar tabs, for his drunken behavior, and for his affairs with young boys soon got back to the Guggenheim Foundation, and Henry Allen Moe, the secretary of the foundation, quickly wrote Crane a reprimand:

> As you know the Foundation is pretty liberal in dealing with its Fellows; and I have never before written any one of them to tell him to drink less and get to work. Those matters are ordinarily their own affairs. But no Fellow has ever been jailed before either, nor raised public Hell, and that seems to me to make all the difference and to justify this letter. . . . I am not asking for any pledges of total abstinence. I am simply saying you must, and I shall insist on that (because I don't want any bullet [or other] holes in your hide and thereby a diplomatic "incident"; and because I am somewhat concerned that the name of the Foundation continue to stand for high achievement) you stay sober, keep out of jail, and get to work.[2]

Shortly after Crane received this scolding from the Guggenheim Foundation, he received news of his father's sudden death, and he left immediately for the funeral in Chagrin Falls, Ohio. His father's death left a great hole in Crane's life, for in recent years, the two had become close after their tumultuous relationship during his adolescence and early twenties. Crane's father had come to believe in his son's work and had become a staunch financial supporter through his son's continual hard times. After the funeral and short stays in Ohio and New York, Crane returned to Mexico in the early fall of 1931, and he was quickly back to his drinking and carousing with young men. He wrote his friend Mony Grumberg that his sex life was more extensive than ever and that it would "take a book" to describe it.[3]

Throughout the chaos of drinking, nightlife, and stints in jail, his visits to the Aztec cultural sites in the mountains were serious occasions in which site and insight were creating intellectual heat. He was effusive with sensory delight in describing the ancient city of Taxco, as he did in a letter to his friends the Rychtariks: "All 10 cathedrals ablaze with candles, songs. My bed heaped with confetti. Dancing, wine, Courvoisier! Heavenly! And the drive through the mountains!"[4] In these moments, Crane was in his bliss and the world was good. He fell in love with native culture, or at least his idea of native culture: "I still (to date, at any rate) harbor the illusion that there is a soil, a mythology, a people and a spirit here that are capable of unique and magnificent utterance."[5] The same impulses that fueled his Native American visions in *The Bridge* were reignited in Taxco.

The Mexican Indian of Aztec descent had become a Dionysian ideal for Crane, and the allure of Aztec culture fueled his passion for history and the exotica of mythic pasts, and so it is not surprising that his experience in Tepotzlan was mind changing. He arrived a day before the annual festival (mid-September) for the ancient Aztec god, Tepoztecatl—god of wine and revelry and analogue of Dionysius—whose partially destroyed ancient temple looks out on the wide valley. Again, Crane's description reads like note-taking warm-up for writing "The Broken Tower."

We knew nothing about the feast, however, until after sundown one evening a light appeared on the roof of the cathedral where a drum and kind of fife began to sound the most stirring and haunting kind of savage summons. I rushed from the bar where I was drinking tequila—up the dark corridors and the stairways of the church and on to the roof, expecting to be thrown over when I got there, but still too excited to resist.

And what a scene it was! Three or four groups of (mostly the older) Mexicans, totaling not more than 20, were standing with lanterns in their midst, talking together and listening to the music, which continued its pagan and barbaric beat for over two hours at intervals between the ringing of the cathedral bells. Can you imagine the strange, strange mixture, the musicians standing with their faces toward the high dark cliff surmounted by the temple of the old barbaric god that they were propitiating, and stopping every 15 minutes while the sextons rang out the call of the Cross over the same dark valley! Sitting there on the top of that church with the lightning playing on one horizon, a new moon sinking on the opposite and with millions of stars overhead and between and with that strange old music beating in one's blood—it was like being in the Land of Oz. Then rockets would be fired from the parapets of the church—and answering rockets would rise from the dark temple miles away on the cliff, as some of the old faithfuls had climbed up there in the afternoon and were holding a wake until sunrise."[6]

For Crane the festival was not only a dramatic mingling of pagan and Christian sensibilities, but also a trigger for his lyrical and mythic interests. He spent the day with the Indians, digging up the remains of artifacts, drinking a special alcohol-coffee tonic, listening to the legends of Tepoztecatl, then drinking tequila and listening to music and to "those elders who still stuck to their ancient rites despite all the oppression of the Spaniards over nearly 400 years," as he put it.

At five AM the next day, Crane woke and went back to the cathedral to have more coffee and watch the sun rise over the valley as the bells rang, and he called it "such a wild music as I never expect to hear again." The beating of what Crane called "the ancient pre-Conquest Aztec drum" he found primal and thrilling, especially as the sun rose over the valley. And then as the light grew brighter, one of the Indians put the drumsticks into Crane's hand and told him to play, and play he did as he managed to keep the rhythm—and to keep drumming until his arms hurt. Then, at the "astronomical hour of six," he wrote, "the whole place seemed to go mad in the refulgence of full day," as the sextons were ringing the bells "like frantic acrobats" and setting off "a bevy of rockets into the sunrise." After the morning ritual, Crane records that he spent the day swimming in a mountain lake with an Indian, eating beans and tortillas, and meeting with the vicar of the Church; summing it up to his stepmother, he wrote that he had "never left a town feeling so mellow and in such pleasant relations with everybody in the place."[7] For Crane, it was an epiphanous, healing, and integrative moment.

Shortly after his Tepoztecatl experience in Taxco, and after returning to Mexico City in November, he met up with his old friend Peggy Cowley. In Craneian fashion, he showed up in front of her apartment, drunk, shouting at a taxi driver over a fare, disheveled, and dressed in a Mexican costume.[8] Peggy, who had just arrived in Mexico City (and was in the process of a divorce), was horrified to see Crane in such a state and feared that his costume could easily be taken as a mockery of the natives. But their reunion led to an unexpected feeling of closeness and nostalgia for their common past. As Peggy put it later, "we were home to each other. . . . Hart represented to me the family life I had just lost."[9]

In mid-December, Crane resumed his exploration of Mexican cultural rituals and went to witness the Feast of Our Lady of Guadalupe just outside of Mexico City. Once again, he was overwhelmed by the theater of it all: ringing church bells, fireworks, dancing, the music of the flutes and drums, the crowds. For Crane, it brought together Indian and Catholic cultural myths, symbols, and histories. Two weeks later, Crane joined a group of people who went to Peggy's in Taxco for Christmas Eve, but only Crane stayed the night. And then the rest of the week. Spending Christmas and New Year's of 1931–1932 with Peggy Cowley turned out to be reviving—"the pleasantist Christmas and New Year's I remember for some time,"[10] Crane wrote to Malcolm Cowley. Then Crane's chaotic behavior gave way to something new. Amid the euphoria of the festival season, he found with Peggy Cowley his first heterosexual relationship on Christmas night in Taxco with the loud and intermittent ringing of bells from the church in the piazza—as sky rockets streaked the night sky, music played, and people in costumes danced. "It's all a poem," Crane wrote after their first passionate night, "and I shall write it, with us right in the middle of it, darling," and the next morning he exclaimed: "I don't believe it for a moment darling, but be good and tell me it's not a figment of my imagination." In a bar the next day, Crane was boasting: "Boys, boys," he said, "I did it," and then went on to relay the joys of making love and the beauty of Peggy.[11]

A week later, on New Year's Eve, as bells, rockets, fireworks, and pinwheels, made the air a synesthesia of a kind Crane imbibed for his art, he and Peggy strolled arm in arm, and Peggy recalled that "His energy seemed inexhaustible. He was keyed to the highest pitch. It was his first experience in loving a woman and it was somewhat frightening to him. He seems to have found something beyond sensuality; he felt purified of a sense of guilt he had always had as a homosexual." Crane wrote to Peggy: "Your letter of this morning makes me ache for you. Why is it you love me so? I don't deserve it. I'm just a careening idiot."[12]

According to Peggy, Crane started "The Broken Tower" during Christmas of 1931 and worked in a frenzy for three days straight. And his friend Lesley Simpson claims that the poem got a giant catapult upon Crane's return visit to Taxco in late January 1932. There he returned to the scene of his earlier exhilaration amid the thunder of the bells in the plaza of the village where he prevailed on one of his Indian friends to take him up to the bell tower at dawn to swing the clapper of the great bell again. Once again he worked for a few days on "The Broken Tower" without interruption.

By February he was sure he was in love and wrote to tell his friends back home the news. For the moment, Peggy was back in Taxco, and he was hoping to finish "The Broken Tower" back in Mixcoac. Insomniac, in his disheveled apartment there, he wrote all night, listening to his records. He sent fragments of drafts to Peggy, urging her to come to Mixcoac: "I'm just beginning to really write again, the first really interesting bit of poetry in two years" . . . "I'll make you a good husband yet."[13]

Elated by Crane's new energy, Peggy agreed to move in with him, and, for a moment at least, Crane felt that he had found a home and wrote to his stepmother that "being with Peggy is doing me a great deal of good . . . her companionship is removing that exhausting sense of loneliness that has been a handicap to me for years."[14] Although Crane and Peggy gave teas for Guggenheim fellows and made the social rounds, worked in their garden, and read and drank and smoked together on their porch, they also quarreled violently and fought with the servants, and their household was chaotic. In moments when he felt oppressed by the domestic chaos, Crane would burst out: "She thinks she can reform me, does she? I'll show her! Why, Goddamn her, I'd rather sleep with a man any day than with her!"[15]

By March, Crane had slid back into extreme alcoholism and

was expressing his paranoia about his literary reputation and his doubts about his projected reception of "The Broken Tower" by friends and editors. He was drunk, on the streets, spending money recklessly—money he didn't have—on Mexican artifacts and booze. He was jailed again, this time for fighting with an Indian friend over an accusation of a stolen blanket. He flew into rages, lived between extravagant highs and lows, trashing his own place and ranting about being betrayed by Mexico and the Mexicans, and falling deeper and deeper into alcoholic dysfunction. But through it all, he was able to finish "The Broken Tower," and he wrote to Morton Dauwen Zabel that he would be sending it to *Poetry* shortly.

>>><<<

In his short life, Crane's aesthetic goals and principles remained well defined. His well-known letter of 1926 to Harriet Monroe at *Poetry* defending or explaining his poem "At Melville's Tomb," which she had just rejected, remains his most articulate statement about his poetics. However disheveled and chaotic Crane's outer life was, his thinking was cogent and often eloquent. He makes it clear to Monroe in his letter that he wants to explain his theory of metaphor and poetic technique and not simply defend his poem. As he put it, "I am more interested in the so-called illogical impingements of the connotations of words on the consciousness (and their combinations and interplay in metaphor on this basis) than I am in the preservation of their logically rigid significations at the cost of limiting my subject matter and perceptions involved in the poem."[16]

He argues in the letter that the "nuances of feeling and observation" demand that liberties be taken, and while he agrees that there is "fine rationalistic poetry" in our tradition, "there is also much great poetry of another order," as the poetics of Eliot and Blake demonstrate. Crane puts forward his argument for what I think can be called an expressionistic poetics in which emotion, mood, and psychology infuse the image or metaphor. He gives the example of Blake's "a sigh is a sword of an angel king," and

Eliot's "every street lamp that I pass beats like a fatalistic drum." He argues for a kind of metaphor that belongs to another order of experience, one that transcends the more familiar, more rational mode of perception. What's left out in the Eliot lines, Crane points out, is the "unmentioned throbbing of the heart and nerves in a distraught man." Crane's expressionism resides in the nexus of what's left out and the strange colliding impacts of sensory seeing that overlay that absence, so there is expansive, often dramatic presence overlaying the absence; and when this is successful, marvelous leaps and openings occur.

In the most inventive poems of his first book, *White Buildings*, Crane made ingenious ways of fusing images with innuendo and associative meanings. Taking off, it seems to me, on Rimbaud, especially in "The Drunken Boat," he deranged the senses the best he could, slicing and twining, and mashing perceptions into sensuous combinations or clusters that evoke new meanings and synesthesias. As he put it to Monroe, "as long as poetry is written, an audience, however small, is implied, and there remains the question of active or an inactive imagination as its characteristic." Active imagination for Crane meant high-octane language configurations—in his impasto forms, in which a sensory overload of careening and colliding image clusters could produce strange, beguiling, dazzling, sometimes brilliant language and thought, and sometimes overwrought, soggy, mythy moments that contributed to those assertions by critics who see Crane's sensibility as ambitious but failed.

Many of Crane's most memorable and inventive images, lines, and passages make him always worth reading. In his expressionistic, dynamic notion of language, Crane is a high-reaching innovator.

> Down Wall, from girder into street noon leaks,
> A rip-tooth of the sky's acetylene.

Here, as in many moments in *The Bridge*, Crane fuses the industrial and natural—an opening in the sky is a violent cut (a rip-tooth saw), and modernity's atmosphere is flammable invisible gas: "acetylene." It's a distance from Whitman's pure "odorless" "atmosphere" of "the riverbank," but it's still a reach for the sublime. Or take his personification, his vision of the Brooklyn Bridge:

> O harp and altar, of the fury fused,
> (How could mere toil align thy choiring strings!)

Crane is a cousin of Shelley here, but the inclination to go for broke—in a very un-Poundian way—is still modernist in its summation of metonyms, extravagant, mythic tropes that fuse and confuse harp, altar, and choiring strings—myth and the social world.

In some moments in his early poem sequence "Voyages," who doesn't feel the excitement of a young poet obsessively conjoining wild evocative images that hook into associative connections with others in the stanza?

> Take this Sea, whose diapason knells
> On scrolls of silver snowy sentences,
> The sceptred terror of whose sessions rends
> As her demeanors motion well or ill,
>
> All but the pieties of lovers' hands.
>
> And onward, as bells of San Salvador
> Salute the crocus lustres of the stars,
> In these poinsettia meadows of her tides,
> Adagios of islands, O my Prodigal,
> Complete the dark confessions her veins spell.

Even if it's adjective-heavy, the idea of "the diapason knell" turning into language as the poet watches the waves churn to "scrolls of silver snowy sentences," or the "crocus lustres of the stars," and "poinsettia meadows of her tides," all open up new apertures of perception as they drip with sensuality.

Or take Crane's vision of "the airplane," just as it was becoming a permanent part of the sky, written a few years later in *The Bridge*:

> Wings emerge from larval-silver hangars.
> Taut motors surge, space-gnawing, into flight,
> Through sparkling visibility, outspread, unsleeping,
> Wings clip the last peripheries of light . . .
> Tellurian wind-sleuths on dawn patrol,
> Each plane a hurtling javelin of winged ordnance,
> Bristle the heights above a screeching gale to hover;
> Surely no eye that Sunward Escadrille can cover!

Crane's metaphor obsessions create dynamo movements in which "space-gnawing," "Tellurian wind-sleuths" and "hurtling javelin of winged ordnance" define a new idea of space. The Italian futurists would have claimed Crane's machine fury, even with some of these agglutinated images. If Crane can overextend his reach or let the paint drip in impasto globs that can clot movement and occlude perception, as sometimes happens, in his final poem (he did not write it believing it would be the last poem), he hits a balance of sensual language, metaphorical reaches, metaphysical tropes and rhetoric that gives this poem a kind of depth that Crane always sought.

>>><<<

The biographical events surrounding "The Broken Tower" create a context that is layered and tumultuous, but still we can't make the poem accountable to the moment in a literal way. The moment is there for our knowledge and it deepens any understanding of this remarkable poem. As I think of "The Broken Tower" and its relationship to this extraordinary moment of Crane's life, I recall John Berryman's admonition to readers of *The Dream Songs*: "I am not writing out my life in verse." "The Broken Tower" is not memoir, but a fantastical vision that emerged from complex circumstances in the volatile final chapter of the poet's life. The poem transforms bits of that lived experience into a torqued language and vision of love and the sublime that is more humane and noble than the sad, quotidian events of Crane's final crash.

In the poem's opening, a lyric density is tempered by a speaking voice, a rhetorical seduction that navigates the self's direction.

The bell-rope that gathers God at dawn
Dispatches me as though I dropped down the knell
Of a spent day—to wander the cathedral lawn
From pit to crucifix, feet chill on steps from hell.

Have you not heard, have you not seen that corps
Of shadows in the tower, whose shoulders sway
Antiphonal carillons launched before
The stars are caught and hived in the sun's ray?

The bells, I say, the bells break down their tower;
And swing I know not where. Their tongues engrave
Membrane though marrow, my long-scattered score
Of broken intervals . . . And I, their sexton slave!

The rhyming quatrains are pushed to the limit with Crane's kind of sensuality; the verbs, "gather," "dispatches," and "water" play off the sharpness of images; "bell-rope," "God," "pit," "crucifix," "hell," with both musical fluidity and upending jolts so that the poem stays in an uneasy motion as Crane meditates on sound as movement and as an emotional force in the mind. Ringing bells are the poem's central trope, and Crane keeps moving between an idea of transcendent meaning and the physical body; the bells are figured as "tongues" engraving "membrane through marrow." He described his own experience of ringing the bells in the tower while he looked out at the valley below during the celebration of Tepoztecatl, and the lines here echo a tone of that moment. But Crane's idea of sound is what is released into space—both a metaphysical idea and a sensual fact—"oval encyclicals in canyons heaping"—the encircling word and oval shape to reify the Emersonian notion of the circle as "the highest emblem in the cipher of the world" and the "flying perfect, around which the hands of man can never meet." In Crane's vision of sound, "the terraced echoes prostrate on the plain" overflow and transcendent sound fills the world.

When the moment of release comes in the fifth stanza, Crane finds an effective balance with an infusion of rhetoric and a self-assertion that releases the poem's human dilemma and conflict:

> And so it was I entered the broken world
> To trace the visionary company of love, its voice
> An instant in the wind (I know not whither hurled)
> But not for long to hold each desperate choice.

Because we know the circumstance of the moment, it's hard to ignore the drama in Crane's life and its animating impact on the poem. Crane has made it clear that the poem was written, in part, as a tribute to his first love for a woman. In celebrating this new dimension of his sexuality, he declares his initiation into the "broken world" and into an ideal of love, which "visionary company" suggests. The broken world of love is fraught with fragility, vulnerability, and mystery, or, as he puts it, "an instant in the wind / (I know not whither hurled)." In Crane's characteristic compounding, metaphoric language, he complicates sexuality with his Chaplinesque sense of humor and plays with language as he makes a metonym for ejaculating:

> My word I poured. But was it cognate, scored
> Of that tribunal monarch of the air
> Whose thigh embronzes earth, strikes crystal Word
> In wounds pledged once to hope—cleft to despair?

His continued drive to find those intersecting nodes between the physical and metaphysical leads him into one of those brimming moments. Crane's trope is an aspiration for an ingenious poetic fusion and a vision of love in which the lover's language, the cosmic force, and the body mingle in a hope to heal the lover's wounds.

Crane slides between the bells ringing their hypnotic power over his imagination and the power of his new love: "or is it she / Whose sweet mortality stirs latent power?" The poem spills into a stanza where voice and metaphor find an affecting balance and the metaphor-drunk Crane merges "angelus" to "wars of his chest." Angelus, the Latin for angel, of course, but also for the Angelus bell that rings a call to prayer for peace and goodwill. In this fragile exploration of new love, Crane gives us his heart, which, for the moment, he holds "healed, original, and pure . . ." before "the tower" ascends into an idea in the mind and a metaphysical force.

Those extravagant image yokings keep driving the quatrains and the conceit, which is correspondingly extravagant, as Crane's tower becomes a metaphysical conduit "(Not stone can jacket heaven)" to those "azure circles" above. Both physical and metaphysical desire leads him to push the body into the cosmos and then into an ideal of love, as the sexual punning ("swells," and "lifts" and "shower") keep the poem oscillating between the body and the vision. The "tall decorum of that sky" meets the beloved's "earth" through the "matrix of the heart," a strangely mathematical metaphor for the tangled complexity of this lover's heart. In that swelling tower, Crane takes us up to the "tall decorum of that sky" that "unseals her earth" (the beloved) and then back down to body and terra firma. Sexual punning and metaphysical complexity is a dialectic of Crane's mad, insistent imagination in which the poem "lifts love in its shower"; it's the up and down—all in one.

In the poem's final gesture, Crane is playful and passionate as he appeals to love as a human force and a transcendent idea. Too much to hope for, too much to have faith in, but lifting love in its shower into the "tall decorum of that sky" from the "matrix of the heart" into "those azure circles" is characteristic of Crane's extravagant reaches, of his high hopes, his expansive language, which, in the end, could not lift him out of his inner struggles and those demons that led to his early death.

>>><<<

I want to return to Crane's end as a postscript to the poem, and not vice versa, because the poem gave Crane a final word that was hard earned and richly made into his best art. His end was sadly too early and unfortunately triggered by immense emotional chaos that he might have worked through in another circumstance or place; and he might have done that only days later if he had made it back to New York—to terra firma and some old friends and haunts.

His Guggenheim fellowship would end a few days after Easter, and Mexican Easter excited his sensory needs once again—with "exploding Judases, rockets, flowers, pappas, delicious and infinitesimal children wearing masks and firemen's helmets, flowers galore and a sky that carries you upward!" as he put it. He bragged to his friend Leon Felipe: "I'm very happy because I have discovered that I am not a homosexual!"[17] Peggy was holding together his imagined world; for the moment, at least, she was a grounding force in his fragmented life of daily struggles.

Writing to Caresse Crosby, he put his reflection about Mexico this way:

> My Guggenheim Fellowship terminates today. But I am remaining a while longer in Mexico on the modest income afforded me by my father's estate, since his death last July. At that time I came north for two months, but was very glad to get back here again as soon as possible. Mexico, with its volcanoes, endless ranges, countless flowers, dances, villages, lovely brown-skinned Indians with simple courtesies, and constant sunlight—it enthralls me more than any other spot I've ever known. It is—and isn't an easy place to live. Altogether more strange to us than the orient. . . . But it would take volumes to even hint at all I've seen and felt. Have rung bells and beaten pre-Conquistadorial drums in fire-lit circles at ancient ceremonies, while rockets went zooming up into the dawn over Tepoztlan [*sic*]; have picked up obsidian arrows and terra-cotta idols from the furrows of corn fields in far valleys; abathed with creatures more beautiful than inhabitants of Bali in mountain streams; and been in the friendliest jails that ever man got thrown in. There is never an end to dancing, singing, rockets and the rather lurking and suave dangers that give the same edge to life here that the mountains give to the horizon. Harry would have adored it—past expression—and I'm sure you would. I should like to stay indefinitely. But I've about

made my adjustment now and am beginning to rap the typewriter a good deal lately. With the world all going to hell—what can one gather together with any confidence these days anyway? . . . Furthermore I've stretched the dominions of Eros a little. Or maybe it should be called "Via Venus" henceforth—with the wife of someone we all know who's here on a mission of divorce. But more's deferred until we meet—or greet again. . . .[18]

By the end of March, Crane had run out of money and began wiring his friends in the States for help. Anxious and desperate, he began to drink heavily and was getting into trouble again and was back in the Mixcoac jail. He was still hoping that he and Peggy would stay in Mexico until at least the fall or longer. His anxiety and depression were such that he left Peggy everything in his last will—Peggy, who he declared was the only person who believed in him and his poetry. He then announced that he had made his will because, as he put it: "this afternoon I am going to kill myself."[19] Believing that he had typed up the "The Broken Tower" and sent it to Morton Zabel at *Poetry*, he was in despair because he had gotten no reply and assumed that the poem had been rejected.

In the ensuing days, he decided to return to the States with Peggy. Although friends urged them to go by train, they both loved ships and booked passage on the steamship *Orizaba*. The Guggenheim people were so fed up with him, they gave him money to help pay for his ticket. As Eyler Simpson put it in his report back to Moe at the Guggenheim Foundation, "It has become apparent to all concerned, including Crane himself, that we must get the gentleman out of the country and that as soon as possible."[20] Peggy and Crane left from Vera Cruz, Mexico, on April 25, and Crane, paranoid and alcoholic as he got on board, was again blaming Mexico for destroying him, claiming his friends despised his work, calling himself a failure, and brooding over the lack of response to "The Broken Tower" from Zabel at *Poetry*.

On their voyage, Crane wanted to show Peggy a bit of Havana, and during their brief stop there they went off on their own shopping and then were to meet in a restaurant for lunch. At the appointed restaurant, Crane waited for her, but she apparently was waiting for him at another restaurant. After an hour or so, Crane realized something was wrong and went back to the ship. When he got on board, he found Peggy at the doctor's quarters having burns on her hand tended to. She told him that while she was waiting for him to return to the ship, anxiously wondering what had happened to him, she burned her hand badly when the matchbook caught fire as she was lighting a cigarette.

What began as a kind of Laurel and Hardy comedy scene turned into something else. When Crane saw Peggy's burns, he became manically upset, chastising her and hovering over her, which angered her and resulted in her locking him out of her cabin. Angry and worried about Peggy, and suspicious and bewildered about why she had not met him at the restaurant, Crane disappeared for the evening. Although the details are unclear, the reports from the ship's guard the next day confirm that Crane had some encounters with various men. Sometime during the evening Crane was beaten up and had his wallet and ring stolen from him. Around four A.M., one of the ship's guards found him stumbling on the deck and hanging dangerously over the railing. He seized Crane, walked him back to his cabin, and locked him in. In the morning, when the cabin guard went to Crane's cabin to let him out, he found Crane drinking heavily out of a liquor bottle. Shortly after, the guard let Crane out, and Crane went to Peggy's cabin in a state of despair, exclaiming: "Everything is lost, I've got to go." Peggy thought he was being melodramatic and convinced him to have breakfast with her. She reports that he ordered everything on the menu, ate ravenously, and then went back to his cabin and began drinking again.

He then put on his pajamas and a topcoat and went back to Peggy's cabin. When she saw him in disarray, she urged him to get dressed so they could have lunch, but he replied bluntly: "I'm not going to make it dear, I'm utterly disgraced." She brushed off his remark and told him he'd feel better after lunch. He responded with a quiet "All right, dear," and then went up on the deck. He stared out at the ocean for a moment, took off his robe, and jumped. It was just after noon. When what had happened was discovered a few minutes later, lifesavers and boats were sent in after him, and the ship circled the area for two hours, but his body was never found.[21]

Overwrought, humiliated, burdened by his conflicted self, part of which was bound up in his sexual identity, discouraged about his work, and the absence of any response to "The Broken Tower" from *Poetry*, and certainly emotionally exhausted from the dramatic intensity of his Guggenheim year in Mexico, he had hit a treacherous moment, a perfect storm in a temporary place of no exit. Days later a letter arrived from Morton Zabel telling Crane he had never received the poem.

It would be a stretch to call "The Broken Tower" what Helen Vendler has called "a last look" or a poet's final encounter with life on the brink of death. But the poem was an inadvertent last look. Although Crane doesn't seem to have premeditated his suicide, he was self-destructive; his suicidal demons were never far away, and in his last episode of implosion he grappled with suicidal impulses. If this is not a self-conscious last poem, it was a last poem, and one that made a grand reach for the life force—in its transcendent vision and sensual embrace—while acknowledging the broken connection between intimate lovers and the self and the world. It was a rare moment of personal release, poetic invention, and a beautiful and risky foray into the joy of love and the dissolution of self.

Poet from Kars: Yeghishe Charents and Armenia's Modern Age

Yeghishe Charents (1897–1937) became a public figure at an early age, in part because of the forces of history—mass violence and political chaos—that shaped his childhood and adolescence. His work defined something about Armenia's harsh journey into modernity. His turbulent life and his art were formed by a dovetailing of personal disaster and political calamity before his untimely death in prison during Stalin's purges of the 1930s. In some ways, his situation as a poet resembles that of Federico Garcia Lorca, Osip Mandelstam, or the less-tragic W. B. Yeats.

Charents is Armenia's most important poet of the modernist era. In Armenia, there is a significant body of scholarship on his work and life, and he holds a particular place in Soviet and Russian literature. In Armenia, Charents also is commemorated with a dramatic monument—Charents Arch—on the highway from Yerevan to the Hellenic temple of Garni. A complex cosmopolitan whose life was defined by violent histories continually colliding and caving into one another, he read and absorbed Armenian, Russian, and various European literatures. It's difficult to think of poets whose lives have been shaped by such relentless political violence, although poets of the Bolshevik era and Stalinist purges, or of the Nazi decimations and the Soviet aftermath, are surely among them.

The larger history that shaped Charents's life and work strikes me as inseparable from the history and predicament of the city— Kars—in which he grew up. In various ways, the fate of Kars is a topos for the violent oscillations in many of Charents's poems and even the shape of his career. For Kars embodies a historical and political drama that is emblematic of some of the predicaments by which Charents's imagination would be pincered and shaped. War-torn, contested by empires, a volatile juncture of both political violence and international trade, Kars, with its dusty horizon, fortress walls, churches, and mosques, would become a resonant symbol for Charents's life and art.

>>><<<

He was born Yeghishe (Elisha) Soghomonian. His father was a merchant who, like his mother, was born in Maku, northwest Iran. His parents later moved to Erzerum (once the capital of historic Armenia) in eastern Turkey, but after Sultan Abdulhammit's massacres of the Armenians in 1894– 1896, especially in eastern Turkey, Charents's father moved the family to Kars, a city at the contested cusp of two empires at the southwest edge of the Caucasus, then just north of the Turkish border. Situated in the rocky highlands, Kars had been a crossroad and trade route for centuries, overrun, pulled, and pushed between empires and countries—and consequently a city of multicultural layers. Its ancient fortress and various Armenian churches have been historic markers there for centuries, and the ruins of the medieval Armenian city of Ani (Armenia's capital during the tenth through eleventh centuries) are only twenty-eight miles to the east. All of it is inside Turkey today, an irony that continues to energize and complicate any reflection on Armenian culture and history and its postgenocide legacy.

Roman historians noted that Kars was the capital of the Armenian Kingdom of the Van region (eastern Turkey today), and by the ninth and tenth centuries the city was a central part of the Armenian Bagratuni dynasty, and its capital for a short time; its famous cathedral, the Church of the Holy Apostles, was built during this period. The city was briefly under Byzantine control until the Seljuk Turks conquered it in the eleventh century, and the Georgians in the thirteenth; Tamerlane stormed the city in 1387, and the Ottoman Turks took it in 1534.

In the nineteenth century, Kars was fought over by Turkey and Russia continuously. After wars in 1828 and the Crimean War of 1854, Kars was captured by the Russians, but the city ended up as part of Turkey after the war treaties. In the battle of Kars of 1877–1878, during the Russo-Turkish war, Kars was taken again by the Russians and then became the capital of the Russian province of Kars. Throughout the continual political turmoil and change, the city retained much of its historic Armenian cultural identity, and Armenians remained a dominant population. By the late nineteenth century, Kars was made up largely of Armenians, Greeks, Kurds, and Turks—an interesting and sometimes tense mingling of Christian and Muslim cultures.

But an acceleration of turmoil ensued as Kars changed hands four more times between 1876 and 1918. At the outset of the Bolshevik Revolution in 1917, the city became a part of a short-lived, independent Federation of Transcaucasia under Armenian rule. Then, in manipulations of German-Russian diplomacy, through which Russia was able to slide out of the war in the Brest-Litovsk Treaty of 1918, a weak Russian government was forced to acquiesce to Germany's demands—at the request of Turkey, Germany's wartime ally—that Kars, along with Ardahan and Batum, be ceded to Turkey.

After a war in 1918 between the short-lived, fledgling Armenian Republic and the Ottoman Turkish army, Kars was in Armenian hands for the two years that the Armenian state managed to sustain itself. After World War I, both the of the Allied treaties with the Ottoman Empire—the Treaty of Mudros and the Treaty of Sevres, as well as President Wilson's award to

Armenia—ceded Kars and its province to the new Armenian Republic. But, Turkish forces refused to leave the region, and in October of 1920 invaded a tenuous Armenia and captured Kars again.

In December 1920, Turkey played out its political power in the region by forcing Armenia to cede all of its territories granted by the Treaty of Sevres. Shortly after that, Armenia, to ensure its survival, became part of the new Soviet Union. By 1921, Turkish control of Kars and the immediate region was solidified by the Treaty of Kars between Turkey and the Soviet Union, and Kars became one of several Armenian cities lost to Turkey in the wake of the politics of the postgenocide, postwar theater. Like Ani, Van, Erzurum, Bitlis, and others, Kars became a cicatrix on the Armenian map, a wound in the collective memory.

>>><<<

It was in this mix and mess of the politics and culture of Kars, "a grim, stifling place at the turn of the century,"[1] as James Russell has called it, that Charents was born and raised. And the turmoil for an Armenian in Kars would have been compounded by the desperate conditions for the Armenians across the border in Turkey. In other east Anatolian places, the Armenian populations of the villages and the cities of Van, Erzerum, Moush, and Bitlis would be decimated by the empire-wide massacres carried out by Sultan Abdulhammit II in the 1890s in retaliation for mostly peaceful Armenian activism for reform for Christians and the other minorities in the Ottoman Empire.

Growing up in Kars in the first decade of the twentieth century, Charents was surrounded by massacre survivors and refugees from across the border; he lived in a culture in the midst of crisis and uncertainty as Armenians in Russia and Turkey faced an uncertain future that would erupt in Turkey's genocidal plan of 1915, when, behind the screen of World War I, Turkey's Union and Progress Party carried out its plan of eradicating the Armenian population of more than two million people.

By April 1915, one of the most dramatic episodes of the genocidal campaign erupted in the city of Van, just 100 miles from Kars, where Armenians took up arms in resistance to massacre and held off the Ottoman army for a couple of months before the Russians came and for a brief time gave them protection. It was this event that led to the first epic impulses in Charents's writing, in a career that would be defined by long, lyrically rich poems with historical perspectives. In the fall of 1915, he joined an Armenian volunteer battalion in Russia and crossed the border, traveling a couple hundred miles through rugged mountainous terrain to Van, a historic Armenian city on a dramatic glacial lake on the eastern Turkish border. An eighteen-year-old who was part of a battalion that had no political backing, scant supplies, and makeshift equipment, Charents found himself in a landscape of ruins and corpses as he and his group attempted to fight off the Turkish killing squads. Out of this experience came his first important poem, "Dantesque Legend"[2]—an epic poem of eight longish sections, in which the persona moves between a diary-like intimacy and an unsettling realism.

Not unlike those British public school boys going off to war on the Western front, these boys with their youthful buoyancy "set out, light headed / with the bright blueness overhead, our souls buoyant, the fresh light soul of the happy traveler / ready and open to the pull of / the unraveling road." Nature is pastoral, almost folkloric: "The golden spikes before us in the fields." But as they walk on, Charents conveys the sense of leaving innocence behind: "Our pasts / vanished without a trace like / a shout exhaled in sleep."

As the poet and his comrades climb a barren mountain in the Anatolian highlands, the language changes. On a barren precipice, syntax tightens, decorative images vanish, language goes stark:

Nothing animate,
but us. Life became something
palpable in each chest. We
breathed. We existed.

On the Anatolian plain, Charents sees the first sign of his murdered countrymen, and it seems as if history has split the poem between two centuries, two eras of the poet's life. The opening, buoyant rhetoric gives way to a language so austere it effaces the self as it sees the real. In these moments, William Carlos Williams's modernist dictum that a poem should be "pruned to a perfect economy" is something Charents arrived at without a push from Western modernism: "We saw there among the vines a body / of an old man, strangled, / fallen under bloodied grapes." "I looked, stiff-eyed, into the clear / water of the pail in which also / half disintegrated parts of a body / rocked calmly." The "stiff-eyed" seeing of this poem owes less to literary irony than it does to an aesthetic of engaging the horror of the real without intrusive sentiment or emotion.

When the poet reaches the Dantesque place—the "Dead City," as he calls it, his trope for Van—the language pushes toward a minimalism, and the restraint in these sections anticipates some of the postatrocity writing that characterizes Primo Levi's clinical-like aesthetic. In this "stiff-eyed" seeing, displacement and disfigurement embody poetry's ability to inhabit the human in the historical event.

> Nothing breathed in the Dead City.
> The windows of the deserted building
> stared darkly like eyes without pupils.
> No, sockets without eyes. And we dared not return
> their stare.
>
> I don't know why we entered a house.
> The wide holes of the windows gaped
> like sunless, dug-out eyes.
> At the threshold a cat's body.
> Who would have killed it?
>
> We entered, and saw the broken bed,
> a woman drenched in blood. Naked.
> The blood-stained mouth holding a laugh,
> open like a hole, smelling of fear.

In this gruesome image, the poet renders the dead body in an ambiguous way so the mouth and vagina overlap—evoking rape but leaving the disfigurement an unsettling part of the descent into the event without any rhetoric. He then reverts to more conventional metaphor to try and take in the traumatic shock of seeing this: "The lid of my skull disappeared then / as if my brain were not mine / and sky and ground danced together. Someone said: 'let's get out of here.'"

By the fifth section, Charents has winnowed the persona down to a diary-like self that is recording details of atrocity. In a nightmare, he probes the traumatized self, and in a kind of insomniac delirium, he sees the dead in a dance of body parts. For a moment, the shattered self loses its own sense of being:

Their dead bodies and blue legs,
yellow breasts, swollen and blood-
splattered buttocks,
danced, staggering before
my terror-filled eyes
in the grave-pit dark.

They sang, moaned, cackled,
almost as if in joy (laughter)
and weeping, and in horrible hollow tones
that gnawed in my ears

In my agitated brain their song
made me feel that I didn't even exist,
that I was a part of some hot, distant dream
in which my soul was floating away

I flew like a ghost
just like them, until another sound
joined their careless song
and I realized it was the sea
roaring in the dark.

In between these arresting moments and the orchestration of a sustained journey toward the "Dead City," the poem has its moments of excess and bald depictions of battle. But the ambition of an eighteen-year-old boy to gather and transform this experience of extremity into a poem is impressive and suggests this early in his career the omnivorous range of his imagination.

PLATE 1. Robert
Rauschenberg, *Monk*
(1955). Oil, printed
paper collage, wood,
fabric, postage stamps,
feather, and vinyl on
linen, 14 × 12 in.
© Robert Rauschenberg
Foundation / Licensed
by VAGA, New York.
Private collection.
Photograph: © Christie's
Images / Bridgeman
Images.

PLATE 2. Robert
Rauschenberg, *Black
Market* (1961). Combine
painting. Oil, watercolor,
crayon, printed paper,
printed reproductions,
wood, metal, metal
box, and four notepads
on canvas, with rope,
rubber stamp, ink pad,
and various objects,
127 × 150 × 10.1 cm.
© Robert Rauschenberg
Foundation / Licensed
by VAGA, New York.
Photograph: © Rheini-
sches Bildarchiv Köln.

PLATE 3. Arshile Gorky, *The Artist and His Mother* (ca. 1926–1936). Oil on canvas, 60 × 50 in. © 2015 The Estate of Arshile Gorky / Artists Rights Society, New York. Photograph: Courtesy the Whitney Museum of American Art.

PLATE 4. Arshile Gorky, *The Artist and His Mother* (ca. 1929–1942). Oil on canvas, 152.3 × 127 cm. © 2015 The Estate of Arshile Gorky / Artists Rights Society, New York. Photograph: The National Gallery of Art, Washington, DC. Alisa Mellon Bruce Fund (1979.13.1).

PLATE 5. Arshile Gorky, *Image in Khorkom* (ca. 1934–1936). Oil on canvas, 35-1/2 × 47-1/2 in. © 2015 The Estate of Arshile Gorky / Artists Rights Society, New York. Private collection. Photograph: Courtesy of the Arshile Gorky Foundation.

PLATE 6. Arshile Gorky, *How My Mother's Embroidered Apron Unfolds in My Life* (1944). Oil on canvas. 40 × 45-1/16 in. © 2015 The Estate of Arshile Gorky / Artists Rights Society, New York. Photograph: Courtesy of the Seattle Art Museum. Gift of Mr. and Mrs. Bagley Wright. Photography by Susan Cole.

Charents's effort to probe the psychological, to get to the traumatic (he was writing in an age before trauma was a social idea)—is tied to the tropes of dream and delirium throughout the poem. After seeing corpses and the dead, raped women, he lies awake at night "in the candleless / dark," imagining "dead bodies with blue legs / yellow breasts, swollen with blood- / spattered buttocks" as they "danced," "moaned," "cackled," in his "agitated brain," which brings him knowledge "that I too did not exist," but was "part of some hot distant dream." Although the poet is a witness, he is a witness at the scene of the crime in the immediate aftermath, and so the idea of traumatic hallucination that is often part of delayed survivor experience, a version of post-traumatic stress disorder, becomes part of the poem's texture. If "to be traumatized is precisely to be possessed by an image or event,"[3] as Cathy Caruth has put it, then "Dantesque Legend" is a poem that emerges from traumatized witness and, through the poet's ingenuity, finds a form in lyric language.

"Dantesque Legend" engenders a journey that unravels with spontaneity and shocks that expose "a satire of circumstance," or "hitherto unimagined reaches of suffering and irony," as Paul Fussell put it in discussing the trench war experience in Western Europe. The poem's experiential and kinetic spontaneity embodies some of Walt Whitman's visceral realism (of a kind that Vladimir Mayakovsky absorbed, too) and Allen Ginsberg's diary-like intimacy. The poet-guide takes us on a journey into a kind of hell that he doesn't understand and for which he has no high rhetorical answer. In pitching the poem between an intensified realism and an allegorical perspective, the poet never mentions a geographical location, never uses the word *Turk* or *Armenian*. Perhaps, then, it is not surprising that Charents closes with a series of metaphysical questions posed to the cosmos: "Oh, eternal mother of mysteries / who in suffering and lust, conceives / numerous lives . . . what is the spring of these eternal rhythms?" Rather than recapitulating or commenting on the empirical, Charents opts for a philosophical reflection at the end as he tries to come to terms with suffering, evil, and the nature of existence;

he sees "the delirium of the universe alive in a dream" and owns up to the ambiguity that his volunteer battalion were both "victims" and "executioners." Having left his boyhood on the other side of the twentieth century, this young poet concludes that "the threat of stupid fate holds / neither meaning nor dread."

>>><<<

By 1918, there were almost no Armenians left in Turkey, and a new Armenian Republic had formed out of Russian Armenia in the Caucasus. Charents found himself caught in political and personal turmoil. In the spring of 1918, he was planning an exotic flight from the region—to head for China with his lover and fellow writer Vivian (Anoushan Jidejian). They packed some books and clothes and set out on foot from Tiflis. Along the way they encountered Armenian survivors, most of them from destroyed Armenian quarters of Erzerum, Mush, and Van, walking along the roadside. When they reached the train station in Tikhoretzk, Charents met by surprise his parents, and in that meeting, which must have been a confrontation between his desire to flee and some sense of obligation to stay, his journey to China ended, and he turned around and went back to Armenia.

One of Charents's moving early poems, "Travelers of the Milky Way," deals with his recognition about staying home, or, to put it another way, to stay in history. There is a clear, open voice here that is more than late Romantic personalism and that anticipates a balder confessional tone that will come to be more prevalent in later-twentieth-century poetry. It's a haunting poem of stoical honesty about how one's dreams of youth have to be relinquished: "I had wanted to sing praises to God, to sing, to sing the glory of love, and bread," even though he and Vivian "started our reverie / of faraway countries, and our life, / our dark absurd life." He acknowledges how the burden of growing up in Kars has shaped him: "Our childhood passed like a mist / floating, gray, sunless, inconsolable," even as he "dreamed on / of far off places." The poem is inflected with a dream atmosphere— "delirium," "vision," and the trope of the "milky way" gives off a disembodied kind of dream-anguish. Amid this, they keep passing figures on the road, wraith-like survivors and refugees, but Charents never once refers to them as victims of a particular event; rather, he shows them passing by, almost passing *through* him, like Whitman's "sleepers":

> Every passer-by passed by
> laughing at our bright eyes,
> scorning their burning want.
> They went their way without
> adding a single light.
> Even the sister laughed, even the friend
> snickered and impatient strangers
> muttered oaths.

Here he acknowledges that staying at home is the beginning of the next phase of his work, and still he is only twenty.

> But never mind, never mind now.
> Our days pass as fever passes.
> Life became an unsoothable delirium.
> And we smile at the dream we dreamed
> That passed as we did.

>>> <<<

In 1918, the year that the Great War ended and civil war tore Russia apart, Armenia, as one historian put it, "backed into his own independence."[4] A nation of refugees ravaged by famine and disease, without adequate means to protect itself and without allies, Armenia had no choice but to declare its independence. But by 1920, Armenia had lost almost half of its territory to an invading Ottoman army that hoped to expunge Armenia entirely. And so, by December 1920, in order to save itself, Armenia became a Soviet Socialist republic.

Shortly after the meeting with his parents at the train station, Charents joined the Red Army in the northern Caucasus and, once again, was a poet in armed conflict and writing about political strife. In the summer of his first campaign as a Red soldier, he began a poem that would change his identity. This new long poem, "The Frenzied Masses," launched him in Moscow and made him the first Armenian poet of stature in the new terrain of Soviet literature. "The Frenzied Masses" is not without irony, as the title suggests, but still, Charents depicts the dawn of the Bolshevik era in an idiom that blends avant-gardist futurism and a kind of Whitman long-line realistic seeing that evolved from his witness eye in "Dantesque Legend."

Charents brings realism and a kind of expressionistic allegory into a strange fusion, as the colors of red and black transform his idea of historical forces into a symbolic drama. In depicting the triumph of the masses over the old order, the urban mob and army and revolutionary battles are rendered in large image strokes that fuse the violent forces of war with the idea of social change. It's an odd blend with a big historical ambition, something almost Pushkin-like in its striving for the epic, and perhaps more expansive than Mayakovsky in evoking the sublime and the grotesque at once—the cosmos shaking with the surging forces of the social world.

> With the evening sun burning the field away,
> in that old field the frenzied masses fought.
> They had come from cities, villages, steppes.
> They had come glowing from their old fires.
> He who had left the city, left its old mists,
> hazes that became dark smoke and stained his past.
> He who had come from distant villages
> left the damp earth which had become disobedient
> and did not sprout life, but refused even a single
>   yellow splinter.
> He who came from the steppes left the stretch
> of limitless horizons which had shrunk
> suddenly onto prison walls.
> And he who was from the city brought his tubercular heart, like a
>   red flag.

There is no named place in the poem, only "the city" of great revolution, as the landscape is depicted in red for blood and Bol-

shevism, and black for the violence and smoke of social and political change:

> It was night, but a burning night, red as a flame.
> The red sun setting in the west
> stained the fog with blood,
>
> as if a red poison were pressed
> from the red heart of the sun.
> The hot sun spit a red incandescent crucible
> spilled a lava of light over the fields.
> And the wavering plains burned with the glow.
> The edgeless field spread fire from the sun
> over a sea without beginning or boundary,
> a red sea in the evening mist.

Unlike the other the poems of the early Bolshevik era that dealt
with revolution, "The Frenzied Masses" maintains an imagistic
opacity that is allusive:

> the old city glittered with a thousand shades of red
> and spread its pyrotechnics
> as if it were swimming on a velvet fog
> as if the buildings hung in the red air
> slowly, dimming, darkening, fading. Not only the glass
> windows floated with distant fires.
> And it was not smoke streaming out of the huge chimneys
> but the thickened evening mist
> covering, slowly hiding the iron chimneys.

Charents transmutes the civil war into urban landscapes of
conflagration. The whole poem is shaded with an apocalypticism
that moves between the earthly world of war and a cosmos on
fire: "a red incandescent crucible / spilled a lava of light over
the fields." It's a wild catapult of Russian futurism, sometimes
bloated with its own symbolism, that doesn't simplistically celebrate the Bolshevik Revolution (although it does lend an affirm-
ing energy to the idea of a new age). In the end, we're left with a
feeling that there is a malignancy in the violence and frenzy, or,

as Charents put it: "A million eyes / spit poison, spit out the salty wrath / skimmed from their hearts." The poem seems to have lent enough epic language to the Bolshevik triumph that, for the moment, Charents passed as a poet of the new age.

During the 1920s, Charents's life was a series of civic performances and personal turmoil. He joined the Communist Party, believed for the moment that the revolution would usher in a new era of literary and social change, and, in 1922, wrote a manifesto-statement, full of the naïve faith of a purported new age, about the end of bourgeois romanticism:

> These are the viruses of our literary disease, the symptoms of which are nationalism, romanticism, pessimism, and symbolism. . . . We oppose bourgeois nationalism with proletarian internationalism. . . . To liberate poetry from the cloistered rooms, bring it into the street and to the masses, out of the books and into the living language. To articulate what is contemporary—movement, class struggle, strength, the zeal. . . . May we be rid of the aristocratic opportunists, the cloistered writers, the books slumbering in the libraries, and the women of the salons.[5]

He was rising in the ranks of the new writers of the new state, and in 1925 he founded the November Union of Armenian Proletarian Writers. By 1928, he had been appointed the literary director of the state press of Armenia. From all appearances, it seemed that Charents was on board in the new Soviet multinational society, a bridge between his country's literary tradition and the new Soviet culture. But, if with one hand he seemed to be trying to please the regime, with the other he was writing poems that were at odds with his own Prolet-cult declarations. In his 1922 poem, "Loveless Romance," he refers to the KGB as a "group that snoops about feelings," and, shortly after, he was condemned by the Writers Union as decadent, inward, and romantic.

>>><<<

Nameh is the Persian word for biography, and this lyrical vision of Charents's life is remarkably contemporary in the intimacy of its voice and its exploration of the psychic life. Written in the same year that *The Waste Land* was published, "Charents-Nameh" couldn't have been further from Eliot's call for the impersonal persona and for the poem to be an escape from personality. In this lyric diary-like poem of twenty-two sections, Charents fuses personal intimacy, myth, and political history in ways that remind one of Apollinaire's "Zone," although in Charents there's a starker kind of realism. The poem moves between places that have defined his life: the sadness of Kars, the sun and roses of Iran (his parents' birthplace in Maku, which he appropriates as his own), and Armenia, which he calls by its mythic name, Nayiri. Kars is both ontology and geography—symbol of weighty origins, childhood of the real:

Again I am in Kars
again, again . . .
wearing the mouth, the lips
of a child.
I see my mother—
the two funnels of her breasts.

My soul is a cold arrow,
ready in the bow of my days.

In the distance a bell
tolls its grief.

My father wears a robe. . .
his face a silver tray.
On it, the hooked knife of his nose.

Time, loveless time, has poured
a white nirvana on his hair.

Here is my mother in a gauze veil
from Teheran, going after water.

His continual recollections of childhood are a long way from those Wordsworthian notions of innocence and "intimations of immortality" that defined much of Western romanticism. In that immovable city wedged between empires, where political violence defined his youth, no "calm existence" is recollected.

In its twenty-two sections, Charents marks threshold ex-

periences: love affairs, childhood memory, names, and dates of
cataclysmic events—Armenian resistance at Van, the Bolshevik
Revolution, and Armenia's war with Turkey to save its borders.
Names of friends, lovers, years, months, and locations skitter
across geopolitical zones in a strange, sometimes artless mix of
historical and personal images in minimalist lines:

> Then flares. Illumination.
> Then exhaustion.
> Suddenly I was free
> breaking the old reins.
> This was 1918
> the year of Soma and
> Lucy Tarayan.
> . . . .
>
> Let me hail now the assemblage on Asdafian Street
> who had joined together,
> crossed the street
> with their red flags
> flaring before Massis . . .
>
> Whoever is ready
> let him join us
> let us burn,
> scream, roar with joyous hearts.
>
> The horses flew,
> zigzagging,
> connecting,
> Evevan to Moscow.
> The iron arm
> crushed the ancient buildings.

In a life without childhood innocence, he calls himself an "or-
phan boy reaching for the / sunburned south," meaning Iran, and
"the warm breath of Aramazt," the Persian sun god. His youth
was defined by his "city without color, Kars," and its traumatic
past: "Grief had grown up in our house long ago. / It had been

there since the time of my grandparents. / And had stayed, weary, old waiting / to go to heaven."

The Turkish massacres of Armenians of the 1890s are alluded to, and throughout Charents marks how history's violence disrupted a boy's growing up. In section 8, he says: "I don't even see / the garden in Kars clearly / anymore. At the end of 1915 / I woke up in the ranks of the army, a volunteer / The Armenian Army," and saw "only corpses / faces of wood / in a country deserted by light." Later: "I reached Moscow" and "was swept along by its terrible shudder." Then his memory of joining the Bolsheviks is spliced by his memory of a love named Karine: "Your charm was sadness, / Karine / fog Karine." History becomes telescoped image and list: "Tro / unfurled a tricolored flag" in Yerevan as "Earth colored ghosts / filled the hungry city"; or, in section 19: "Kars / 1919," where "the sun was digging out the eyes / of the buildings in vain." In the poem's closing, we find Charents in Moscow with all the contradiction of his life as a poet:

> In my head, a Robert Owen
> stands vigil
> while I write
> and dream of what is to come.
>
> I love you Nayiri
> and my incendiary Iran.
>
> And am I far away from you?
> No. I am nearer. As the tensed arrow
> pulled back
> from the gazelle running before it.

It's clear from "Charents-Nameh" that, by 1922, Charents was already coming apart; his romantic sensibility, erotic desire, the fixation on lost Iran, and his passion for the new Armenia—all were impulses, orientations, and ideas for poetry that were at odds with the demands of Stalin's stifling program of social realism.

Charents's poems continue their anti-elegiac depictions of

childhood, which bears some resemblance to the confessional remembrances of Robert Lowell, Theodore Roethke, and Allen Ginsberg that defined post–World War II American poetry. In "Childhood," the incunabula phase is always tainted by Kars ("the very gray city / at the edge of the world"), where childhood was defined by genocide, war, revolutionary violence—anything but Wordsworthian or Emersonian innocence:

> Before me stretches the past,
> a gray city, without myth or mystery.
> My throat closes in, choking
> as I prepare to sing
> old, nostalgic sweetness with
> exotic, imprisoned softness.
> But instead of elegies, laughter
> bursts forth.

"Let others sing of the mother's kiss / while I begin with charmless / primary odors," Charents confesses, as he makes his childhood parable that one can take as a psychological and political initiatory moment. The poet recollects being ten and showing off his new blue shirt to the landlord's boy, who had "often stung" him with "curses, while showing off his new finery." When the landlord's boy tells the proud ten-year-old to wait a minute for him to return, Charents believes he has gone to fetch his sister (who will be impressed by his new attire); when the landlord's boy calls to him from the upstairs window, he looks up and is doused with a bucket of piss—"the yellow liquid pouring over me," the "stench flooding my gold / braided shirt," as he wryly puts it. Among other things, it's a poem about power and cruelty, a history of bitterness, a suitable allegory for the Armenian boy in Kars. In a short poem of 1929, "How Soon You and I Matured," he wrote: "Villon mourned his colorful / younger days once / but ours should be cursed / the wicked wind-blown youth / which slipped away."

Charents's introspective inclinations continued to lead him away from the Soviet aesthetic that he had tried to affirm and toward aspects of Russian acmeism, European symbolism, which now found a new energy in the Armenian literary tradition. Vahan Derian, an Armenian poet half a generation his senior, whom Charents had derided a decade earlier as a hopeless, decadent romantic, he now embraced in his poem "Midnight Sketches" (1928), in which he depicts himself "mumbling Derian's rhythms." He also wrote an homage to Armenia's leading early modern poet, Hovhannes Tumanian, and as late as 1933 endangered himself by praising the book of poems for which his friend Gorgen Mahari (1903–1969) would be later exiled to Siberia. In what was a brazen defense of Mahari's "nationalistic deviations," Charents wrote: "Let these flowers you raise / from our field bloom forever." In his verse biography of Armenia's great modern composer Komitas Vartabed, who suffered a mental breakdown after being arrested and deported from Constantinople (Istanbul) by the Turkish government on April 24, 1915, Charents relived some of his own Dantesque experience:

> Like splinters, like dry thorns
> driven by wind over the roads, you saw
> people and hovels eaten by fires.

It is not surprising, then, that in his "Ars Poetica" of 1927–1929 he expressed his predicament as a poet, who, like Mandelstam during the same years, could not serve propaganda and art at the same time. His Brechtian humor is playful: "Start with greetings to Lenin and Marx / and then get to work and rework the new art form. / . . . Give greetings now to Lenin and Marx and / to Shakespeare's and Dante's nobleness. / Let the hours go simply. Let them / pass knocking at doors." As the poem unfolds, Charents is unstinting about the Soviet program: "the machine gun or bayonet cannot help / you find the road to the ingenious." In the end, he invokes a pantheon of Western writers—Baudelaire, Poe, and Verlaine—and celebrates notions of poetic imagination (Persian and European) that surely were not lost on Stalin and his culture bureau.

In the garden the mimosa light will show
the popular in Heine's shape ready to let in
the ghostly moon to leaf through my sad Rubaiyats again.

After some traveling in Europe and Turkey in 1925, Charents
returned to Yerevan, and with a decade of cataclysmic violence
behind him, an arc of catastrophe continued to define his life.
On a September afternoon, on a main avenue of Yerevan, Charents pulled a gun out of his pocket and shot a woman, fortunately only wounding her superficially. The cause seems to have
been part of a romantic conflict between him and the woman,
who apparently had spurned him. He was sentenced to eight
years in solitary confinement, and a journalist who covered the
trial described him as being in a state of mental collapse from
depression, insomnia, and alcoholism. It is no alibi for his violent
behavior, but it's not surprising that a man in his late twenties
who had lived through a decade of genocide, war, and two civil
wars was coming undone.

In prison, Charents began to write immediately, and his
memoir, *Yerevan's House of Correction* (1927) is a social and psychological portrait of a troubled society in transition. "It's not as
awful . . . as it was in Uncle Dostoyevsky's *House of the Dead*,"[6]
Charents remarked about his first night in jail, and his portraits
of the victims and outcasts of a threadbare world convey some of
the impact of surviving the past decade. When Charents's wife
died unexpectedly only months after his sentence had begun,
he fell into such severe depression that the doctors persuaded
the authorities to let him out of jail to convalesce. After his jail
sentence was commuted, his stature as a writer enabled him to
reemerge as the literary director of the state press in Armenia,
and in 1931 he was elected secretary of the Armenian Writers
Union. But ill health continued to plague him, and in the same
year severe pain from kidney stones forced him to go to Moscow
for surgery, where he was treated with morphine and, during his
convalescence, became addicted.

>>><<<

As the decade of Stalin's campaign of terror commenced, Charents found himself in near poverty, hooked on morphine, increasingly disaffected by Sovietism and the communist literary culture, and anxious about the future of Armenia. It was timely, then, that when Osip Mandelstam and his wife Nadezhda made their famous trip to Armenia in the summer of 1930, Mandelstam and Charents became friends. In the fall of 1930, when the famine created by Stalin's policies, which would take the lives of millions in Ukraine, had begun to affect life in the Caucasus, Charents used his street knowledge of Tiflis to help the Mandelstams get food and cigarettes.[7] "You have a book in you," Charents told Osip in Tiflis, after Osip had read him his new cycle of poems about Armenia. Nadezhda recalled how much this encouragement meant to her husband after his long creative dry spell, for which he had come south to the Caucasus in hope of breaking.[8]

Mandelstam had come to see Armenia in the hope of finding there an easterly civilization of classical and Christian culture, part of a geographical continuum that he believed followed a contour from the Caucasus to Crimea, across to the Peloponnesus, and then to Italy. Armenia—with its Hebraic mountain symbol of Ararat and its ancient Christian culture, and especially its unique sixth- to twelfth-century churches, wedged into its recent bloody past—for Mandelstam promised an idea of world-culture that he was seeking. His essay "Journey to Armenia" angered Soviet critics because it was not a patriotic appraisal of Stalin's First Five-Year Plan in Armenia but rather a complex, lyrical essay about imagination and the cultural layers of Armenia's history and land. Charents, who had already translated Pushkin, Mayakovksy, and Gorky into Armenian, now helped bring Osip Mandelstam into an Armenian conversation.

Between 1928 and 1932, when Soviet writers were enlisted in a cultural Five-Year Plan to write social realism that would serve the state, Charents's poetry became increasingly subversive. When the centralized Union of Soviet Writers was formed in 1932, his position as secretary of the Armenian Writers Union was taken away, and he found himself at the mercy of a more virulent centralized power. As Stalin's purges unfolded, things only got worse for Charents. In December 1932, when Maxim Gorky, the Writers Union's first director, made plans to celebrate Charents's twentieth anniversary as a poet, Charents was elated. But when the celebration was mysteriously canceled, it was a foreshadowing of things to come.

By May 1933, Charents was having difficulty publishing what would be his final book of poems, *Book of the Road*, which included poems dedicated to Armenian figures such as Komitas, Tumanian, and Mahari; a long poem, "At the Crossroads of History," a historical view of Armenia's fate; and love poems and religious poems that showed the breadth of his evolving imagination. The publication of the book was surrounded by a blundering mess of politics that even involved the intercession of Armenian politburo member Anastas Mikoyan. When the book was finally released in 1934, several of the poems had been deleted, and it was derided by the critics. Charents's fate could not have been any different in an intellectual climate that one critic has described as so "padded with the fluffy cotton of optimism, lack of conflict, official slogans, and bombastic patriotism that its propagandists looked twice their natural size and resembled Mme Tussaud's wax figures."[9] The literary bureaucracy called *Book of the Road* ideologically unstable, nonconformist, and defiantly nationalistic.

As Stalin's purges continued, Charents became, for one last time, a visible force in Moscow. In the fall of 1934, he gave an enthusiastically received address at the first Congress of the Soviet Writers Union. He was greeted warmly by Gorky and went to his summer house for a party, where he became friendly with Pasternak, with whom he later spent time in Moscow. Shortly after, Pasternak translated into Russian one of Charents's later poems, "The Curly Haired Boy"—a poem that satirized the idea of the steel rod of progress—but before the poem was published in *Pravda* in the fall of 1935, Charents had been expelled from the executive committee of the Writers Union and then from the Writers Union itself.

In the summer of 1936, Lavrenti Beria, chief of the secret police, shot and killed the first secretary of the Armenian Communist Party, Aghasi Khanjyan, in Beria's office. Outraged by the assassination of Khanjyan, Charents wrote a series of sonnets, and the closing lines of one of them addresses the age of new terror:

> In a forest darkened by one small shade
> we are doomed forever to have you raped
> and hear your cry without giving aid.

Answering his conscience and his art, he continued to write openly about Soviet society. The age, he wrote, belonged to "thieves who steal water" and "plunder land." Any lingering hope he may have had for the Marxist-Leninist revolution was extinguished, for the hoped-for liberator had become the state that executes those who love "the small field" of their homeland.

In many of his final poems, Charents turned to God, and we can hear an anguished voice betrayed by his own hope. His new model became the tenth-century monk Gregory of Narek, Armenia's greatest poet of the premodern era. And Charents's "Prayer to God from the Depths of My Heart" takes its title and impulse from Narek's most famous poem, "Conversations with God from the Depth of My Heart." In this late poem, Charents addresses God as if he were a religious man. In the face of overwhelming odds, the poem is a bald cry from the dungeon:

> Now I stand here
> like a scorpion under the head of a sun-bright
> hatchet, deprived even of merciless bread.

Like many of Stalin's targets, Charents was never told why he was arrested, and in prison he lashed out at the state, and in his poem "The Prayer on the Mount," he continued to address God—who seemed to be his only imagined audience:

Until today, O Lord, I have been
in the dark, a savage apprentice
to my art, in the desert, surrounded
by peasants and sons of shepherds

living for centuries in valleys
subject to torrents and floods.
I watched salvagers fishing for trees
from strategic posts.

At the end, Charents lived by poetry in the face of diminishing odds. About two months before his death, he wrote a poem, "For Avedik Issahakian," on a handkerchief to his friend and fellow poet, Avetik Isahakyan, after hearing a prisoner sing one of Isahakyan's songs in a neighboring cell (the handkerchief is now in the Charents House-Museum in Yerevan). On this handkerchief he affirmed his faith in the poet's work:

All my life, my impossible
aim was to finish
a song to charm children
that old men could cherish,

just as all hearts quicken
with the tempo of yours.

From his cell, he wrote about "daylight" thickening "into dusk" and "fine mold" falling "from the sky," and the downward spiral continued. Having no idea that his second wife, Isabella, had been arrested and incarcerated in the same prison, he wrote a letter to her about a month before his death, urging her to be strong in his absence, "even if they throw you out on the street." She, too, had no idea that they were in the same prison. In late November 1936, when he died after sustaining head injuries against his cell wall, a poet in a neighboring cell wrote, "it seems impossible that I should stay sane after hearing his heart piercing voice, his shout."[10] When Isabella was exiled to Siberia months after her husband's death, she still had no idea that he was not alive, or that he had died perhaps a hundred yards from her.

>>> <<<

In his short life, Yeghishe Charents lived and wrote through successive historic eruptions: the Armenian genocide of 1915, the dovetailing of the Bolshevik Revolution with the Turkish-Armenian wars during years of the failed Armenian Republic (1918–1920), the rise of the Soviet Union with its repressive culture of social realism during the 1920s, and the violence of the Stalin purges of the 1930s. To have come of age during such a period of history was for this poet an entry into a cultural, political, and aesthetic space that affected his language and poetic orientation. Out of it, he made a language that was passionate, but not sentimental, keen in its ability to witness history in motion and in ways that opened up taboo territories, and flexible enough to evolve and absorb political change without becoming polemical. Charents's idiom was influenced in part by an avant-garde Russian futurism of a kind that Vladimir Mayakovsky had begun to forge in the years preceding the war, before the paralyzing Soviet realism ruined the lives of the genuine poetic imaginations of the era—Anna Akhmatova, Mandelstam, Mayakovsky, and Charents among them.

Charents's first major poem, "Dantesque Legend," is an important part of the literature of World War I and shares some of the orientations of Wilfred Owen, Siegfried Sassoon, and Isaac Rosenberg, who became known as "the trench poets." In the literary moment of late Victorian and early modernist transitions—as Georgian genteelism with its inclination toward the generically beautiful and the uplifting was giving way to a new concrete and quotidian realism—Charents was already, as an eighteen-year-old, working in this vein and finding an even more expansive way of wrestling with it. Russian futurism, especially Mayakovsky's political version of futurism, and the violence of the genocide in Turkey, led Charents to an idea of the lyric in which the intimately personal melded with the violent witness experience.

The resistance mission in 1915 opened him up to a language that was, in various ways, modern in its concreteness and deromanticized and antiheroic in its representations. In the most disturbing moments of "Dantesque Legend," the poetics of metaphor are eschewed, and Charents creates a stark language—a "stiff-eyed" seeing, as he put it—that allowed him a vision of the real that refused to aestheticize the horrible and so achieved a kind of compression that forces us into confrontations with extreme violence and death in raw and naked ways—ways that are different from what the British poets of the World War I trenches often did, as they overlay the experience of violence with metaphoric strategies and conceits.

It's unfortunate that Charents's poems are so little known outside of Armenian and Russian literature. A fine translation by the poet Diana Der Hovanessian (with Marzbed Margossian), *Land of Fire: Selected Poems of Yeghishe Charents* was published in 1986 and has been out of print for a quarter of a century now. The range of Charents's major poems and their use of language in engaging exile, displacement, political repression, genocide, and mass violence in relation to a self caught in the wilderness of such histories seems more familiar to us in the twenty-first century than it might have at the time. In our particular literary climate, we can see how both modernism and the antiromantic historicism of postmodernism afford readers a better context for assessing how Charents forged a small piece of modernism, in part out of his predicament as a witness to atrocity on the eastern front of the Great War in which the Armenian genocide was embedded. Although he wrote a long way from avant-garde New York, London, and Paris, he made a piercing voice for modernism that could swallow and articulate "the world men talk in and go to war in," as William Carlos Williams put it. Whitman, Yeats, Wilfred Owen, Allen Ginsberg, and some of the post–World War II American confessional instincts are recognizable in Charents, which should give readers in English today a broader literary context in which to engage this poet from Kars.

Charents's poems embody a struggle against the defeat of the most fundamental structures of civilization. The body of his work, from "Dantesque Legend" through "The Frenzied Masses," "Charents-Nameh," "Childhood," and his final spiritual poems, represents a counterforce to the dissolution of culture that Eliot and Yeats also fought against in their different contexts. Charents's poems articulated a force that, as Yeats put it, "could hold in a single thought reality and justice."

Charents created an important body of poems out of unremittingly harsh political events and personal suffering. He carved on large-hewn stones with big, well-sharpened tools, and his poems sometimes show seams and cracks and sometimes lapse into a raw language of confrontation with dark predicaments. But even when emotion overtakes lyric transformation, his "stiff-eyed" seeing shocks the reader back into an acknowledgment that the poem is bigger than its parts. It is not surprising that Mayakovsky, Pasternak, and Gorky all thought Charents was a commanding voice of his generation.

7

Collage and Its Discontents

From such chaotic, mish-mash potpourri
what are we to expect but poetry.
« T. S. ELIOT »

There is in the most compelling collage-works a restless energy
that is torqued to undermine any neat containment that form
might imply or impose. The kinetic force of the collage-work is
pitched toward an idea of motion that resists linearity and formal
closure and maintains a desire to go beyond its own boundaries.
In this way, the collage pushes beyond itself in the force of its accretion of materials and its nonlinear syntactical strategies. The
collage-work is intrinsically driven by its failure to rest in closure
and resolution; it's always bigger than the sum of its parts, but its
parts are energized by their relationship to the other parts of the
work, and so the work generates an energy and dynamism that
draws the reader into a swirl or vortex of motion. In the most
compelling collages, the parts accrue meanings from the relation
they bear to one another.

The collage isn't interested in resolution or closure, and there
is something organic in this, and something similar to the kind
of thing that Emerson once articulated about organic form in
poetry: that "meter making argument," in which form and mean-

ing are snaked into each other and grow out of each other. Although collage is often highly conceptual, it is also driven by open-endedness and incompleteness that articulate an organic dimension to the larger whole, which allows us to see the parts and the whole differently. In its resistance to closure and resolution, collage appeals to an epistemological orientation that asks us to be self-aware about how we know what we know, about the process of making meaning.

The rich tradition of collage, montage, and assemblage in folk art and popular culture that precedes modernism is vestigially alive in modernist and postmodernist collage art. The genealogical registers of late medieval Europe made with cut-out paper and parchment and silk; seventeenth-century Dutch silhouettes; Russian icon collages; eighteenth-century devotional paper collages of German prayer books; nineteenth-century English valentines; Victorian "memory chests"; German *kladderadatsh* (kit and caboodle) assemblages; and nineteenth-century photo montage in the early evolution of photography all remind us how rich and multifarious the collage tradition is and how richly it's been appropriated.

In the twentieth century, the collage has been central to modernism and postmodernism. The drive to bring disconcerting entities together, to make a form out of seemingly disparate materials has been essential to literary and visual forms across genres. In part, collage has been defined by the construction of intersecting materials, forms, and discourses, and in this way the collage is always defining new and myriad relationships between fragments and an idea of a larger concept, or something that alludes to a whole. Collage-works challenge genre boundaries, traditional parameters, and, as Brandon Taylor has put it, they embrace "indecency, paradox, and perplexity."[1] A subversive potential is always emanating from the strange combinations of collage inventions that have the potential to usurp the idea of traditional genre, linearity, and the determinedly rational.

The evolution of collage from early cubist modernism through late surrealist adaptations defined the collage as aspiring to surpass its antecedents, to making claims to the perpetually new. The range in that era is expansive: Braque and Picasso's early papier colle and cubist collages; Umberto Boccioni, Carlo Carra, and Giacomo Balla's three-dimensional constructions and "free word pictures"; Hans Arp's decontextualized paper fragments; the media mixing of Swiss and German Dadaism; Kurt Schwitters's use of metal and wood on board; Max Ernst's superimposing multiple images in pursuit of the surrealist unconscious; Russian constructivism's photomontage, political realism, and commercial design; Dada's love of fusing high and low culture in its bricolage inventions; and the conceptual collage ideas in Magritte and Tanguy's juxtapositions of incongruous metonymic signs.

Picasso and Braque and Gris found in their inaugural modern collages of 1912–1915 a way of rejecting not only traditional painting but a whole notion of perception and ordered experience. Among other things, their collages came to embody uncertainty, just as later postmodern collages would embody a collation of fragmentary forms and layered explorations of disunity. And, for both modernists and postmodernists, the collage was also about either analytic or nonrational perception, or the kinetic shocks and dramas of the modern metropolis. The impulses behind both modern and postmodern collage are driven by an immersion in the kinetic and turbulent modern urban landscape—which is, as Walter Benjamin noted, defined by excess, overstimulation, and shock; the unexpected, the disparate, and constant boundary crossing; bombardments of materials and alterations of time and space—and a constant heterogeneity of fields in motion.[2]

For the Italian futurists, collage was made on canvas or board, or perceived as occurring right then and there—in the world. The futurists were so engrossed in collage as motion that they extolled the work of art as a manifestation of modern life—as moving parts, as speed, light, heat; so obsessed were they with modernity that they celebrated war (misguidedly, I would say) as a grand expression of modern action.

In creating emblems of kinetic energy, the collage creates objects in motion in visual, symbolic, and metonymic ways, and the viewer is compelled to engage in what Whitman once called "a gymnast's struggle," as he or she moves with the jumps, leaps, and juggles that the materials and perspectives generate. Motion, then, is intrinsic to the subject of collage, and if the conversion of the energy of motion is not always completely efficient, the heat it gives off is eponymous to its form and its aspirations. Because the collage spurns being a well-wrought urn, part of the drama of its articulation resides in the intersecting arcs and the motion that define its parts.

I want to suggest that whether collage-works are conceptualized by radical social visions or vanguard aesthetic impulses (Dada's subversive and antibourgeois visions or surrealism's engagement with the nonrational and the unconscious), I find the form is most energized and rich when it finds a dialectical balance (and dialectical is everything in the collage kinetics) between the inventiveness of its disparate yokings of materials and an inner coherence that generates depth through layering. In more quixotic and whimsical collage forms, the work can be sapped by a lack of cohesion, a random floating of forms, or a mechanical arrangement of fields. As successive generations of twentieth-century writers and artists see themselves as wrestling with unfolding zones of modern chaos, the collage has been a form to engage disorder while embodying a kind of order as it makes a form for an aesthetics of open-ended dynamism and epistemological challenges.

I want to look at three collage-works in different genres and at their achievements in their different forms at different moments in twentieth-century upheaval. T. S. Eliot, Robert Rauschenberg, and Joan Didion created collages that have expanded the canvas, the poem, and the nonfiction essay. Eliot's *The Waste Land* and Didion's essay "The White Album," in her book of the same title, continue to open possibilities for literary form, and Rauschenberg's combines of the 1950s and early 1960s created inventive pathways for the shape of the text and the text's relationship to the reader and the world. I also want to suggest how aspects of their collage forms created new notions of consciousness, self-directed ways of reading and seeing, and surprising visions of the social and political world.

>>><<<

From its epigrammatic opening, *The Waste Land* is defined by mixed idioms, shifting planes, intersecting textual notations, and linguistic textures. The epigram from Petronius's "Satyricon" is in Latin and the words of the Sybil at Cumae are in Greek, and there are no text citations given. The reader is, as Whitman once put it, "to do something for himself"—in this case, to find the sources. One is drawn in by two classical languages and then quickly to the dedication that follows directly under the epigraph: "For Ezra Pound / il miglior fabbro" so that one is forced to both bring Pound into the poem and to negotiate another language, modern Italian.

In an era that was defined by traditional Anglo-American forms of the kind practiced by Thomas Hardy, A. E. Housman, and John Masefield in England, and E. A. Robinson and Robert Frost in America—the concept of *The Waste Land* was redefining and beguiling. Eliot, a conservative in religion and politics and a traditionalist in intellectual taste, had been shaped by Pound's new idea of the lyric poem as intellectual collage and repository of cultural texts and sources.

The opening section, "The Burial of the Dead," can be seen as a series of intersecting cubist-like planes that move without ligatures or narrative rationales. In five scenes and five voices, we move seamlessly from the elegiac opening of April as the cruelest month (a riff on Chaucer) to the spoken voice of the young girl, Marie, who recalls the privileged life of her Central European childhood in the Starnbergersee Mountains of Bavaria. Her nostalgic, prewar memory of staying at the archduke's and sledding in the carefree mountains is deepened by lines of German that inscribe her cultural identity. The poem shifts with no set-up or rationale to a mythic voice situated in a biblical landscape that is inflected with allusions to Ezekiel 2:1 ("What are the roots that clutch, what branches grow / Out of this stony rubbish? Son of man") and Ecclesiastes 12:5. But the poem pivots on a dime to the voice of the drowned lover of Wagner's *Tristan und Isolde*, and again a bit of German inflects the poem, creating another texture and intertextual kinesis:

> Frisch weht der Wind
> Der Heimat zu
> Mein Irisch Kind,
> Wo weilest du?

"You gave me hyacinths first a year ago;
They called me the hyacinth girl."
—Yet when we came back, late, from the Hyacinth garden,
Yours arms full, and your hair wet, I could not
Speak, and my eyes failed, I was neither
Living nor dead, and I knew nothing,
Looking into the heart of light, the silence
Oed' und leer das Meer.

As section 1 continues, Eliot keeps cutting and splicing, this time to the fortune-telling, Tarot card–reading Madame Sosostris, through whom we get a biting perspective of the "famous clairvoyante," before Eliot cuts abruptly montage-like to another urban scene in which the allusion to Baudelaire ("Unreal City, / Under the brown fog of a winter dawn") morphs quickly into a voice that speaks from the thronging crowds of the London streets with postwar trauma:

There I saw one I knew, and stopped him, crying: "Stetson!
You who were with me in the ships at Mylae!
That corpse you planted last year in your garden,
Has it begun to sprout? Will it bloom this year?"

While Eliot's scenes move without syntactical set-ups or rational contexts, they are not without nuanced linkings of meaning and their sometimes mythic threads. In its kinetic organization by titled sections ("The Burial of the Dead," "A Game of Chess," "The Fire Sermon," "Death by Water," "What the Thunder Said"), the poem moves in large pieces that embody metaphoric meanings and tones, keeping the poem in constant flux and generating a collage force that allows Eliot to generate zones of surprise and disorientation.

Not unlike like a shift in a surrealist montage, in Section 2, "A Game of Chess," Eliot splices two disparate scenes in the lives of women in London. In scene one, with its baroque, Jamesian interior in which a pampered woman is cloistered in her neurotic world as she sits in her "Chair . . . like a burnished throne," he sets up one of several moments of sexual sterility. The spiraling literary allusions—to Shakespeare's Cleopatra, the "laquearia" from Book 1 of *The Aeneid*, "the Sylvan scene" from Book 6 of Milton's *Paradise Lost*, and the Philomel myth from Ovid's *Metamorphosis*—make the layering of myth essential to the kinetic movement that is then strategically interrupted with the woman's voice: "'My nerves are bad tonight. Yes, bad. Stay with me. / Speak to me. Why do you never speak. Speak. / What are you thinking of? What thinking? What?'"

In the other half of the montage, Eliot takes us to a pub in working-class London where a woman is recounting her conversation with her friend Lil amid the theatrical interruptions of the pub keeper's last call: "HURRY UP PLEASE ITS TIME" (with its double entendre on time passing). Eliot splices the scene at intervals as his dramatic dialogue pushes the montage. Lil looks "antique" because, she claims, the effects of the pills she took to have an abortion (she already has five children, the last of which almost killed her) have taken their toll. Eliot's version of working-class dialogue isn't cockney, but he makes clipped phrases that bring us into his vision of still another variation of sexual sterility: "He's been in the army four years, he wants a good time, / And if you don't give it him, there's others will, I said." And then the scene ends abruptly, with its mocking playful riff on Ophelia's departure in Act 4 of *Hamlet*: "Goonight Bill. Goonight Lou. Goonight May. Goonight. / Ta ta. Goonight. Goonight. / Good night, ladies, good night, sweet ladies, good night, good night."

Eliot gives us a social texture, closing time at the pub, as well as a metaphysical hint about time passing and passing time, all twined together in the kinetics of Eliot's lyric theater.

In Section 3, "The Fire Sermon," he pushes the shifting movement into an even more layered, kaleidoscopic poetics that is closer to that "chaotic mishmash, potpourri." Had there ever been a poem or section of a poem with such cutting and splicing, such frenetic movement that, formally at least, it seemed closer to Italian futurism's love of mixing and combining the unexpected. In a section held together by the image of the Thames River, the movement of the mythic omniscient Tiresias voice moves around like a shaky handheld camera. The opening lines press hard on the idea of desolation in language and seem stilted and overdrawn, even with the sweet lines from Spenser's *Prothalamion*:

> The river's tent is broken: the last fingers of leaf
> Clutch and sink into the wet bank. The wind
> Crosses the brown land, unheard. The nymphs are departed.
> Sweet Thames, run softly, till I end my song.

The following stanzas make another cinematic-like montage of scenes along the river in which past and present London are jostled together in a mode that Eliot, Joyce, and Pound all believed the mythic method could accomplish. We go from "empty bottles, sandwich papers / Silk handkerchiefs, cardboard boxes, cigarette ends" to a big dramatic voice: "By the waters of Leman I sat down and wept . . . / Sweet Thames, run softly till I end my song," which echoes the elegiac exile of Psalm 13, "By the rivers of Babylon, yea, there we sat down, we wept," and the *Prothalamion* again. Back and forth between myth and contemporaneity, the sterility of sex and sexuality obsess Eliot: "The sound of horns and motors, which shall bring / Sweeney to Mrs. Porter in the spring." With his witty play, things move from an allusion to Marvell's "To His Coy Mistress" to a scene closer in a line from Verlaine: *"Et O ces voix d'enfants, chantant dans la coupole!"* before the stanza spills into an onomatopoetic interlude in which allusions to bird sounds evoke rape as well:

Twit twit twit
Jug jug jug jug jug jug
So rudely forc'd
Tereu

And then we're spun once more into a kinesis of montage with another Baudelairian allusion of an "Unreal City" that introduces us to "Mr. Eugenides, the Smyrna merchant / Unshaven, with a pocket full of currants," whose homosexual assignation defines another part of the Eliotic sexual landscape. And when Eliot shifts again to the "violet hour," Tiresias finally appears by name, witnessing the tawdry modern urban work world. The long scene of the office secretary having her indifferent sexual encounter with the "carbuncular . . . clerk" continues Eliot's meditation on failed sex, and as Tiresias keeps watching the world turn, we move to a scene in a kind of Rauschenberg combine-like way made of playful one- and two-beat lines. In those staccato lines, we continue to see the Thames through Eliot's Thames nymph— his riff on the Rhine daughters in Wagner's *Gotterdämmerung*. Once again, the mythic past propels the scene—this time with its evocation of Queen Elizabeth and her supposed lover the Earl of Leicester as they float down the river to "the peal of bells," and "White towers," and the nymphs echo the Rhine daughters in a further indented stanza, "Weialala leia / Wallala leialala." The ensuing stanzas take us back to tawdry, working-class London and repellent sex (in real life, as we know, Eliot was struggling with his sexuality and his marriage to his soon-to-be ex-wife), and then to another one of those abrupt shifts as the poem's mythic voice assumes Saint Augustine's Christian confession about lust: "To Carthage then I came / Burning burning burning burning / O Lord Thou pluckest me out / O Lord Thou pluckest / burning," as those incantatory lyric lines move the whole wild spliced section to a close.

Section 4, "Death by Water," is like a small inset photo in a larger collage of big forms; a quiet, haunting lyric poem, it abuts two wild, mythy sections and gives the poem the kind of asymmetry an interesting collage structure does, as it catches us off guard and comes as thematic continuation of the focus on death that has haunted the poem from the opening lines of "The Burial of the Dead." It's like a small insert in, say, a Hans Arp collage.

The final section, "What the Thunder Said," is a big swath of landscape that, like the earlier sections, is made of spliced pieces; but here the predominance of the spiritual topography dominates. Eliot's ability to imagine a desert landscape of the final days of Christ is an evocative myth-history moment that sets up the spiritual drive of the final section. From the evocation of Jesus being betrayed in the garden at Gethsemane, Eliot's successive stanzas are defined by that parched landscape that embodies the spiritual hunger of the poem. The repetition of rock and water becomes almost hypnotic in the short one- and two-beat lines of the fourth stanza: "And no rock / If there were rock / And also water / And water / A spring," before the section slides into another desert landscape that evokes Christ's return at Emmaus, "Gliding wrapped in a brown mantle, hooded." As dry sterile thunder hovers over the section, Eliot's image of "hooded hordes swarming / Over endless plains" brings us the dislocation of upheaval in the wake of war and the fall of empires and decline of civilization:

Falling towers
Jerusalem Athens Alexandria
Vienna London
Unreal

With the evocation of Baudelaire again, Eliot cuts the scene, cinematic-like once more, to a surreal sexuality as a woman lets her hair out as bats are flying and hanging in a church bell tower. Then more dry bones, empty chapels, desert rocks of Eliot's Levantine desert, until he shifts the scene in the middle of a stanza, startlingly, to India. Eliot's spiritual hunt now drives him to the holy water of the Ganges. In this inset segment, Eliot shifts landscape as if a camera were panning scenes, as we now leave the Levant's biblical topography for the holy water of India: "Ganga was sunken, and the limp leaves / Waited for rain, while the black clouds / Gathered far distant, over Himavant. / The jungle crouched, humped in silence. / Then spoke the thunder / DA."

When the poem opens into a penultimate piece of its final part—a prayer meditation demarcated, as if flashcards were inserted, by the instructions in virtue from the Brihadaranyaka Upanishad: "Datta. Dayadhvam. Damyata."—meaning Give. Sympathize. Control. With Sanskrit wisdom enmeshed with biblical scenes from the life of Christ, the poem spills into a frenetic, futuristic whirling of small pieces—a montaging of fast scenes, as the section closes with an allusion to Jesse Weston's book *From Ritual to Romance*, which then spills into a line from Dante's Purgatorio, and then moves to a phrase from the fourth-century Latin poem *Pervigilum Veneris*, which enjambs to a line from a sonnet by Gérard de Nerval and then to a line from Kyd's *Spanish Tragedy* and back to the Upanishad commands of virtue, and then—can it be?—to a formal closing from the Upanishad "Shantih shantih shantih"—the word for peace that passeth all understanding. Notwithstanding those words of peace, the splicing and piecing of this chaotic closing has some futuristic collage-like swirling or Rauschenberg combine motion to it. As Eliot closes, are we closer to order or entropy?

> I sat upon the shore
> Fishing, with the arid plain behind me
> Shall I at least set my lands in order?
> London Bridge is falling down falling down falling down
> *Poi s'ascose nel foco che gli affina*
> *Quando fiam uti chelidon*—O swallow swallow
> *Le Prince d' Aquitaine à la tour abolie*
> These fragments I have shored against my ruins
> Why the Ile fit you. Hieronymo's mad againe.
> Datta. Dayadhvam. Damyata.
> Shantih   shantih   shantih

If the reader thinks the last collage piece has been set in motion, she will have one more segment to navigate: the Notes. The Notes, which Eliot added at the urging of his editor, comprise, really, another section of intersecting sources, and so the reader is forced to engage and presumably consult Eliot's sources such as Ezekiel II, i, *Tristan and Isolde*, verses 1, 5–8, *The Tempest*, I, ii, Verlaine, *Parsifal*, and so on, for several pages. The Notes create another kind of mishmash that is designed to push the poem into a self-reflexive modern-ness and send the reader both out into the world of literature and history and back into the poem with myriad ways of making meaning while bringing the poem to a new kind of multiplicity.

The Waste Land has given scholars fits of joy for decades, and its built-in scholarly appeal and its impact on the English department curriculum bears that out. The poem's intellectual lures are many, and it is the kind of poem scholars feed on because it engages an intellectual sleuthing process that can be fun and rewarding, even if at times necessarily incomplete. Sometimes there seems something comic about the degrees to which scholars have treated *The Waste Land* as if it were a continuous narrative, an almost seamless continuity of symbols and images and poetic telling that isn't all that different from Tennyson's "In Memoriam" or Wordsworth's *Prelude*.

In his controlled, well-conceived (with the great aid of Pound) "mish-mash potpourri," Eliot created a modernist collage as no other poet before him had. In its continual cuts and shifts, pivots and leaps, informed, as well, by the end notes that lead the reader into the poem's forest of intertextuality—providing both coherence and some desired obscurity. Without surrendering to the collage-like movements that embody fragments and fragmentation, disconnects, wild and shaky jumps, the reader misses the meaning of the poem that is generated by its formal and coherent disunity and its collage dynamism. The poem embodied a new age in which Pound's poetics, Picasso's and Braque's collage rebellion against the canvas, and Dada's and futurism's immersion in the dynamism and fragmentation of the new urban-technological world were all part of a context and moment. It is Eliot's appropriation of these idioms combined with his intellectual classicism that continue to give the poem its appeal to both experimentalists and traditionalists, so that perhaps he did succeed, in some way, in shoring those fragments against his ruin.

>>> <<<

Joan's Didion's opening essay, bearing the same title as her book *The White Album*, suggests collage in its title. If *album* derives from the Latin word for list, it has come to be subsumed by the LP or CD album as a collection of songs, or the photo album or scrapbook that suggests a collection of artifacts of disparate layers, hybrid, of a polyglot nature. Didion's chapter is an album of a time of turmoil, both inner and outer for her, in the late 1960s—a time of bewildering change, chaos, violence, uncertainty. She articulates her ars poetica early in the chapter: "We live entirely, especially if we are writers, by the imposition of a narrative line upon disparate images, by the 'ideas' with which we have learned to freeze the shifting phantasmagoria which is our actual experience." Narrative as imposition on disparate images is one way of seeing how a nonfiction writer might take on the prismatic intersections of the real—as they collide and intersect in ways that give off something about the state of reality she's compelled to engage. So radical was Didion's sense of a break with her previous notions of the real that she refers to the time "when I began to doubt the premises of all the stories I had ever told myself." It seems fair to assert that the years between 1966 and 1971 in the United States were years of turmoil and change of an unprecedented kind. The antiwar movement, the civil rights movement, a new pop culture that included psychedelic drugs, a more subversive rock 'n' roll, and a new sexual liberation, which intersected at times with cult violence, group movements, and political assassinations, were defining a new American landscape. As Didion put it, "certain of these images did not fit into any narrative I knew."

Confronted with these realities, Didion's appropriation of collage techniques in "The White Album" enables her to get hold of a sense of "the shifting phantasmagoria" of "our actual experience." And her choice of phantasmagoria captures the collage nature of her seeing. In using the trope of the phantasmagoric, that late-nineteenth-century form of theater in which a magic lantern was used to project frightening and nightmarish images in kaleidoscopic forms on a screen, she encodes another trope for collage-seeing, as colliding, kinetic, nonlinear perception becomes the central way of taking in the real.

"The White Album" opens its meditation on confusion with an autobiographical accounting of family life, personal events, political occurrences, and her confessions of bewilderment and uncertainty. Didion continues to address her sense of the rupture in the narrative: "I was meant to know the plot, but all I knew was what I saw: flash pictures in variable sequence, images with no 'meaning' beyond their temporary arrangement, not a movie, but a cutting-room experience." She tells us that she "wanted still to believe in the narrative and in the narrative's intelligibility," but there has been a break in the narrative, and so experience seemed like a flash cut—abruptly shifting images "with no 'meaning' beyond their temporary arrangement." The abrupt shifts in reality that hit Didion in the year 1968 needed another kind of form to absorb it. "The White Album" offers a form and an approach to capture the phantasmagoria of violence, political chaos, jolting new social arrangements, and relations that bring us into the realm of the American grotesque. Her essay is made up of textual flash-cut layers, and, not surprisingly, many of them are texts of testimony. I'm reminded here of Shoshana Felman's claim that we live in the age of testimony, which has supplied us with a new sense of crisis.[3]

In "The White Album," we enter into a more intimate kind of testimony in which we open with a text Didion pulls from her confidential file; it's a psychiatric report about her near collapse in June 1968, when she was an outpatient at Santa Monica hospital:

A thorough medical evaluation elicited no positive findings and she was placed on Elavil, Mg. 20, tid. . . . The Rorschach record is

interpreted as describing a personality in process of deterioration
with abundant signs of ailing defenses and increasing inability of
the ego to mediate the world of reality and to cope with normal
stress. . . . Emotionally, patient has alienated herself almost entirely
from the world of other human beings. Her fantasy life appears to
have been virtually completely preempted by primitive, regressive
libidinal preoccupations many of which are distorted or bizarre. . . .
Patient's thematic productions on the Thematic Apperception Test
emphasize her fundamentally pessimistic, fatalistic, and depressive
view of the world around her.

Rendered in italics, and as a longer report in her essay, the narrative hinges on a flash cut in which we—as readers of Didion's
report on her medical trauma—enter into her intimate sense of
struggle. In this way, the impact of cultural chaos on the life of
the self becomes part of Didion's personal voice, one in which
self and world are enmeshed. As the chapter turns on flash cuts
and fragments, overheard voices, song lyrics, street slogans, and
more testimony from various sensational trials, we are pushed
into the chaos of American culture, California style. We move in
and out of narrative as we intersect with planes of jarring texts
that push us both in and out of chaos and the self's struggle with
chaos. The text of a sentimental framed "house blessing" on the
wall of Didion's mother-in-law's house in Connecticut is pure
irony in the opening, "God bless the corners of this house," and
its closing, "And bless each door that opens wide, to stranger as
to kin." This kitsch is followed by the transcript of a murder trial
of two boys convicted of killing a sixty-year-old man who had
read their fortunes at his house (not far from Didion's house in
Hollywood) and who turned out to have been a former silent
film actor:

Q: Did you talk after you ate?
A: While we were eating, after we ate. Mr. Novarro told our fortunes
   with some cards and he read our palms.
Q. Did he tell you you were going to have a lot of good luck or bad
   luck or what happened?
A. He wasn't a good palm reader.

Between murder trial transcripts, encounters with cult murders (Linda Kasabian of the Manson cult) and taking sedatives for vertigo or migraines (25 mg. Compazine), from which Didion suffered, pop songs on the radio float through her consciousness: "Midnight Confessions," "Visions of Johanna," "Do You Wanna Dance." There are conversations with women private detectives and prophets of Scientology, and then she is at a recording session of the new rock Dadaists, The Doors, with their charismatic leader Jim Morrison. She captures the sound bites of dialogue between Manzarek and Morrison with a Raymond Carver–like minimalism, and then a block of lyrics by rock's new prophets of "apocalyptic sex":

Come on baby, gonna take a little ride
Goin' down by the ocean side
Gonna get real close
Gonna get real tight
Baby gonna drown tonight—
Goin' down, down, down.

As the essay swings back and forth from rock music to trial transcripts, the scene cuts to the Black Panthers trial of Huey Newton up north in Alameda County in the East Bay region, where Newton was charged with killing police officer John Frey. Didion's flash edit of the scene captures the street chants of fellow Panthers outside the Alameda County Jail:

Get your M-
31.
'Cause baby we gonna
Have some fun.
BOOM BOOM. BOOM BOOM
. . .
Bullshit bullshit
Can't stand the game
White man's playing.
One way out, one way out.
BOOM BOOM. BOOM BOOM.

Testimony—"that crucial mode or our relation to events of our time,"[4] as Shoshana Felman puts it—continues to be Didion's approach to crisis, and again we get a Huey Newton transcript from a journalist:

Q. Tell us something about yourself, Huey, I mean your life before the Panthers.
A. Before the Black Panther Party my life was very similar to that of most black people in this country.
Q. Well, your family, some incidents you remember, the influences that shaped you—
A. Living in America shaped me.

As Didion investigates the trial, she gives us another testimony, this time of Corrine Leonard, the nurse at the emergency room of the hospital (Kaiser) where Newton was brought after being shot in the stomach during the gunfire with officer John Frey:

> I heard a moaning and a groaning, and I went over and it was—this Negro fellow was there. He had been shot in the stomach and at the same time he didn't appear in any acute distress and so I said I'd see, and so I asked him if he was a Kaiser, if he belonged to Kaiser, and he said "Yes, yes, get a doctor, can't you see I'm bleeding? I've been shot."

With confessional snippets set into parts of the narrative, Didion grafts the intimacy of the testimony of others into a larger portrait of a cultural moment and her own journey through it. No detail of intimacy is too private or irrelevant, and so we move from a moment at Eldridge Cleaver's apartment with his parole officer on the day of the publication of Cleaver's sensational book *Soul on Ice* to a list of things taped on the inside of her closet door that gives us a view of her life as a traveling journalist:

To Pack and Wear:
   2 skirts
   2 jerseys or leotards
   1 pullover sweater

2 pair shoes
stockings
bra
nightgown, robe, slippers
cigarettes
bourbon
bag with:
    shampoo
    toothbrush and paste
    Basis soap
    razor, deodorant
    aspirin, prescriptions, Tampax
    face cream, powder, baby oil*

The narrative continues to scissor between the swirling events of Didion's personal life and the phantasmagoria out there. She finds herself on the San Francisco State campus, where the Black Panther revolution is playing out as police and mace mix with camera crews, militant black students and bourgeois white students trying to be revolutionary. Then we cut to the shallow end of her sister-in-law's Beverley Hills swimming pool, as news comes over the radio about the murders of eight people by the Charles Manson cult at Sharon Tate Polanski's house on Cielo Drive. As this phantasmagoric piece of the collage emerges, Didion takes us from the social real as she interviews Linda Kassabian—one of the Mason cult who was a witness to the murders on Cielo Drive—to the state of her nervous system:

> Certain organic disorders of the central nervous system are characterized by periodic remissions, the apparent complete recovery of the afflicted nerves. What happens appears to be this: as the lining of a nerve becomes inflamed and hardens into scar tissue, thereby blocking the passage of neural impulses, the nervous system gradually changes its circuitry, finds other, unaffected nerves to carry the same messages. During the years when I found it necessary to revise the circuitry of my mind I discovered that I was no long interested in whether the woman on the ledge outside the window on the sixteenth floor jumped or did not jump, or in why. I was interested

only in the picture of her in my mind: her hair incandescent in the floodlights, her bare toes curled inward on the stone ledge.

We then catapult from being with Didion at the fashionable I. Magnin in Beverly Hills, where she is picking out a dress for Linda Kasabian to what I would call a small insert like something out of a 1970s Rauschenberg collage, in which she recalls being in a motel near Pendleton, Oregon, doing a piece for *Life* about the storage of nerve gas at an army arsenal. She recalls the motel manager, a Mormon, abruptly saying to her: *If you can't believe you're going to heaven in your own body and on a first-name basis with all the members of your family, then what's the point of dying?* From this "koan of the period"—a startling non sequitur that functions like a counterintuitive aphorism of the cultural moment—she moves us back to her neurology report and her vision disorder and the doctor's conjectures about her having multiple sclerosis. In her closing, she takes us back to her departure from her house in Los Angeles to a house on the ocean, where she ruminates on the chaos swirling around her.

If she comes to a place where she acknowledges the limits of writing—"Quite often I reflect on the big house in Hollywood, on 'Midnight Confessions' and on Ramon Novarro and on the fact that Roman Polanski and I are godparents to the same child, but writing this has not yet helped me to see what it means"—the essay affirms the power of collage. The mosaic pieces, fragments, and splicings that she orchestrates bring us into a deeper sense of the reality of unfolding historical forces. Her assemblage of sensations and encounters and disruptive images (violent events, pop-song fragments, court testimonies, street chants, personal medical reports) intersect with her desire to get at something about 1968 in California. The collage-album becomes a record of witness and an idiosyncratic confession about writing and living in personal and cultural chaos. If they are "fragments shored against ruins," it is not a ruined Didion we encounter, but a writer who wants to collect and render the fragments so cultural confusion can come into whatever focus it might—the way shards, rapid cuts, and edits bombard consciousness.

>>><<<

I want to close by reflecting on the combines of Robert Rauschenberg—in particular, his combines of the 1950s and 1960s, which took the idea of collage to a new place, and perhaps a place that is unique in its range and goal and expansiveness. During the early 1950s, Rauschenberg was obsessed with the idea of remaking the barriers between life and art: "Painting relates to both art and life. Neither can be made. I try to act in the gap between the two,"[5] that similar impulse which also drove both the Beat and confessional poets of the same 1950s moment.

Rauschenberg's technique of combining objects—scraps of metal, street signs, license plates, photographs, diverse materials (paper, cloth, plastic, wood, metal), taxidermied birds and animals, pieces of furniture, industrial scraps—within and on the surface and perimeters of a canvas created an idea of collage that, as the word *combine* suggests, brings wild and radical combinations of forms, textures, concepts, and materials together. What marks Rauschenberg's combines of the 1950s is their explosive fullness, their baroque excess, their entanglements, fusions, and combustions. Rauschenberg's breakthrough into what he named his combines is inseparable from post–World War II American culture and the aesthetic energies of the 1950s. The combines embody a kind of bebop spontaneity and freedom and a sense of motion that evokes the Beat idea of the American road (a mid-twentieth-century extrapolation of Whitman's "Open Road"). This sense of freedom—both metonymic and literal—defined the Kerouac-Ginsberg highway of *On the Road* and *Howl* of the 1950s as well as the Rauschenberg combine with its kinetics of possibility and surprise.

Whether Rauschenberg's combines are autobiographical, as some are, or less personal, they embody a field in motion where things merge, converge, and intersect as they give off explosive

energies. As collage, they challenge notions of formal containment and aesthetic assumptions about the beautiful, the elegant,
the decorative, and they hold in balance something of Jackson Pollock's idea of action painting—the fluidity of abstract
expressionism—earlier modernist notions of collage, and a new
notion of space and materiality.

Whether one is interested in finding iconographic meaning
in the combines or seeing abstract formalisms, Rauschenberg's
collages allow us another perspective on the collage as a mode
of remaking and extending form beyond linear expectations and
closed or contained parameters. His passion for the bric-a-brac
layers of American material culture (was there a more plentiful
culture of materialism and commerce than the postwar United
States at the time?) enabled him to create collages of singular
hybridity and intertextuality, often inflected by his neo-Dadaist
(as Rauschenberg termed his own sensibility at the time) mixing of postwar jazz and abstract expressionism. His omnivorous
eclecticism and his brilliant sense of design (he was a set de-
signer for Merce Cunningham for years) were also essential to
his inventions.

In his 1955 combine, *Monk*, which evokes and plays with the
work of the jazz innovator Thelonius Monk, we're overwhelmed
with colliding images, textures, and materials (Plate 1). A newspaper fragment, a comic strip, a reproduction of a serene Hudson
River School water landscape, a piece of a record with the half-
legible title "'Round Midnight," a filmstrip of sequential images
of Charlie Chaplin, a postage stamp, a piece of an airmail envelope, wood, fabric, swaths of paint, and some gooey drippings in
red and yellow. The materials are quintessential Rauschenberg,
but it is the motion created by their intersections—the animated
fury of their coming together—that creates a challenging and
compelling aesthetic with its signifying layers of objects. We are
pulled into looking at images, materials, textures, gestures, and a
multiplicity of interpretations.

Not unlike Ginsberg's wild image juxtaposings in part 1 of
Howl (which was written the same year that *Monk* was made),

Rauschenberg asks us to look freshly at things with a new visual syntax. What are we to make of the seven sequential film frames of Charlie Chaplin in relation to a photocopy of a Hudson River School image and a scrap of Monk's classic 1944 record "Round Midnight"? Is the traditional Hudson River School image undercut by the Monk record label? Do the pop-culture images (the cartoon frame, the frames of Chaplin) intersect with the more genteel image of the Hudson River School landscape in order to ask us to consider the nature of American art and imagination? Rauschenberg's perspectival openings are also inflected by the values of the paint—red and yellow that are dripped and dashed across the canvas and over the Hudson River School image. In the hot and excitable tensions created by the gestural brushstrokes, Rauschenberg also asks us to look at relationships between textures and color as they overlay the images within his compositional form.

One of the arresting images in the combine is a hunk of polka-dot fabric that pops near the center of the canvas; it brings you through the clotted images of newspaper and comic strip to the filmstrip of Chaplin. To get there, you have to travel through layers of transparency and opacity as you view the comic strip and the newspaper fragment through washes of white paint. The dynamism of the design is as compelling as the syntax of the images and materials. The action-spilled red paint over the staid Hudson River School image, and the swirling red, blue, and orange impastos of paint over cloth at the top, from which a postage stamp emerges, force us out of any easy metonymy into oblique relationships between color and form, image and idea.

If you take Monk's famous jazz piece "'Round Midnight" as a trope for the combine, then Rauschenberg's mode of collage play has a more self-aware sense of riffing about its movements and strange mixes. From one perspective, it's a riff on American forms of art and compels us to ask: What is American culture? What strange elements make up the landscape of the American imagination? What do we make of the relationship between the Chaplin film, the Hudson River School image, and the Monk jazz piece? How do they intersect with one another, and how do they exist in relation to textures, colors, and other materials: a fragment of a map of West Virginia, a comic strip, a newspaper fragment, a piece of cloth, the translucent white wash?

In the yoking of such images, genres, color, and materials, *Monk* also leads us by composition, by the juxtaposing of images, by strange intersections, by an idea of motion that resists linearity and goes beyond its own boundaries. In this way, Rauschenberg's combine is open-ended, bigger than the sum of its parts, as it generates motion. Hybridity and intertextuality drive its fabulous fusions but also keep it working with its disparate parts so that the collage doesn't lapse into arbitrariness or slackness but stays torqued to its own inner workings, to the parts speaking to one another as they animate the whole.

Monk forces the viewer to participate in the kinetics of collage, to negotiate meaning from image to image, from texture to texture, from color to color. In doing so, the viewer engages in a jumping and leaping and in negotiating meaning across image representations of genres of music, painting, and film. The intensity of visual movement is part of the intellectual drama that activates our signifying process and is also congruent with the compositional structure, which is—in its spontaneity—also formal. Rauschenberg creates, in this way, interpretative perspective out of a visual language of hyperexcitation. In his visual dynamism, we're led lyrically into a vision of culture and aesthetics that can also resist iconographic interpretation while it leads us to contemplate an idea of potentiality and of meaning making as a process that is incomplete and open-ended. This kind of collage kinetic opens us to an idea of dialogical thinking that Matthew Leone has called an epistemology of potentiality—in which the relationship between the parts generate "an interconnectedness" and an "interanimation" that keep the dialogue between the viewer and, in this case, collage in constant motion.[6]

In his 1961 combine *Black Market*, Rauschenberg takes the collage to an even more expansive place (Plate 2). Working in New York at the time, Rauschenberg was immersed in the culture of industrial America, or junk culture, in another sense. The collage owes something to his living in Lower Manhattan for over a decade during a time of urban transition and change.[7] Mounted on a framed canvas, Rauschenberg's assemblage of industrial junk includes an Ohio license plate, Plexiglas clipboards affixed and hanging from the canvas, a piece of found metal, a magazine photo of the U.S. capitol over a gray wash, crumbly poster fragments, finger-applied impasto paints, a bright white stamp-pressed lettering, a news photograph, a rusted panel, billboard posters, a thick silver X over a clean canvas piece, metal file card dividers, and other mass-produced objects. And then there is a large wooden "ONE WAY" sign.

The collage starts in a flat plane and morphs into something else as the affixed clipboards hang like translucent windows through which vague shapes of color show. The clipboards pop the canvas and push it into a three-dimensional space. They are the white windows that break up the dark industrial materials. But Rauschenberg pushes the spatial play further, as the wooden "ONE WAY" sign disrupts the flat surface as well as the idea of containment. The sign is a formal gesture as it sends the collage into another dimension, out of its perimeter and conceptual containment; but it's also a signifying image that marks a moment in Manhattan urban planning, which had just been redefined by the creation of one-way avenues on the East Side, transforming the traffic flow of the city, which is also the flow of space, the kinetics of machines in the confines of an urban grid, the way consciousness now experiences the formation of human-techno movement, and the desire to remake the city as a systematized place of order and flow.

The "ONE WAY" sign also disrupts the already intersecting chaos of materials; nailed on wood that is affixed to the canvas, the sign's black-and-white boldness is not only three-dimensional but it then breaks out of the frame, undermining the idea of containment and closed form. But Rauschenberg takes it even further: From the arrow point of the "ONE WAY" sign, he drops rope down the length of the canvas to a wooden suitcase on the floor. As the combine pushes toward what will come to be more popularly known as *installation* by the 1980s—the suitcase, still attached to the canvas through the tip of the extruding "ONE WAY" sign—extends the idea of space and object play. The rope casts a shadow line on the wall as it drops to the valise, and it is through the valise (an old wooden suitcase) that Rauschenberg invites the viewer's participation.

Here the viewer is invited to put items of his or her own in the suitcase in exchange for objects already in the valise. It is not only a black market of gift exchange but a way for the viewer to give meaning to ordinary objects, meaning that could only be ascribed by the viewer. Through this process of participation, Rauschenberg pushes the collage to engage the viewer both physically and intellectually and through a sense of materiality—as the viewer contributes a material object to the collage and takes one away with her. The implications of *Black Market* are, in part, about open-endedness, expansiveness, continuousness. Dialectical tensions between meaning and materiality keep the idea of conceptual and formal dimensions energized in *Black Market*; stasis and motion keep pushing each other into new planes or spaces of meaning. As the image is allowed its own formal presentation, it's also enveloped by shifting contexts that are set in motion by planes of color, texture, materiality, by stasis and motion—free and attached. As the materials break out of the perimeter of the canvas, *Black Market* resists closure, and in this way Rauschenberg's kinesis recalls Whitman's notion of open-endedness at the closing of "Song of Myself," when the poet reminds us that the meaning of the poem supersedes any conventional idea of form and that the poet is outside of the parameters of the text, as text diffuses in a wider world: "If you want me again look for me under your boot soles. . . . Failing to fetch me at first keep encouraged, / Missing me one place search another."

>>><<<

The Waste Land's collage configuration inscribes T. S. Eliot's sense of social change from sexual mores and spiritual decline to post–

World War I human dislocation and historical trauma. Robert Rauschenberg's combines raise issues embedded in social meanings and material forces that are part of an emerging post–World War II American culture of explosive power, rapid motion, and material and cultural capital that are coming to shape some of the new empire's modes of cultural production and signification. Joan Didion's phantasmagoric collage vision of California in 1968 embodies both her personal crisis and something of the psycho-social-sexual pop-cultural revolution and political upheaval that defined U.S. culture at a time of explosion. Collage thrives on the continual potentiality of its elements, which are redefined as they are seen in relation to the other fragments of the whole. In this way, collage not only eschews traditional formalisms of the autotelic text, it also allows us to see the imagination taking on historical moments of shifting meanings that define the dynamics of social change and historical disruption.

Arshile Gorky: From the Armenian Genocide to the Avant-Garde

When my essay "Arshile Gorky and the Armenian Genocide" appeared in *Art in America* in 1996, there was a surprising absence in the scholarship on Gorky. Amid the quite considerable criticism and scholarship (although not yet one full, scholarly biography), Gorky's Armenian historical and cultural context were largely missing. There was acknowledgment that Gorky had come from Van, a city in a province of the same name in eastern Turkey, part of historic Armenia, in what was sometimes referred to as "Turkish Armenia." There was some mention of his mother's death in tragic circumstances, and some general note that Gorky's childhood was lived in an Armenian village and agrarian setting. But most of this so-called background was relegated to biographical detail or exotic backdrop. Scholars and critics noted that he was an exile, as were many of Gorky's fellow painters—Willem de Kooning, John Graham, Mark Rothko, and Raoul Hague among them.

Yet the absence of any more deeply probed Armenian context and its possible implications for his work struck me as a lacuna, a missing piece in the attempt to understand Gorky's art. I felt that, for all the explication and praise from critics, the paintings had been seen through a lens of dominantly formalist critique that belonged to an almost exclusively and more narrow aesthetic disposition of modernist art historical and critical practice. It would take another essay to summarize many of those mostly good critics and scholars and their opinions.

Although some critics, such as Melvin Lader and Ethel Schwabacher, were more attentive to the Armenian context of Gorky's life and work, it wasn't until Gorky's nephew, Karlen Mooradian, in his self-published books of the late 1970s and early 1980s wrote about his uncle that the richness of the Armenian context emerged; and even if Mooradian was not able to bring that context into a way of viewing Gorky's art very clearly or perceptively, at least he had pointed to something significant. Unfortunately, Mooradian's eccentric, overwrought, and somewhat disjointed prose and his deeply private musings on his uncle, whom he deified, both shed light on and obscured Gorky's past. This was further complicated by the swatch of letters that Mooradian unearthed and published—letters that Gorky had supposedly written to his sister Vartoosh. These letters were full of reflections on Armenian genocide trauma, Gorky's childhood, and assertions about the supremacy of the Armenian aesthetic tradition and culture. They were full-bodied and lyrical, and because most of Gorky's other letters were yet to be translated and were in archives, there was little to which to compare them. But decades later, Gorky scholars could not find the letters anywhere (Mooradian committed suicide in 1990) and came to the conclusion that Mooradian had constructed the letters either from interviews he had done with his mother about Gorky or from his own imagination. The letters were part of my original essay, but I excised them as soon as I discovered they were not able to be validated, and I would note that, although they provided texture and biographical excitement for my earlier essay, they were not necessary for my arguments.

In 1996, I argued that to read Gorky deeply, one had to understand something about the Armenian aesthetic and cultural tradition from which he had emerged and something about his experience as an Armenian genocide survivor, which had traumatized him in complex ways. In revising my essay several years after its publication, I hope that I've taken my sense of Gorky's work further in exploring how the Armenian cultural and genocidal contexts of Gorky's life allow deeper and fuller insights to the paintings. Since "Arshile Gorky and the Armenian Genocide" was published, there have been three full biographies, a monograph, a collection of letters, and exhibition catalogs, along with scholarly articles. And, although all these studies have enriched our understanding of Gorky, his childhood in Van and in the early days of the Armenian Republic, there is still something missing regarding the relationship between historical and cultural context and the art, and a failure to grasp fully the role of Armenian aesthetics and history in Gorky's work.

In reading the paintings as I do, I in no way mean to suggest that there is only one way to read them, nor do I suggest that the formalist dimensions that have been so well treated by other critics, and by myself, are not important. The aesthetic formulations and executions are always essential dimensions of any work of art. Without the particular nature of those formulations and executions, there is not a distinctive work, and the text (painting or poem or play) does not pass into the wider view of the world—and, of course, does not gain critical reception. My own readings of Gorky's paintings are enmeshed in my own aesthetic engagement with Gorky's style, painterly forms, and constructions. Otherwise, why write about his work?

It is hardly radical to note at this moment in critical thinking that cultural forces and historical events that inform an artist's life and work might also be important to a deeper understanding of the work, or to assert that what informs and enters a painter's work might also emanate from various domains of personal experience and cultural and historical influence. In reading the paintings as informed, in part but not solely, by the traumatic experience of loss—the death of his mother as a result of famine and death march that were part of the Armenian genocide, the loss of and uprooting from home and homeland, the saturation in death that genocide always leaves with the survivor—I hope to bring the context of history and biography to bear on the formal nature of Gorky's art.

>>><<<

When my essay first appeared in 1996, it elicited an array of responses. I heard from the aesthetic formalists who were offended that I would suggest that both abstract forms could embody meanings that were iconographic or representational and might even encode biographical and historical meaning. Conversely, the then new generation of art historians, cultural studies scholars, and new historicists responded with affirmation, claiming that my essay had opened up Gorky's work in a new way. As one art historian colleague put it: "I knew there was something else going on in Gorky's work, and could never put my finger on it." Susan Sontag wrote me a letter expressing her excitement about my bringing the Armenian genocide and Gorky's art together.[1] Among the most vocal critics of my essay was Matthew Spender, a sculptor and the husband of Gorky's eldest daughter, Maro (also a painter), who subsequently wrote a biography of Gorky, *From a High Place*, and later edited a collection of Gorky's letters. I realized that Spender's response was, in part, the result of my taking him to task in my essay for having curated an impressive show "The Breakthrough Years of Arshile Gorky," which was then traveling around the country in 1995, because there was no mention of Gorky's childhood experiences as a survivor of genocide in either the text of the catalog or the museum wall text. Even a sentence would have contributed some honesty to the narrative and context of Gorky's complex life and art.

It became clear to me quickly after some exchange of letters in *Art in America* and in other correspondences with Spender that he believes in the aesthetic autonomy of the work of art in an absolutist way, and that he is hostile to those who navigate artistic meaning from any nuanced intersections between history, biography, cultural context, and the work. At the conclusion of his biography, Spender exclaims: "Gorky was not an Armenian painter. Neither Armenia nor America was enough. He was searching for an identity which lay beyond anyone's land, and from his solitary pinnacle he bequeathed an eloquent example of how one individual can renew the language of art and himself, entirely from within."[2] I'm not convinced Gorky was searching for any identity other than one as a painter. Some painters are more deeply aligned with a national aesthetic or a national cultural ambiance, but I think it's an obvious truism to note that Gorky was, as a painter, neither Armenian nor American. He referred to his own works as hybrids, and he was clearly a painter who was a cosmopolitan—an international, who owed dimensions of his craft and sensibility to Armenian culture, European culture (especially French and Spanish surrealism), and American modernism. Spender's assertion that Gorky created his art "entirely from within" is as romantically naïve as it is apparently ignorant of the fundamental impacts of culture (artistic and intellectual) and history on the self.

In his introduction to Gorky's collected letters, Spender also claims that, because Gorky didn't articulate in writing or interviews any Armenian perspectives about his work or about the impact of his childhood experience, his art couldn't possibly embody any meaning that might pertain to his Armenian past or its culture. It's true Gorky resisted making any narrative statements about the meaning of his forms, and it seems clear that he would have been uncomfortable with iconographic readings of his paintings. Because he did his best to bury his Armenian personal and cultural past by claiming he was a Russian from the Caucasus and a cousin of the Russian writer Maxim Gorky, it seems also that Gorky had no desire to say anything about Armenian origins or sources, except through one important technique: the titles of his paintings, which I discuss later.

Furthermore, Spender's antipathy toward meanings or contexts that are Armenian seem to have led him to make statements that sound quite bigoted. For example, he writes: "Gorky is the most famous Armenian artist of the twentieth century. His success enables Armenians to claim 'external validation' for their national identity. Karlen's letters are still quoted because they fulfill a profound need, especially in the United States, where immigrants sometimes face indifference to the question of who they are and where they come from."[3] It's strange to read in humanistic discourse such an unsubstantiated statement, and such an essentialist depiction of Armenians or any cultural group. Putting aside whether Gorky is more "famous" than, say, William Saroyan, Aram Khachaturian, Aivazovsky, or Parajanov, to claim that scholars would exploit the cultural history and context of Gorky's life for "identity building" or nationalist subtexts is as intellectually and ethically offensive as it would be to suggest that any number of scholars of Jewish heritage are distorting the work of Jewish writers or artists (Chaim Soutine, Marc Chagall, Paul Celan, or Philip Roth, for example). Replace Spender's statement with any national or well-defined culture group (English, Irish, French, African American, etc.) and one gets a sense of what Spender's assumptions about art and culture are, and his apparent lack of understanding of what culture (the more expansive term for ethnicity) is.

His assumption here is also that cultural and biographical contexts—regardless of authorial intentionality—contribute nothing to our understanding of art, artists, and imaginations. To imagine the study of literature and art without the various engagements with cultural, historical, and biographical context in the past 400 years—say, from the British Renaissance to the present—is to imagine something quite different than what in fact exists in the period discourses over the past four centuries. Spender seems unaware that scholars have long discarded anxiety surrounding authorial intentionality. If we were interested only in what writers and artists believed they were doing, or said they were doing, there would be very little far-reaching criticism or probing analysis, and certainly much less detached perspective on all works of imagination.[4]

In a postformalist age, reading deeply is often the result of discovering how various contexts—historical, social, cultural, and biographical—allow more nuanced understandings of the texts. It would be difficult to imagine writing about Paul Celan, an inventive poet whose life was shaped in various ways by the Nazi era and the extermination of the Jews and the death of his parents in concentration camps, without exploring the Holocaust as context. Nor would one write about Marc Chagall's early work without delving into the climate of anti-Semitism in Russia during the first decades of the twentieth century; or about Picasso's paintings of the 1930s without a consideration of how the Spanish Civil War figured in his life and work. Similarly, the history of the Armenian genocide, and all the complex layers of experience that left with Gorky, should be necessary context for thinking about Gorky's life and art.

I'm not the only scholar who sees iconographic associations in Gorky's forms, but my own assessments differ in that they emerge from bringing the formal dimensions of the work (composition, color, form, etc.) into a relationship with biography, culture, and history, and noting that the titles of the paintings and drawings are important aspects of technique and make certain demands on us as viewers.

>>><<<

Arshile Gorky was born Vostanig Adoian on April 15, 1904 (though Hayden Hererra and Nouritza Matossian are more inclined to put his birth year at 1900), in the Armenian province of Van (pronounced *vahn*) in eastern Turkey, part of the Ottoman Empire. He was somewhere between eleven and fifteen in 1915, when the political party in power (the Committee of Union and Progress) began its final solution for the Armenians of Turkey. Even before the events of 1915, Gorky's family had been scarred by the empire-wide campaign against the Armenians in the 1890s. Sultan Abdul Hamid's massacres were retaliation for Armenian protests against deep-seated and institutionally entrenched discrimination and violence against Christian and Jewish minorities in Turkey. Gorky's maternal grandfather, Sarkis der Mardirossian, a priest, was nailed to the door of the church in Van city, where he served, by local government forces. And Gorky's mother Shushan's first husband, Tomas Prudian, a political activist, was either shot or stabbed and beheaded in front of her at their house in a village near Van city. Shortly after, her uncle Nishan was abducted by Kurds or Turks and disappeared.[5]

Beyond the violence to the family, the Adoians lived through an extraordinary period of mass violence against the Armenians in the region around Van and would have received the news and reports from all over Turkey that Armenians had been subjected to massacre at the hands of the Sultan's private army, the Hamideye, and by local Kurdish and Turkish vigilante groups, which resulted in the deaths of more than 100,000 Armenians and the decimation of their property, land, and churches throughout Turkey. When new reforms were initiated after the Sultan was deposed in 1908, and non-Muslim minorities were now drafted into the Ottoman army, many Armenian men left Turkey for Europe or the United States—among them Gorky's father, Sedrak Adoian, who emigrated to Watertown, near Boston, in 1908 to escape the draft and the decaying conditions for Armenians in Turkey.

As World War I broke out, Gorky's mother, Shushan, and her three children (one of the daughters from her first marriage) found themselves in a vulnerable position, living now in Aikesdan just outside of the city of Van. After a tense winter, thousands of Armenians of the region had been killed by orders of the new governor of Van province, Djevdet Bey, who had been appointed by his brother-in-law, Minister of War Enver Pasha, to purge the region of its Armenians. The American missionary physician who ran the mission in Van heard Djevdet Bey exclaim about killing the Armenians of the region: "I won't leave one, not one so high," and pointed to his knee.[6]

By mid-April, a politically flammable negotiation between Djevdet Bey and the Armenian community broke down because of the Armenian community's refusal to hand over 4,000 men for conscription into the Ottoman army, at a time when Armenians in the army were being slaughtered in an organized way by Ottoman soldiers throughout Turkey. Refusing the governor's orders with an offer of 300 men, the Armenians now prepared to defend themselves in the old quarter of the city of Van as Djevdet Bey's squads attacked the city. About 1,300 Armenian men with pistols and rifles held off the Turks until the middle of May, when, unexpectedly, the Turkish forces withdrew.

The Armenian defense of Van is one of the most dramatic events in the history of the gory brutality of the Armenian genocide. It was a strange interlude in which Armenians—a subjected minority with no state or military—managed to defend themselves and a piece of their historic city for a short time. Gorky's experience in the siege of Van must have been a dramatic, traumatic, and a somewhat mythic experience, especially in retrospect. Nouritza Matossian calls it his "rite of passage to boyhood"[7] or one might say, to manhood. For more than a month, Gorky lived in the crossfire of cannon fire, gunshot, and hand-to-hand combat; he witnessed mangled bodies, dead children and babies, razed houses, and burnt swaths of the city. This was amplified by the unimaginable idea of Christians fighting back against their Muslim rulers after decades of unmitigated violence against them.

Although Gorky left no personal reminiscences of this period of his life, his sister, Vartoosh, in interviews recalled and stated vividly that Gorky was a part of the battalion of boys who helped in the defense of the city by bringing water and food to the men fighting on the barricades, and who helped gather materials for munitions and various other tasks amid the killing and chaos. The resistance demanded an intensely orchestrated community organization. Women mended clothes and cooked; in the orphanage workshops, children made ammunition; school bands marched around the Armenian section of the city playing patriotic songs to camouflage artillery fire and anger the enemy.[8]

The American mission at Van headed by the physician Clarence Ussher quickly became a ground of refuge for the Armenians, and Ussher and his staff were often heroic in dealing with the Turks to protect the Armenians. As surrounding villages were destroyed, Armenian refugees piled into Van and Aikesdan. The terrain was full of corpses and people dying of dysentery. Several weeks into the fighting, Gorky was sent by his mother back to their house to get vegetables from their garden, and he found the empty house gouged with bullet holes and partially destroyed by cannon fire. He gathered some vegetables and even a bouquet of flowers for his mother and returned to the city. But what impact did this image of his house have on him? What meaning did the siege of Van leave with Gorky? How did he carry privately the trauma of the event for the rest of his life?

For a month, the Armenians of Van survived conflagrations and shellings, and then, in a surprising moment in mid-May, the Turks retreated. Shortly after, the Russian army (with some Russian Armenian soldiers in its ranks) crossed the border into the province of Van with the hope of occupying it. But by June, the Turkish army returned and retook the city, which sent most of the remaining Armenians into exile or quick death. On June 15, 1915, Shushan and her children (Gorky, Vartoosh, and their two half-sisters), like nearly all Armenians who weren't slaughtered outright, were put on deportation marches that were like walking concentration camps, where men were tortured and shot, women and girls raped and killed, and children abducted and murdered. Gorky's family was marched north to the Russian border. Vartoosh remembered that they left with "nothing but a few days' supply of bread . . . [and] a little money" and that they "marched along the east end of Lake Van, a very mountainous area, and . . . passed Bergri Dasht where later the Turks massacred 50,000 Armenians."[9] Subsisting on grass and fruit, they walked day and night, shoeless much of the way, through harsh mountain terrain. Finally, they crossed the border into Russian Armenia. At Etchmiadzin, the seat of the Armenian Church, the roads were piled with corpses, black from cholera. The family reached Yerevan, their destination, on July 16. This region of precarious geopolitics in Russian Armenia was the setting of Gorky's early adolescence.

In Yerevan, the family lived on the brink of starvation. Gorky and his sister did odd jobs to keep the family alive, but as famine and disease worsened, his mother died of starvation in March

1919 at the age of thirty-nine. The world of their childhood destroyed and family and friends dispersed or slaughtered, Gorky
and Vartoosh, like many other Armenian refugees, fled to the
West. The two made their way along the Black Sea to Constantinople in the fall of 1919, and then to Athens and Naples before
arriving at Ellis Island aboard the SS *President Wilson* in February 1920.

After unsuccessful stays with his father, Setrak, in Providence,
Rhode Island, and his half-sister, Akabi, in Watertown, Mas-
sachusetts, and factory jobs in both cities (one with the Hood
Rubber Company in Watertown and one at the Iron Winding
Company in Providence), Gorky decided that art was his calling
and enrolled in art school in Boston, where his skills at drawing
were so impressive that he soon became a teacher at the New
School of Design there. By 1924, he was offered a teaching position at the New York branch of the New School for Design, and
he left for the city that was to become the new center for the
avant-garde.

By 1924, Gorky was living in the Village, making and teaching
art and gaining a new identity. In Providence and Boston, he had
already begun to pass himself off as a Russian from the Caucasus, and it seems clear that being openly Armenian was complex
and, in some way, traumatic and unappealing to him. With his
Armenian friends, he was comfortable being who he was, but
with his non-Armenian friends, he cloaked his identity and his
past in mystery and myth and fiction. In New York, he also took
his new name, and so Vostanig Manuk Adoian became Arshile
Gorky. The new name evoked Greece and Russia: Arshile, Russian for Achilles, Homer's great warrior; and Gorky, meaning
bitter, and also recalling Maxim Gorky, whom Gorky claimed as
kin more than once. Achilles the Bitter, then, was a name with
historical force and symbolic resonance, and was the painter's
way of christening himself a new man in a new world.

>>><<<

The town where Gorky grew up, Khorkom (the family moved
to Aikesdan on the outskirts of Van city in 1910), was a tradi-

tional Armenian village along the southeast shore of Lake Van, a glacial lake surrounded by farmlands and vineyards where the agrarian society had changed little in a thousand years. His mother Shushan was devout, and her father had been a priest in the Armenian Apostolic Church, as had other members of her family in previous generations. Shushan often took her children to the churches and monasteries of Van, including the impressive tenth-century Church of the Holy Cross on the island of Aktamar in Lake Van.

Gorky's childhood was a strange brew of trauma and cultural richness. He grew up in an agrarian community of farmers in the fertile region around Lake Van, a dramatic glacial lake distinguished by its high salt content, its milky foam, and changing colors. His childhood was shaped by traditional customs of Armenian agrarian life within a context of decaying stability for Armenians in Turkey, marked by continual terror and massacres of Armenians in the Van region from the 1890s and through the siege of Van and the ensuing genocidal deportations and massacres.

But life was also defined by religious rituals, mythic tales, and ancient, nature-oriented traditions. Gorky recalled the mythic presence of a sacred rock near his house in Khorkom, where women would come to gently rub their breasts for healing and fertility purposes. And he recalled vividly a sacred tree— *Khachdzar*, meaning Tree of the Cross—where pilgrims and others would tie strips of cloth to the branches. He remembered vividly his house "made of clay blocks" and "a roof of rude timber" and how, during Lent, an onion with seven feathers plunged in it was suspended from a wooden cross, and how each Sunday a feather was removed, marking the passage to Easter.[10] The landscape had its sacred demarcations both in organic forms and in art and architecture; layers of decorative arts defined Armenian village and city life, and for a young boy who was obsessed with drawing, carving, whittling, and making decorative objects, it was significant.

As a five-year-old, Gorky made a drawing on slate that so impressed his teacher, he assured him he would be an artist. From a very young age on, Gorky drew compulsively on various surfaces, even on the pages of the church Bible. He made soldiers out of the yellow clay of the region, carved shepherd's flutes for his friends, and painted Easter eggs with homemade pigments from crushed flowers and other plants, egg yolks, and fruit peels.

Armenia's art historical tradition and its aesthetic and decorative arts culture has evolved over more than 2,000 years, but the forms and genres that most fully defined the culture began with the conversion to Christianity in 301 and the invention of the alphabet a century later. Van province and its capital city were a cultural center for much of the Christian period, and there were more than 1,500 monasteries in the province. Gorky spent much of his childhood roaming around churches and monasteries— with their fine stone carvings on the façades, frescoed interiors, and ornately worked silver artifacts: Bible covers, oil lamps, censers, and reliquary boxes.

The early medieval churches, made of colorful (tan, coffee, chocolate, gray, ruddy) volcanic tufa stone, are elegantly proportioned and small enough to create an intimate space. Their conical domes were innovative, constructed with squinch buttressing, and the elongated window niches were spiritually evocative. Gorky certainly spent time gazing at the bas-reliefs and stone carvings on their façades, with their graceful, decorative motifs that are curvaceous and spiraling or meandering like the vines of pomegranates and grapes, or garlands and wreaths they depict. The churches were, as well, the equivalent of museums, because they were the repositories of the culture's prized, sacred, and aesthetic art and artifacts that had accrued over the centuries.

Armenian illuminated manuscripts and Bibles were displayed and used in churches and monasteries. They embodied the historical continuity of Armenian Christianity, and they were essential works of painting and ornate calligraphic design and writing. Their illuminations were made of rich colors and gold leaf: aubergine/purple/magenta, hues of lapis, and blues, delicate greens, yolky yellows, and rich lampblack are among the colors that define the manuscripts. Masters of illumination such as Toros Roslin and Sarkis Pidzak worked in the twelfth and thirteenth centuries, and the manuscript illuminations of every region were achievements of considerable painterly skill. These miniatures, as they were often called, were embodiments of abstract form and color, especially with their flourishes of peacock tails, winding vines, halos, and rays of light.

Gorky would have also encountered regularly in his village routines *khachkars*, the carved stone crosses that were prevalent in the landscape and in the churchyards and cemeteries. The *khachkars* were creations of obsessive artistic work, which included the carving of ornate, lace-like filigree. Carved patterns of meandering vines and fine netting are wound throughout the cross shape and convey spiritual meanings and devotional work; the crosses often commemorated the completion of a church or the death of a loved one.

Gorky also grew up in a culture of textiles, especially rugs and carpets (although silk and lace covers and woven utilitarian bags were part of daily life), those prized weavings that could be sacred or utilitarian and often both. The forms on the rugs of eastern Anatolia and the Caucasus were abstract, geometric, often with curvaceous, winding, and spiraling forms. Unscrolling running vines with mannered leaf and berry shapes; *botehs* or scarab shapes, and other abstracted zoomorphic forms, and lattices, hooks and diamonds. The wool was rich and thick and the color saturation brilliant and deep. The rugs and carpets were a cultural equivalent to paintings in the West, and they were hung on walls, stored in chests for special occasions like weddings and christenings, and used as covers for couches and beds in wealthier homes. Miró, Picasso, and Matisse all learned aesthetic lessons from rugs of these regions, as their paintings reveal. Furthermore, the palette of the rugs was rich and layered. The dyes were made from berries, leaves, roots, stones, and soil. A wine deep red-purple, known as cochineal, made from the crushed insect of a bug found in the wetter lands of the Ararat plain, a lavender purple, shades of apricot, shrimp and coral colors, greens and yellows, chocolate and tan browns are some of the tones and colors produced by the dye makers and woven into rugs. Looking at some of the eastern Anatolian and Southwest Caucasian rugs, one cannot help but see versions of what would come to be called abstract expressionist art.

Amid this landscape of artifacts, design, decoration, and form, there was another form: the Armenian alphabet. Any alphabet is an assumed, almost unconscious background to life in a given culture. But perhaps when one becomes an exile, assimilates to a new culture, those native letters assume another property or even aesthetic value. The letters of the Armenian alphabet are exceptionally curvaceous, sinuous, and calligraphic; and they are made of dramatic flaring shapes as well as squiggles, curlicues, loops, hooks, and curves. If you assemble dominant Armenian aesthetic and decorative forms—*khachkar* carving, rug iconography, church façade bas-relief and wall carvings, ornate silversmith work on hanging silver lamps and church relics, and the omnipresent alphabet—you can see an interesting design paradigm. The Armenian design and decorative aesthetic and tradition is dominated by curvaceous, curvilinear, compulsively ornate arabesque forms and twisting, snaking, and turning shapes.

That Gorky's art of the 1940s, his breakthrough work, would be defined by compulsively ornate, meandering, curvaceous, curling, snaking, twisting forms and shapes of a kind never seen before in Western painting does not seem accidental, nor does it appear to have a context in European or American art. If one searches for works that are defined by such shapes, there is no antecedent. Miró made free forms and big circles, Matisse had smooth edges and curves in his representational figures and in some of his design motifs, Kandinsky is more geometric and color-field oriented, Chagall's magical realism is tied to representations, Tanguey's forms are stiff, metallic, and a bit sci-fi like. Van Gogh's animated brushstrokes curve and writhe but always in the service of representational figures and forms. I think one can say with some nuanced discernment that there is nothing like Gorky's ornate, curvaceous, compulsively ribboning, spermatozoa-like forms anywhere else in Western abstract painting before him. And it seems fair to suggest that this visual iconography has its sources in these long-standing layers of Armenian art and design.

To a young, burgeoning artist who is pried loose from his Armenian Anatolian culture, and resettled in the thick of the avant-garde art scene in New York in the second quarter of the twentieth century, might not those Armenian forms reemerge, like the return of the repressed, in a new idiom inflected, in this case, by surrealism, cubism, and an emerging abstract expressionism? Might not those old Armenian forms come to be a source for the new forms made out of a hybridization of Armenian traditions and new American and European movements in the dynamic art culture of America in the 1940s?

Of course, I mean only to suggest that the Armenian aesthetic tradition is one source—but a significant one—that Gorky used in developing his hybridized forms and style—in which he fused and mixed, blended and mashed various orientations and traditions to make the kind of imaginative universe he came to inhabit. Ingres, Cézanne, Picasso, Miró, Kandinsky—all are well-known sources, and a great deal has been written about their impact on Gorky. About the significance of the Armenian decorative and design tradition on Gorky, much too little has been noted about the confluence of the forms of the Armenian aesthetic tradition on the art and imagination of a painter who studied at the feet of his modern masters: Cézanne and Picasso.

>>><<<

In some of Gorky's most dynamic paintings, representations of grief and loss aren't separable from the calligraphic intricacies of his draftsmanship, his symbology and iconography, and the encoded tones of his palette. Gorky's first major paintings are the two portraits of the artist with his mother. The two canvases titled *The Artist and His Mother*, the first dated ca. 1926–1936, the second, ca. 1929–1942 (Plates 3 and 4, respectively), mark some emancipation from his cubist-influenced beginnings to a style and tonality, whether representational or not, that drive to an expressionism that characterizes his emotional palette. Both of these paintings are based on a photograph for which he and his mother had posed in Van city in 1912. The photograph was then sent to his father, already living in Providence, and Gorky found it in 1919 when he lived with his father. When he left the next year, he took it with him and kept it in his studio for the rest of his life. It was one of the few objects he rescued from the fire that burned down his studio in the summer of 1946.

In the photograph, the eight-year-old Gorky, dressed in a dark overcoat and holding a flower in his hand, stands next to his mother. Shushan is seated and wears a large kerchief around her head and an apron covered with embroidered flowers, which dominates the foreground.

Both portraits transfigure this photograph and create what might be seen as a continuous meditation on something that happened to the two of them over there in that lost place of Van. Biographical and historical context become essential dimensions for analysis. Knowing such a particular context about the photograph affects how we read the painting. We know that she was a casualty of the later phase of the genocide, and her deportation march to Russian Armenia and her subsequent death from starvation in famine and disease-ravaged Yerevan in 1920 left its permanent mark on Gorky's life. Now, in recollecting her through this photograph in some tranquility thousands of miles away, it seems an organic assertion to suggest that both paintings deal with the son remembering his mother, their relationship, and her death as a genocide victim, and, correspondingly, his survival. At the time I wrote this essay (in the late 1980s), it was fair to say that critics and scholars viewed these paintings in very general terms, and only pointing out the European influences of Cézanne and Picasso, Vermeer, and cubism, without any sense of the central reality from which both paintings emanated. Even though recent scholars (Herrera, Matossian, Taylor, Spender, and Theriault) steer away from seeing the portraits as situated in a historical moment, the photograph offers an unambiguous autobiographical source that is located in a time and place and in relation to the catastrophic event that would shape Gorky's life.

In the first portrait (Plate 3), the two figures, constructed in single-point perspective, are composed of large planes of color. Mother and son are frontal and formal, imposing as they stare at us. It is worth noting that the iconography of Madonna and Child images in stone relief on Armenian churches and in manuscript and fresco painting had a central place in Gorky's imagination and, as others have noted, most likely contribute to the perspective. The dominant earth colors give the portrait an organic tonality: Grays and umbers, puce and yellow ocher convey something of the dry, highlands feel of Van in eastern Anatolia. As in the photograph, the boy stands next to his mother, who is seated. In the background, a gray wall and dark portico frame their heads. Before our eyes fully meet their faces, they are stopped by the hands of both figures. Except for the boy's right hand, which holds a flower, the hands have been expunged by white paint. In this picture, mother and son still seem to be in the land of the living, but the melancholy look on the son's face seems to bestow an intimation of something else to come. Nearing thirty, Gorky seems to be looking back to his boyhood self, at a moment of foreboding. The events of 1915–1920 that followed affected Gorky profoundly, and the paintings are one manifestation of that trauma. Here in his New York studio in the late 1920s, the portrait is an interpretive view of a piece of his past with his mother.

Although other paintings of the period, such as *Self Portrait* (ca. 1937) and *Portrait of Master Bill* (ca. 1937), also have hand erasures, and this technique has various and playful meanings in the various paintings in which it's used, here the context of the painting allows a more nuanced interpretation. The painterly effacements of his mother's hands are emblems of disconnection and erasure, suggesting the fragility of their lives and the incompleteness of the relationship. These handless figures are more than post-cubist or surrealist-influenced forms; they are images of separation and loss. But with his one hand, the living hand, the son offers his mother a pink flower, an offering of beauty, life, their garden, evoking the bouquet of flowers he picked for her from their garden after their house was decimated during the siege of Van. The sallow side of his face is lost in inward grief, and the almond-shaped eyes seem sunken with sorrow. Grief and melancholy define the portrait, though there are still signs of life in the remembrance.

The son's tilted head and hairline lead us to his mother, whose eyes bulge like black cherries beneath the lids that hood them. The painterly solidity of her form can't mask the expression of fatigue and worry on her face; her pursed lips hold a quiver of defiance, and her expression embodies some force of will to protect her child. The painting is a trope on and a vision of the photograph that was taken to be sent to his father who was then living in Providence, Rhode Island, as an emblem of their existence, to say: "Here we are back in Van." It seems to have demarcated a moment of some stasis before things turned bad again.

In the second portrait (Plate 4), the change is dramatic. Mother and son no longer confront us with their massive foreground stances, and they seem less accessible. Although the paintings were begun and finished at different times (1926–1936, 1929–1942), Gorky worked on them simultaneously, and the similarities of the pictures dramatize Gorky's obsessive need to wrestle with memory, the absence of his mother, and the violence that took her life. And if we view them side by side, as a kind of diptych, the congruencies between them are less obvious and the differences more haunting. Gorky once remarked: "I never finish a painting, I just keep working on it, re-painting it."

The colors in Plate 4 have a shock value that creates a dramatic contrast with the softer earth tones of Plate 3. Mother's head is now a more abstracted form and is mannered, and the chalky blue-green color of her face evokes something disembodied, more death-like. The face seems more like a death mask. Those once-defiant big eyes are now glazed as if they are looking into nothingness. Her mouth has lost its sensuality and is now a flat, grim, red line. The massive white apron of the first portrait, an image of domestic solidity, is now an odd flesh color, shaded red, and it's hard not to see it as the color of blood, and then as a lap of blood that evokes death by violence; one can roll with the rich associations of those blood colors in that expressionistic rendering of her body: menses, womb, placenta, the source and origin of the boy's life, or a survivor's torn place of origin.

From the edge of her apron, a violet hue spreads to the picture's perimeter (a deeply sacrificial Christian color in the Armenian palette), and then to a more burnished blood-red that seems to stain the world as it fills the window behind them. Whereas his left arm is partially whited-out in Plate 3, in Plate 4, it is entirely whited-out; and, unlike in the first portrait, where his arm hangs from his side apart from his mother, in the second portrait, his arm is expunged by white brushes against his mother's shoulder, which is painted red. The arm is lifeless like a plaster cast, and it is chalky colored like his mother's face; it is difficult not to see that the death of her face has rubbed off or into a part of him. He, too, is streaked with red—shoulder, ankles, eyebrow, ear—so that he looks tainted by the violence that defines her image. Like Grunewald, who painted green flesh blistered with blood on his crucified Christ in the Isenheim altarpiece, Gorky creates here expressionistic colors with brushstrokes that evoke a pathology of suffering.

The boy's face has gone from its deep sadness to a shocked and traumatized expression; his almond eyes are frozen and bulging, his mouth pursed shut, his ear blood-red. Given all the context we have and the extreme expressionism of this red-drenched portrait with its chalky white body parts, and these faces of shock and disembodiment, it seems organic to suggest that the portrait embodies memory's mediation on loss and death by violence—in this case, the genocidal violence of 1915. And as the stump of flowers the boy holds in his hand is the color of his mother's chalky face—does this not seem like an offering to a world destroyed? That bouquet of flowers that Gorky picked at their destroyed house in Aikesdan and brought to his mother in May 1915 make an interesting biographical context.

>>><<<

Image in Khorkom (ca. 1934–1936) (Plate 5) is a pivotal painting in Gorky's career, and it opens the way to the fluidity of his biomorphic and swirling works of the 1940s. (The painting was followed by two related paintings, with alternative spellings of the name, titled *Image in Xhorkom* and a third titled *Khorkom*.) It was in this painting, a 33-by-43-inch canvas in which diverse biomorphic forms are configured around a central gourd-like shape, that Gorky found a way of imagining his lost world of childhood. By the late 1930s, Gorky had absorbed various modern masters, especially Picasso, Miró, and some dimensions of surrealism found in Tanguey. In his "Nighttime, Enigma and Nostalgia" series of the 1930s, Gorky obsessed over the idea of estranging objects from their contexts and exploring a new playfulness with abstract forms. Although the forms in those drawings are a bit academic and stiff, in comparison with the freedom and organic energy of *Image in Khorkom*, they were important to the evolution of his new style.

It's difficult to ignore the title and the degree to which Gorky's titles are key dimensions and techniques of his paintings. Khorkom—*khor kom* meaning "deep stable" in Armenian—was Gorky's home village on the southeastern shore of Lake Van in historic Armenia, a place that had been populated by Armenians for more than 2,000 years. It was situated on a bluff overlooking the lake, and the villagers who practiced Armenian Apostolic Christianity were steeped in ancient pre-Christian rituals, so rich was the historic continuity of the region.[11] The other thread of historical context that intersects with the painting is what happened to Khorkom. Like scores of other Armenian villages of the region, it was destroyed, and its population was mass-murdered or deported.

In some way, *Image in Khorkom* discloses Gorky's vision of the place that bore him, a way of seeing the Armenian agrarian world of his childhood. The titles of Gorky's paintings are pithy, lyrical, and instructive, and they encode meaning. Perhaps spelling the name of his village with an X in some cases instead of with a K is a playful way of putting some distance between himself and his lost homeland, or perhaps it indicates in some encoded way that Khorkom has been x-ed out. If Gorky did not advertise his Armenian past or discuss his life in Van during the genocide and the transitory Republic of Armenia in 1918–1920 where his mother died, he did use his trauma as a source of creative energy.

So what is happening in *Image in Khorkom*? Four areas of color create a broad backdrop for the dance of curvilinear shapes: a muddy brown slope at top and bottom, terra-cotta in the left foreground, a section of black with a teal triangle on the right. It's an earthy and elemental world in which shapes join and glide— biomorphic: human and vegetal. The shapes resemble and evoke body parts: a green heart modeled in black and white with a trickle of crimson across it; putty-white breasts hanging in black, from which a kind of clavicle shape leads to more breasts (one flesh colored with a nipple, the other with a red eye and black pupil); more organ-like shapes lead to a red mouth and an eye shape in dark amber. In *Image in Khorkom*, the feminine seems embedded everywhere. Breast, eyes, stomach, heart, and mouth are curvaceous and animated. The title directs us to Gorky's lost village, and to that mythical garden that he recalled in a poetical piece of prose he wrote in 1942 for Dorothy Miller, when the Museum of Modern Art in New York acquired *Garden in Sochi*. He recalls a fertile, mythic Armenian garden of his youth:

About 194 feet away from our house on the road to the spring, my father had a little garden with a few apple trees, which had retired from giving fruit. There was a ground constantly giving shade where grew incalculable amounts of wild carrots, and porcupines had made their nests. There was a blue rock buried in the black earth with a few patches here and there like fallen clouds. But where came all the shadows in constant battle like the lancers of Paolo Ucello's paintings? This garden was identified as the Garden of Wish Fulfillment and often I had seen my mother and other village women opening their bosoms and taking their soft and dependent breasts in their hands to rub them on the rock. Above all this stood an enormous tree all bleached under the sun, the rain, the cold, and deprived of leaves. This was the Holy Tree. I myself don't know why this tree was holy but I had witnessed many people, whoever did pass by, that would tear voluntarily a strip of their clothes and attach them to the tree. Thus, through many years of the same act, like a veritable parade of banners under the pressure of wind, all these personal inscriptions of signatures, very softly to my innocent ear used to give echo to the sh-sh-sh-sh-h of silver leaves of the poplars.[12]

The ambiguous relationship between eros and dismemberment in the painting is unsettling and evocative. The feminine shapes appear simultaneously as both a dance of images in the earth and as a dispersed body in a landscape. Without wanting to intrude on the lyrical freedom in the forms, the name of the village and the history that transpired there, at least, lead us to ask whether the images that resemble body parts dispersed in a landscape evoke atrocities, killing, and death—which Gorky witnessed as a teenage boy aiding in the defense of Van in 1915. At the same time—and this is what is lyrically rich about Gorky's playful forms and their layered evocations—the female forms in the field of the painting also make a dance that evokes birth and rebirth and an idea of place that is, in memory, fertile and dynamic.

In style and concept, the Garden in Sochi paintings follow the Khorkom paintings, and because Gorky often falsified his identity and childhood to his friends and even his wife, claiming he was Russian, the Sochi painting might be seen as further meditations on east Anatolian landscapes, and as efforts to find lyrical forms in that imagined lost place. Like Khorkom on the shore of Lake Van, Sochi was also a place on water, the Black Sea, north of Van, in the Caucasus.

>>><<<

By 1944, Gorky was advancing his new idiom with expansive confidence. He was painting whirling forms, calligraphic designs, glandular shapes, and intricate swirls, and his palette had achieved a new sensuality and richness. In the pictures of his last four years, a tension governs the relationship between representation and abstraction. His attachment to the sensuality of nature and the body allows his pictures to be poised between chthonic origins and transcendent realities. Emerson's notion that in apprehending the sublime one becomes like a transparent eyeball is alive in Gorky's vision. In the final paintings, the organic world—animal, mineral, and vegetable—is drawn into a kind of syntax that brings the metonymous layers and metaphoric dances.

How My Mother's Embroidered Apron Unfolds in My Life (1944), one of the most moving paintings of Gorky's high period, reveals how deeply personal history could be embedded in abstraction (Plate 6). Once more, the 1912 photograph of mother and son is a generative force. In the photo, his mother is seated, dressed in a dramatic dress/apron with cascading leaf and floral shapes; it's an ornate, decorative artifact and likely of needlework. Again, personal history, an Armenian decorative tradition, and a broader cultural history enter the painting. And, again, the title situates us in an autobiographical and historical context. We know his mother died as a result of genocidal violence, that she was the nurturing source of his life, and that he was the beloved son she doted on. His mother's apron becomes here a domestic trope for her presence in the family and home, and it is as well an Armenian artifact of quotidian and aesthetic value, a reminder of her absence and his lost world. In Gorky's reimagining, the apron and mother become a source of continued sustenance that unravels in his imagination and life, the gorgeous forms, washed and dripped with turpentine (a technique he learned from his surrealist friend Matta), move toward the color field of later abstract expressionism. As the title notes, his mother's apron is endlessly unraveling into his imagination and life.

In making a white backdrop, the whole canvas gains a sense of transparency. Gorky's technique of diluting and washing colors by using turpentine on the canvas creates a flow of colors pouring, as if they have come loose from their source. Entwined with his disciplined draftsmanship runs a freedom of color, so that the picture can also seem to be about the making of itself. Out of labial and ear shapes and petal forms come these warm yellows and amber (blotches of daylight), lichen green, lavender. The canvas appears like a grid—and because of the notation of the textile in the title—it seems like a warp and weft that have been broken but have not come undone. Broken, but still holding in fierce tension the erotic flow of color; hence, sorrow and painterly happiness, love and loss.

For a culture that has been centered on a tradition of decorative textiles for millennia, an embroidered apron embodies artistic traditions that involve color and design and Gorky's own initiations into art. The painting surely suggests itself as a kind of ars poetica in which the folk art of the mother's Armenian apron encodes an aesthetic palette from which the boy learned. In the weaving tradition of his culture, the dye makers performed an alchemizing act as they made color from roots, plants, stones, and dirt, from which they produced intense reds and blues, various greens, and golden ivories and yellows. Gorky's first lessons in color came from those woven artifacts and the other forms of Armenian art around which he grew up. In some way, *How My Mother's Embroidered Apron Unfolds in My Life* is a tribute to his mother and the mother culture that nurtured him, an encoded vision of origins looked back upon from middle age.

>>><<<

The final two and a half years of Gorky's life read like a diary of disaster, as misfortune stalked the heels of happiness. He found much grounding in his (second) marriage to Agnes Macgruder in 1941, whom he called by his affectionate Armenian nickname, Magouch, and the birth of their two daughters, Maro and Natasha, in 1943 and 1945. He had broken through with his work to a new distinctive style and had found, at last, a permanent venue in Julian Levy Gallery in midtown New York. He had also left the city to find new energizing and peaceful places in which to paint, and especially paint nature. At Magouch's parents' Crooked Farm in Lincoln, Virginia, he did some of his most productive painting in the summers of 1944 and 1945, and when David Hare lent the Gorkys his house in Roxbury, Connecticut, in 1945, Gorky found it such a welcome respite from the city, Magouch recalls that "he was turning out paintings like butter cookies."[13]

But in the spring of 1945, the chronic abdominal pain and rectal hemorrhaging that had initially been misdiagnosed by his physicians was finally diagnosed as rectal cancer, and Gorky had a colostomy in March 1945. The procedure was traumatic psychologically as well as physically, as his sexual performance seems to have been hindered and his fastidious sense of order and cleanliness were upbraided by the new rituals of body care. The surgery and its aftermath acerbated growing tensions in his marriage. In the summer of 1947, Gorky's mishandling of his wood-burning stove in his studio barn resulted in a fire that destroyed his studio and all of his new work (some twenty to thirty paintings) and supplies. In June 1948, Magouch began a brief affair with Gorky's good friend, the painter Roberto Matta, which devastated Gorky and led to his sense that the marriage was through. At the same time, in June, Julien Levy, Gorky's friend and gallery owner, driving drunk in a downpour with his wife and Gorky from his house to Gorky's across town, skidded off the road; the car turned over, and Gorky broke a vertebrae in his neck, temporarily paralyzing his painting arm. In great pain and forced to wear cumbersome head and collar gear to stabilize his neck, he was terrified about the prospects of losing his painting arm and despondent because Agnes had left him, for the moment at least, for her parents' house in Virginia, taking their two children. On July 26, Gorky hanged himself in a shed on the grounds near his studio.

But through the turmoil of the final years, he painted with great intensity, only running into a dry spell in the final weeks. *Making the Calendar, Agony, Charred Beloved, The Orators,* and *The Scent of Apricots* are some of the finished pieces of 1946 and 1947, and some of his best. There's an interesting blend of pain and joy, grief and celebration in these works. *The Scent of Apricots* is a synesthetic celebration of the fruit and tree that are a national symbol of Armenia. He remembered pilfering apricots from trees in Khorkom as a boy and called the orange-colored fruit "flirts of light." The image of apricots is as universal as any fruit or flower (though they are not plentiful in the northeast of the United States, where Gorky lived), yet, knowing the meaning of apricots for Armenians, the painting takes on a richer layer of meaning. It's a painting that embodies a visionary notion of nature in which a conglomerate of swirling circles, egg shapes, and spiraling forms coalesce in a flowing movement. In the painting's contagion of color, the scraped and washed rose tone at the top of the canvas and the yolky and darker yellows descend on a fusion and diffusion of oranges, reds, umber, faded lavender, tainted whites, and washed greens. It's a wild, choral celebration of some natural force that emanates from Gorky's vision of the apricot. It's not an Armenian painting, but a painting that owes something to a memory of childhood on the shores of Lake Van.

In a similar way, one of his final grand achievements, *The Plow and the Song* (1947), owes something to the lost agrarian Armenian village life. Friends attest repeatedly to Gorky's love of breaking into dance and song in the middle of parties and his pride in grilling shish kebabs over roaring fires at picnics. In these performances, Gorky was holding on to traditional Armenian rituals as well as having fun being the exotic exile from some faraway place. Some friends knew it was Armenian dance and song, and others thought it was Caucasian Russian, as he had put it. *The Plow and the Song* is painted in oil on burlap, and the coarse burlap creates a chthonic texture. His agitated brushstrokes of brown and amber over the coarse hemp fibers give the picture its earthy, sculptural sense. Again, there is a kind of visionary dynamism in the composition, and its materials create a continuous flow of form and convey a wild dance of objects with the earth.

The Armenian poet Daniel Varoujan's pastoral poems provide another perspective on the painting. Varoujan, who was perhaps the finest Western (Ottoman) Armenian poet of his generation, wrote his final poems at the age of thirty-one, in April 1915, in prison after he was arrested by the Ottoman government along with the other 250 Armenian cultural leaders in Constantinople (Istanbul) on the night of April 24, at the start of the genocide. In some of Varoujan's final poems, he remembered his boyhood and the communal agrarian life of Armenia. Here, from his poem "Tillers": "tillers of my village, spawned from soil. . . . The lymph of seasons sings in their blood; / their hands are anointed by the ox, / their coats by myrrh of barns." And in "Sowing": "Sow, ploughman. . . . / Tomorrow the body of Christ / will ripen in each milky spike."[14]

Like Varoujan's vision, Gorky's *The Plough and the Song* captures a fusion of a pastoral world with a spiritual piety. Once again an Armenian artifact—not a butter churn, a slipper, a photograph, or an apron, but a plow—becomes a source of vision. Gorky transforms the image of a wooden plow of a kind he saw daily in the fields of the villages around Van, a technological artifact that would have been closer to the Bronze Age than to the modern Western world of farming. The archaisms of the title bear no correspondence to farming life in America with its tractors and technology and engine sounds that would hardly allow for song. The title instructs us where to go, though it doesn't limit the painting, but allows for an interesting layer of meaning that takes off on the painter's Armenian childhood and becomes a trope for the mothering earth of one's origins.

The forms of the painting are driven by a white diagonal shape in the middle of the canvas, and the forms are interlocked in some kind of dance movement—some raucous sensual romp, as if that white diagonal with its pale blue melon-shaped horn at the bottom is activating the forms of the painting. There's a flow of visceral and anatomical shapes across the canvas: eggs, heart, kidney, gland-like heads, that inimitable Gorky slipper, horn-like shapes like bodily orifices. As these Gorkeyesque shapes come to life, the picture brims with its organic, earthy celebration. The place of song in traditional Armenian life is fact and metaphor here. Village songs, folk songs, work songs, festival songs, songs of mother singing as she did her chores were rudiments of village life among Armenians in the Anatolia of Gorky's childhood. The colors of *The Plow and the Song* are as beautiful as anything he ever made: magentas, royal and teal blues, amber, pink, lavender. A sense of layered depth emanates from these colors, and that wild vision of a plow—that ancient anchor of Armenian agrarian life—is a catalyst for the sensual dynamism of the painting and for Gorky's memory of village life in Khorkom.

>>><<<

At the closing of his biography, Matthew Spender notes that Gorky was a loner and a lonely man in several ways. He remained an outsider to American art movements of his time and was not a joiner of groups or organizations. It seems clear that most of the time Gorky kept the truth about his Armenian childhood, the genocide survivor experience, and his time spent in the early Republic of Armenia a secret, even from those closest to him, including his wife, who was shocked and saddened to learn years later that he was born Vostanig Adoian in the village of Khorkom in the Van province of Ottoman Turkish Armenia. Spender concludes that Gorky needed to either reinvent himself so he could be the artist that he became or, consciously, at least, erase the trauma of the Armenian genocide experience because of its debilitating pain. Although Spender doesn't examine either of these theories in his biography, they lead him to conclude that neither Armenia nor America were big enough to define Gorky and that most certainly, "Gorky was not an Armenian painter." For Spender, Gorky is an example of the artist who "from his solitary pinnacle . . . bequeathed an eloquent example of how one individual can renew the language of art, and himself, entirely from within."[15]

What strikes me about this conclusion is how driven it is by the idea of self and the rather extreme notion that art is made "entirely from within." No one would argue that art—in all its forms and genres—is not made by a self, and that the inner life is crucial to that process. But it's the absoluteness of the phrase and the concept that is so inadequate. I agree with Spender's sense that Gorky is neither Armenian nor American. He is indeed more than both of those signifying cultural notions. What does it mean to be an artist of or defined by any national rubric? Two of the great Armenian painters of the twentieth century, Martiros Sarian and Minas Avedissian, made paintings that belong in any major museum (although their works are mostly hanging in Russian and Armenian museums), but their techniques owe less to Armenian aesthetic traditions than do Gorky's. In part, I think this is true because, as an exile, Gorky felt freer using Armenian aesthetic elements, thousands of miles away from a place to which he would never return and rarely acknowledge.

Notwithstanding Spender's unexamined notion of what an Armenian painter might be, I think it's worth underscoring that artists don't emerge solely from within the self, nor do they live on a "solitary pinnacle"—notions that are far too romantic for the complexities of any artist's situation. Gorky, like most artists, is a multiheaded hydra of a person and painter whose best work—mostly his exciting inventions of the 1940s—is the outgrowth and manifestation of numerous complex aesthetic, cultural, historical, and deeply personal realities that he tapped into and which tapped into him. The recipe of any body of art is never fully understood, nor is it only a rationally conceived concept; nevertheless, many of the pieces can be traced and seen, tracked, and opened up so that more understanding and more meaning may emerge from the work. And why would we *not* want deeper understanding?

Gorky was an international, hybridized painter for whom European masters such as Ingres, Cézanne, modernists and surrealists like Picasso and Miró were important, as were the Armenian purples of medieval illuminated manuscripts, the decorative work on Armenian stone crosses, the iconography of Anatolian village rugs, and the squiggling shapes of the Armenian alphabet. If living in Lower Manhattan in a current of avant-garde atmosphere of the 1930s and early 1940s was transformative to his art, so was his childhood in an Armenian village on Lake Van and his traumatic experience as a survivor of the Armenian genocide.

Whether he was comfortable talking *openly* about the impact of the Armenian past on him, the impact of the Armenian past on Gorky's imagination was significant. And Gorky is on record recalling how his family garden and surrounding landscape fed his imagination. Even if he only articulated the tip of the iceberg, the rest of it was down there in him and kept bubbling up in his obsessions with human anatomy and nature, in the evocative autobiographical and place-anchored titles of his paintings, and in many of the unique, formal qualities of those curling and writhing shapes.

9

The Anatolian Embrace: Greeks and Armenians in Elia Kazan's *America, America*

Shortly after *Tom Jones* won the Academy Award for best film in 1963, Henry Miller wrote to Elia Kazan: "I don't think the film [*Tom Jones*] deserved so much. It was good but not great. Yours was great, but not always good."[1] Kazan later referred to *America, America* as his favorite film because it was "the first film that was entirely mine."[2] Not only was *America, America* the first full screenplay he had written, but he had first written the story as a novel, *America, America*, published in 1962. It was a novel that was memoiristic in its grounding in his family's passage out of Turkey in the late nineteenth century. In the film, Kazan takes the story into the personal, doing the voice-overs of his narration himself, and he pushes the film closer to memoir than any dramatic nondocumentary film could be. Eli Wallach called it Kazan's "last great film," and the critic Foster Hirsch called it his greatest achievement and "one of the greatest films ever made in this country." Although it was nominated for three Oscars and won one for best art direction, it opened to no box office and was a commercial failure.

Kazan's voice-over in the film's opening sequence articulates an immediate, essential historical context and a clear direction to the viewer that we are returning with him to a dramatic time and a complex place: 1896 in central Anatolian Turkey. Kazan's personal-confessional narration runs for about sixty seconds over a black screen: "My name is Elia Kazan." And then images of the Anatolian landscape (a snowcapped mountain, a plateau, wheat fields) as a voice cries, *Allahu Akbar* over the mountains, and Kazan continues: "I am a Turk by birth, a Greek by blood, and an American because my uncle made a journey. This story was told to me over the years by the old people of my family."[3]

The camera keeps panning images of the Turkish interior: agrarian scenes, fields with animals being herded, a village of stone houses, a marketplace, Ottoman cavalry on horseback riding through a village. Behind Kazan's narration, there's the plaintive sound of a bouzouki, and then a ballad by Manos Hadjidakis—the words by the poet Nikos Gatsos ("And you, my lost, distant homeland / You will remain a caress and wound as the day breaks on the land"). Even if the words are lost in translation, the sadness and nostalgia of the song augment the poignancy of Kazan's opening narrative:

> My name is Elia Kazan. I am a Turk by birth, a Greek by blood, and an American because my uncle made a journey. This story was told to me over the years by members of my family. They remembered Anatolia, the great central plateau of Turkey in Asia. And they remembered the Mountain Aergius standing over the plain. Anatolia was the ancient homeland of the Greek and the Armenian people. But five hundred-odd years ago the land was overrun by the Turks. And from that day the Greeks and Armenians lived here but as minorities. The Greeks, subject people. The Armenians, subject people. They wore the same clothes as the Turks, the fez and the sandal, they ate the same food, suffered the heat together, used the donkey for burden. And they looked up to the same mountain, but with different feelings, for in fact, they were conqueror and conquered. The Turks had an army. The Greeks and the Armenians lived the best they could.

Kazan's opening is not only unconventionally memoiristic but it's a narrative that articulates a political reality situated in a history of colonized Christians in Ottoman Turkey at the end of the nineteenth century. His voice frames a story that will emerge in *America, America* as a boy's epic journey out of a crumbling empire—a story about trauma, survival, and political oppression. And "its greatness," to use Henry Miller's words, emerges, I think, from Kazan's ability to blend a highly stylized cinematography with frequent long, slow tracking shots of psychological intensity with expressionistic mise-en-scènes of unusual historical and anthropological texture. (The scenes and mise-en-scènes of Anatolian Greek life, the complex aerial shots of the Anatolian landscape, the camera angles that bring us into the densely layered urban culture of Constantinople are as brilliant as anything that Kazan has done.) Among the many rich color films of 1963, such as *Tom Jones, Lilies of the Field, Cleopatra, Irma La Douce, The Birds, How the West Was Won*, the film's severe black-and-white cinematography was anomalous.

Foster Hirsch, who did a two-hour-and-forty-five-minute analysis of the film, almost scene by scene on a recent Warner Home Video DVD (2010), calls himself the "world's number one champion of the film" and extols *America, America* as "the greatest achievement of the twentieth century's greatest director of actors in American theater and film." In this film, Hirsch goes on, "all of Kazan's skills come to fruition." It's "a film that should claim its place in the American canon as an American masterwork." Of all Kazan's extraordinary films—and there are many, including *Gentleman's Agreement, On the Waterfront, A Streetcar Named Desire, A Face in the Crowd, Splendor in the Grass, East of Eden*—Hirsch asserts "this is the work he is proudest of—the work that represents all his dreams of being a filmmaker."

Although it opened to "no audience," as Hirsch notes, and was a commercial failure, fifty years later *America, America* has been rediscovered in the wave of celebration of Elia Kazan's work, and Martin Scorsese's documentary, *A Letter to Elia*, was shown as part of the PBS *American Masters* series in May 2011. With its evocation of American exceptionalism, the film seems to have become a metonym for the American immigrant narrative. Scorsese calls it "the story of the passage of the old world to the new." In some very basic way, *America, America* corroborates this metonym as it celebrates the idea of the United States as land of hope and new beginnings. Close to the end of *America, America*, there's even a heart-wrenching sea voyage of poor immigrants crossing the Atlantic by ship and coming into New York Harbor, where that great indexical image of the Statue of Liberty rises up out of the fog. The TV film channel AMC recently ran the film on the Fourth of July—as one of those classics that depicts the heroism of the immigrant story and the epic journey to Ellis Island.

Although the final scenes bring us to Ellis Island and New York for the American dimension of the story, the place and location of *America, America* is Turkey, both the rugged Anatolian interior and the great capital, Constantinople (now Istanbul). For all the praise and scrutiny the film is now receiving, and from formidable figures like Scorsese, Wallach, Jonathan Lehr in *The New Yorker*, and even a film scholar like Hirsch, there is something odd and perplexing about the failure of any of its critics and champions to explain what the fundamental and boldly depicted historical story and circumstance of this film is about.

>>><<<

America, America opens in 1896 in the mountainous terrain of the Anatolian plateau, near the city of Kayseri, where we encounter the protagonist, Stavros, a young Greek man in his early twenties who lives in a small village under Mt. Aergius, near Kayseri. From Kazan's opening voice-over and the song by Hadjidakis, we cut to the ice-piled flank of Mt. Aergius, where Stavros and his best friend, the Armenian, Vartan Damadian, are hacking ice and loading it on their wagon to sell it over the mountain in their village. Kazan continues: "But the day came here in Anatolia as everywhere where there's oppression, when people began to question. There were bursts of violence, people began to wonder, and some began to search for another home."

As we encounter the Ottoman militia harassing Stavros and Vartan, who are carting the ice back to their village, we learn the news of a political event that has rocked the country: Armenian activists have taken over the Ottoman Bank in Constantinople, protesting the long-standing mistreatment of Christians by the government and the deep-seated discrimination in the Islamic infrastructure of Ottoman Turkey. The event, known as the Ottoman Bank Incident, results (in the film and in history) in a second round of Sultan Abdul Hamid II's massacres of the Armenians throughout Turkey in the mid-1890s—an episode known as the Hamidian Massacres.

This violent history is both context and text for *America, America,* and that history generates the darkness of the film that is embodied, symbolically and aesthetically, in Kazan's cinematic landscape of relentless, tenebrific lighting and dark mise-en-scènes. Kazan's stylized lighting and long, slow, sometimes handheld camera shots deepen an expressionistic and psychological complexity. But darkness is the film's modality, and it defines the texture of scene after scene in which the inner turmoil of the characters is interwoven with the oppressed condition of Christians in Turkey. Stavros is continually moving through a landscape of shadow, chiaroscuroed faces, and dark interiors in which social and psychological meanings emerge. Stavros's family, the Topouzoglus, are a comfortable, middle-class provincial Greek family, and if conditions had been difficult for them as Christians, now the massacres of the Armenians have convinced Mr. Topouzoglu that it is time to leave Turkey.

In the early scenes, we see close-ups of Stavros and his family, their intense stares, brooding looks, dark eyes, and contorted faces, all modeled by dark shading. Darkness encompasses psychology throughout the film, and in the mottled darkness we encounter the faces of Stavros's mother's anguish, his father's repressed pain, and the stoical anger of his Armenian friend Vartan. In many ways, the film is defined by Stavros's many gazes and facial gestures of pain, anger, sadness, humiliation, and brooding; his face is haunted, scowling, silent, pained, and repressed. Over and over, and perhaps excessively, Stavros's face is shadowed, mottled, shaded, cradled, framed by darkness—in his house in the village, in the Turkish governor's office doorway, in his grandmother's cave in the mountains, in raki houses and brothels, and in the hull of the ship going to America.

Dark (and sometimes black) interiors dominate the mise-en-scènes: the rooms in the Greek village house where Stavros moves in and out of his mother's anger and his father's fear; the almost black interior of the basement of the house where, amid the hidden family wealth, Stavros meets with his father, who exclaims: "I've made up my mind. We're going to send you to Constantinople. Our family is going to leave this place and you're going to go first"; the raki club where Stavros and Vartan dance in half dark, half light as Turkish men smoking hookahs look on; the shadowed streets of the village where Armenians are running into the dark interior of a church where they will be burned alive; the half-black interior of a brothel where the prostitutes dance as Stavros broods; the darkness of the sewers underground in Constantinople where the *hamals* (human pack animals for cargo) have their labor meetings; Stavros's face encircled in darkness as he sits next to the shadow that encapsulates Mrs. Kebabian at a dance club in Istanbul; Stavros's face, like a Caravaggio portrait, amid the dust and light of a strange basement room, where he tells his fiancée, Thomna, that he must leave her and "this land of shame" for America.

Aboard the ship, there are more dark interiors: the cabins, the passageways of third-class steerage; night through a porthole on Stavros's face; the dramatic conversations on board happen in darkness; Stavros's cathartic dance at night on deck; and, at Ellis Island, masses of people are slumped in half darkness inside the bars of the waiting stations.

>>><<<

Once the narrative unfolds with Kazan's opening voice-over, Armenian-Greek relationships are crucial to shaping the plot.

While driving their ice cart off the mountain, Stavros asks Vartan if there are mountains bigger than this one in America, and Vartan answers: "In America everything is bigger." As Vartan stares at the mountain, he exhorts Stavros: "What are we waiting for? Come on you, let's go you. With the help of Jesus." Here and later, the intense relationships between Stavros and his Armenian friends deepen both the mythic and political dramas that underscore much of the tension in the film. Both personal and cultural relationships between the Greek protagonist and his Armenian friends are enmeshed, reciprocal, and symbiotic, and his rebellious soul is drawn toward their vulnerable condition.

Vartan—the older friend whom Stavros regards "in a worshipful way" (as Kazan's script directions indicate)—is the catalyst for what becomes Stavros's obsession with going to America. And for Vartan, the idea of America will soon become inseparable from the political oppression of Christians in Turkey. The repeated phrase, "for the sake of Jesus" or "with the help of Jesus," passes between Stavros and his Armenian friends as not only a prayer but also a cultural signifier that embodies both an idea of hope and the issue of religious difference that defines much of the predicament for Greeks and Armenians in Turkey.

From the time we meet the earthy, disaffected Vartan in the opening scene, Armenians become a topos, sometimes allegorical, sometimes fully realistic, and always a source of agency for Stavros's journey out of Turkey. Armenians—even more so than Greeks at this flammable historical moment in the late 1890s—are a pariah minority, a tainted group. If Kazan has already noted in his opening voice-over that "a time comes when people begin to question," we discover in the next scene that the Armenians have pushed the political envelope for reform by creating a national incident in setting fire to the national bank in Constantinople. Kazan has dramatized history a bit here by turning the incident into a conflagration. In fact, the Armenian activists in late summer of 1896 did not burn the bank, but they took it hostage with no intentions of violence and with the goal of calling on the European powers to intervene against the Sultan's mass killings of the previous two years, which took the lives of more than 100,000 innocent Armenian civilians. Although a shoot-out with the Turkish authorities resulted from the bank takeover, the bank and its possessions were untouched. But, the Sultan's response to this act of protest was to perpetrate more massacres of Armenians throughout Turkey.

Within the first three minutes of the film, Kazan has cut to a scene in the office of an Ottoman provincial governor who reads to his staff of bureaucrats a telegram from the Sultan. The voice-over tells us that the year is 1896, as the governor, an avuncular-looking man in a fez and glasses, says:

> This came an hour ago over the wire from the capital. "Your Excellency on this day, the eve of our national feast of Bayram, the Armenian fanatics have dared to set fire to the national Turkish bank in Constantinople. It is the wish of our Sultan, Abdul Hamid II, the resplendent, the shadow of God on earth, that the Armenian subject people throughout this empire, be taught once and for all, that acts of terror cannot be tolerated. Our sultan has the patience of the prophet, but he has now given signs that he would be pleased if this lesson would be impressed once and for all on this dangerous minority, how this will be affected will be left up to each provincial governor and to the army post commanders in each provincial capital."

In a scene that must have perplexed (or perhaps bypassed) most viewers in 1963, as perhaps it still does today, Kazan brings a dramatic, historical moment back from the mothballs. What did viewers make of this? Armenians? Burning a bank in Constantinople in 1896? Constantinople? Or is it Istanbul?

Kazan recalled his grandmother's stories about hiding Armenians in her basement during the 1890s massacres. "One of the first memories I have is of sleeping in my grandmother's bed and my grandmother telling me stories about the massacre of the Armenians, and how she and my grandfather hid Armenians in the cellar of their home."[4] Here, too, Kazan has mined the traumatic memory of his family's experience in creating a story that involves inextricable ties between Armenians and Greeks in Turkey. The viewer who knows the broader arc of this history knows that the massacres of the 1890s were a prologue to the genocides of the Armenians and the Pontic (Black Sea region) Greeks between 1915 and 1920, and to the ethnic cleansing of Greeks from their historic homelands of western Turkey, especially Smyrna and Constantinople from 1913 through the Turkish burning of Smyrna in 1922. Kazan's memory of his grandmother's narrative had left its mark on him.

Stavros and Vartan must continually navigate the racism and infrastructural prejudice that define their public identities as Christians. On their way back to the village, Stavros and Vartan are harassed by a group of Turkish soldiers who mock them and then help themselves to the ice they're hauling. Only when Vartan reveals to the Turkish captain Mehmet that he had been his orderly in the army years ago does Mehmet's tone change. Calling him his "little lamb," Captain Mehmet embraces Vartan, in the way a plantation owner in the American South might have gone nostalgic upon meeting a long-lost house slave. He warns Vartan that because of the Ottoman Bank seizure, "today no Armenian will be forgiven for being an Armenian" (Figure 1). Here, as in various scenes throughout the film, Kazan captures the nuances of racism with facial gestures and body language that are quintessential to his method-acting idiom. The Turkish captain then urges Vartan to stay with him in the mountains, but Stavros explains that Vartan must go to help protect his family in the village.

When Vartan and Stavros arrive in their village of Garmeer (the word means "red" in Armenian), Armenians are running through the streets in terror, flocking to their church for protection, and the Greeks are closing their doors and shutters. In Kazan's passion for facial expression, he captures the terror in the haunted faces that are running, watching, hiding. Stavros is admonished by a woman to whom he is selling ice, "Don't be seen with this Armenian." When he returns home, he is scolded by his mother, who tells his father "he's been with the Armenian again." When Stavros's father tells his friends in the family parlor that his son is close with an Armenian, he says defensively,

FIGURE 1. Elia Kazan, still from *America, America* (1963). "Today, no Armenian will be forgiven for being an Armenian," says a Turkish captain (far right) to Vartan (far left) and Stavros.

"It's not our affair. They are Armenians and we are Greeks. It's their necks and not ours." Stavros overhears this, pokes his head in the room and retorts: "True, they're saving the Greeks for their next holiday." The older men are made uncomfortable by the boy's remark; Stavros has hit a nerve and has disclosed his political astuteness about the relationship between Greeks and Armenians in Turkey.

In a melodramatic scene in a raki club where Stavros and Vartan do a macabre dance as the local men stare at them from the dark corners of the tavern, Vartan repeats his mantra, "Come on you, let's go you." Stavros answers, equally transfixed: "America, America." Those words, uttered in a kind of haunted trance, are epithets for hope, emancipation, new life—and just then there is a cry from the street and Vartan whispers, "The jails are emptying," signifying that the criminals have been released to start the massacre.

In an extraordinary scene and perhaps a historic representation of government-sponsored mass killing in the history of film, Kazan's depiction of Armenians being burned alive in a village church brings his probing political realism together with his expressionistic aesthetic. When the men in the raki club shout, "It's beginning," we understand that the idea of massa-cring Armenians has a ritualistic aspect to it and that the local population has been waiting for the sign to be given. Kazan then cuts to the inside of a church where Armenians are congregated, candles and incense giving the interior a sensual mystery, as a priest is leading them in prayer. The Armenians in the church are chanting *Devormyah* ("Lord Have Mercy"); there's a cutaway to Turkish gendarmes and locals surrounding the church, carrying torches and brush; then a cutaway to the interior of the church, where men, women, and children are singing as the church fills with smoke and the icons and crosses and altar are enveloped. Outside, a priest is humiliated; he fights back, and a gendarme puts a lit torch in his hand and throws the priest into the burn-ing church. As flames engulf the church, we watch smoke fill the narthex; Armenian words and screams dissolve into flames, some people escape, and Vartan is embroiled in a fight to defend his people. Then images of smoke and fire are juxtaposed in such a way so that the scene swirls and fades to a vortex of flame and black sky, and the music crescendos in an atonal flourish (Fig-ure 2). Kazan cuts to the smoke-covered remains of the church, the dead scattered in the streets, and Stavros sitting next to Var-

FIGURE 2. Elia Kazan, still from *America, America* (1963). Armenians burned alive in a church set on fire by Turkish gendarmes.

tan's corpse. Foster Hirsch asserts that this scene is indicative of how "the Christian religion has failed its believers." When I first heard his comment on the on Warner Home Video aftermath commentary, I replayed it several times to see if I heard correctly. I wondered if in viewing an image of a synagogue being burned during Krystallnacht, Hirsch would have said that it revealed how the Jewish religion had failed its believers. I think it is fair to note that this scene is not about how the Christian religion has failed its believers. Rather it is a depiction of the calculated mechanisms of state-sponsored mass killing and the assault on religious identity of a targeted minority group, and it gives us various insights about human rights atrocities.

Grief-stricken, Stavros drags Vartan's body away to bury it, only to be arrested by Turkish soldiers. Forced to leave the corpse, he snatches Vartan's fez, and after that, only his father's bribe to the governor can buy him out of jail. Although Vartan is dead, he has become the first source of agency in Stavros's journey, and his fez will remain an emblem of his friendship with Vartan and a symbol of his quest for America.

Almost immediately after Vartan's death, Stavros meets a frail, tubercular, coughing young man walking barefoot on a mountain road. The man, whose name is Ohannes Gardashian, is mumbling as he walks along, begging, "I will pray for you when I get to America." Horrified, but with pity for this waif wandering in the mountains hoping to escape Turkey, Stavros asks him how he expects to make it to America without shoes or money, and Ohannes retorts, "With the help of Jesus." Irritated, bemused, drawn to the Armenian, Stavros gives him his own shoes and then asks him where he's from. Ohannes gazes upward, points to the sky: "Beyond those clouds are the mountains of Armenia. I'll never see them again." He keeps coughing as he bids him farewell: "I'll remember you."

After the massacre, in an ensuing scene in which Mr. Topouzoglu must go to the governor's office to beg for Stavros's release, during which the governor extorts a bribe from him while lecturing him about the virtues of being a "good"—meaning

subservient—Christian. Stavros looks on in horror at his father's submissiveness, then takes off to find his grandmother in
the mountains. In a scene of primal intensity, Stavros finds his
grandmother in her cave-like house in the side of a mountain.
She looks like a weathered crone, a tough, witty woman who
disparages her son (Stavros's father) for being a Greek coward
in the face of Turkish oppression. She gives her grandson a dose
of her wit: "The Turks spit in your face and they say it's raining."
Desperate for her to help him get to Constantinople, he begs
her for money, but instead she gives him a knife, which he tries
to refuse until she gives him another piece of Greek wisdom: "It
will remind you that no sheep ever saved himself by bleating."

Shortly afterward, to Stavros's shock, Mr. Topouzoglu decides
it is time for the family to leave Turkey. In a dramatic scene in a
dark basement room of their house, father gives son permission
to leave the village for Constantinople with the family's entire
material wealth and possessions. He confesses to his son the humiliation he has endured as a Christian in Turkey: "From time to
time, I have had to do things . . . well, we live by the mercy of the
Turks. But I have also kept my honor safe inside me. Safe, inside
me. And you see we are still living. After a time you don't feel
the shame." Stavros stares at his father, his face half swallowed in
darkness—smooth and cherubic, hardened and sour as his father
whispers, "It's our last hope."

>>><<<

In sending Stavros by donkey to Constantinople with the family
wealth to join his cousin in the rug business before he makes his
passage to America, Kazan commences the picaresque sequence
of the film. Stavros is not unlike Pip or Huck Finn in his initiation into adult complexity as he navigates a sinuous, obstacle-
laden path that tests his character and courage. Episode after
episode, his journey across Anatolia to the great capital city is
a baptism into violence, thievery, extortion, and corruption—a
journey into the bowels of Ottoman society and its institutions.
At one point near the end of the film, as he explains himself in a

moment of crisis, Stavros exclaims: "I have been beaten, robbed, shot, left for dead. I have eaten the Sultan's garbage, and driven the dogs off to get at it. I became a hamal."

And from the start, he is robbed by a Turkish ferryman, befriended by a Turkish con artist, Abdul, who calls Stavros "brother" as he extorts his money and family possessions, spending it on prostitutes and raki in exchange for protecting him. After Stavros is fleeced by a prostitute at a brothel, Abdul accuses him of having stolen *his* possessions and takes him to an Islamic court because, under Ottoman law, by swearing on the Qur'an his word is sacred against a Christian's; in court, Stavros is fleeced of everything. As in *Gentleman's Agreement* and *On the Waterfront*, Kazan's interest in corruption, bigotry, and social infrastructures is explored with uncanny power.

Again and again, Kazan depicts the harsh realities of being Christian in Ottoman society with his documentary and psychological realism. In the next scene, Abdul taunts Stavros: "I envy you—you Greeks have learned how to swallow insult and indignity and turn around and smile." The legacy of shame that Stavros's father articulated (and that Kazan noted about his own father) keeps building, and after trying to steal Stavros's last coins, Abdul continues to taunt him ("are you any different from sheep, they won't fight for their lives either"). This finally provokes Stavros to use the knife his grandmother gave him, and he attacks Abdul as he kneels for his evening prayers; a fight ensues, and the murder happens below the cliff and off camera.

In Constantinople, Stavros is plunged into a world of cruelty and poverty. Because he's arrived penniless, his cousin refuses him a place in the business and tries to convince him to court a young Greek girl from a wealthy family. Stavros rejects the idea and is then forced to become a hamal. After more calamities befall him, his fellow hamal, Garbed, convinces him to join an underground labor movement, and when Garbed exclaims, "The main victims of the Turkish Empire are the Turkish people," Kazan deepens his political vision to encompass subaltern life in Turkey and the conditions of the working class. Kazan's ability to get hold of the edgy undersides of poverty yields a sequence of scenes among the devastating conditions of Constantinople's hamals and prostitutes and other marginal segments of Turkish society. After Stavros miraculously survives the Turkish police massacre of the members of the labor movement at their secret meeting underground in the sewers, he takes his cousin's advice; he gets himself a suit of good clothes and becomes a suitor of one of the daughters of the wealthy Greek rug merchant, Aleko Sinnikoglou.

As the texture of the mise-en-scène changes radically, Kazan takes us through elaborate rituals of courtship in a wealthy Greek Constantinople family, where we witness the stratification of power and gender roles between patriarchal men (especially the pasha-like father) and encounter Kazan's rich mise-en-scènes of bourgeois life. The cinematography of Haskell Wexler and the editing of Dede Allen are inventive and scrupulous in ways that give the film a gritty realism that is enmeshed with lyrical, symbolistic, and metaphoric meanings. Stavros is betrothed to Sinnikoglou's eldest daughter, and although he appears to be headed for a life of affluence and familial comfort, at a crucial moment and in an uncharacteristic burst of passion, he confesses to his fiancée, Thomna, that an inner vision compels him to leave all this good fortune for America:

> I don't want to be my father. I don't want to be your father. I don't want to have that good family life. That good family life! All the good people they stay here and live in this shame. The churchgoers who give to the poor live in this shame.

In what is an evolving trope that began with his father's confession about the humiliation and shame that are inseparable from being a Christian in Turkey, here Stavros breaks through the mask and confesses that he can't live in this society where Christians live in terror or, to use Ralph Ellison's trope—in invisibility. On the threshold of inheriting the prosperous Sinnikoglou carpet company, his quest for America is reignited and, once again, Armenians become sources of agency.

At his prospective father-in-law's rug store, Stavros meets Harutiun Kebabian, a wealthy Armenian American rug merchant, and his wife, Sophia, who was born in Constantinople but left at eighteen to marry. Elegant and sensual, Sophia, married to an elderly husband whose only interests are money, lives in frustrated desperation. She tells Stavros: "My twenty-second year is still inside me waiting like a baby to be born." In initiating an affair with Stavros, she pulls him closer to America. At her apartment he looks longingly at catalogs of American fashion; he tries on her husband's straw hat, fantasizing about New York. After Sophia has helped Stavros secure passage aboard the ship to New York, her husband learns of their affair, and an altercation erupts between Mr. Kebabian and Stavros. Stavros is charged with criminal assault and ordered to be deported upon arriving at Ellis Island.

As desperate as Stavros's situation seems, there is still an Armenian in the wings to bail him out. That mysterious tubercular man, Ohannes Gardashian, to whom Stavros gave his shoes on the mountain road in Anatolia, has made it to Constantinople, and Stavros befriends him again, becoming his protector, giving him money and food. Ohannes has boarded the ship to America as one of the shoeshine boys who are being sponsored by a Greek American businessman. Aboard ship too, Stavros takes Ohannes under his wing, getting him food and coaching him on how to suppress his tubercular cough so he won't be sent back to Turkey by the Ellis Island health officials.

After the altercation with the rug merchant Kebabian, Stavros knows his future is jeopardized, and he tries to join Mr. Agnostis's shoeshine boys but is rebuffed because he has no sponsorship. When Ohannes butts in, saying: "Take my name. I beg you. Take Ohannes Gardashian," Mr. Agnostis reminds him that there can't be two Ohannes Gardashians on board. In an ensuing moment of carnivalistic apotheosis, Ohannes and Stavros find themselves on the ship's prow at night with the lights of New York in the distance. When Stavros threatens to jump overboard and swim ashore, Ohannes, knowing the impossibility of his surviving, implores him not to. Kazan then cuts to a scene of young wealthy Americans celebrating the ship's arrival; party lights, a band, cocktails, and dancing create a counter scene to the immigrant drama going on near the railing. Stavros looks on from a shadowy corner of the deck, then leaps into the celebratory arena and does a wild, gyrating dance in which he screams a primal scream—what might be seen as a cathartic unburdening of the cumulative pain (and perhaps a cry of collective historical rage, too) he has endured through his journey from his village in Anatolia to this liminal place on board a ship approaching Ellis Island.

The Americans look on, bemused and ignorant, like characters in a Fitzgerald scene, laughing in their evening attire with drinks in their hands. And while all this is happening, Ohannes has silently walked to the railing of the ship and jumped. From the moment we were introduced to this gentle, ethereal young man walking in the Anatolian highlands—pointing to the clouds and the Armenian mountains to the east—he has seemed a sacrificial figure and, to use the cliché, but one that works here in a larger Christian context, a Christ figure.

When we see Stavros next, he has joined Mr. Agnostis's shoe-shine boys and is in line at Ellis Island's immigration desk, now using the Armenian name Ohannes Gardashian, whose papers have been given to him by Agnostis. With some comic Ellis Island realism, Kazan has the customs official Americanize the name from Ohan-nes to Joe Arness, and so, through the agency and sacrifice of his Armenian friend Ohannes Gardashian, Stavros Topouzoglu is reborn Joe Arness—a new American in the land of hope. However, Armenian agency is not over, and as Stavros walks off the dock, Bertha, the Kebabians' maid, comes running up to him with an envelope from Sophia that contains a substantial sum of cash to aid him in his first weeks in the New World.

As the movie closes, Kazan splits the screen between the old and the new—a Turkish village and Manhattan. In New York, Stavros/Joe is shining shoes; then Stavros's family, in their village, receive a letter from him. "In some ways it's not different here," Stavros writes, and as his father looks around with a sense of paranoia, he says to his wife, "How quickly he's forgotten what it is here!" "But let me tell you one thing," Stavros writes. "You have a new chance here! For everyone that is able to get here, there is a fresh start. So get ready. You're all coming. I'm working for that. To bring you all here, one by one."

The scene shifts back to Manhattan, where Stavros is shining shoes and tossing a newly earned coin in the air, saying, "Come on you, let's go you," and now the words "people waiting" replace Vartan's epithet, "with the help of Jesus." In another cutaway back to the Topouzoglu home, the camera pans the faces of the family looking out on the town as a squadron of Turkish cavalry ride past their house. The sound of the hooves is loud, the force of the militia echoes loudly, and Stavros in a voice-over is saying, "people waiting, people waiting." Kazan intercuts an image of the Flatiron Building in Manhattan, then to Stavros hurrying up his customers in that mode of American entrepreneurial hustle. Then Kazan cuts to Mt. Aergius in the Anatolian highlands, as the juxtaposition of the land of shame and the land of possibility create a metonym for the whole story.

>>><<<

Why has the central historical structure of the film been left out, ignored, or possibly self-censured by critics, admirers, and journalists alike? The persecution of the Greeks and Armenians by the Ottoman Turkish government is the animating force that propels the story, makes the film's concept possible. It's curious that none of the cultural, journalistic, or commercial framing of the film, whether it be on AMC, in *The New Yorker*, or in the new Warner Home Video package, even notes, let alone represents, this history. Warner video presents a narrative on the DVD cover stating that Stavros "leaves his war-torn homeland behind to begin a new life." Even the most uninformed viewer might ask: What war was this? The informed viewer might ask: If the film's subject were the pogroms of the Jews in eastern Poland

and western Russia in 1900, would Warner Home Video present the historical event as a war? John Lahr in *The New Yorker* quotes Kazan's memorable opening voice-over about Armenians and Greeks being subjugated minorities, and then notes that the Kazan family left the capital of Turkey (it was still Constantinople then) for New York but never mentions *why* the family left. Lahr goes on to note that Kazan's father was intensely anxious and once told his son, "Say nothing, don't mix in." And he quotes Kazan recalling, "I was kept segregated . . . it's the segregation a minority imposes on itself . . . but it was really the result of terror."[5] Wouldn't it seem an organic continuation of Lahr's narrative to mention something about "the terror" that inflected Kazan's father's behavior and the terror that Elia makes explicit note of? Why did this Greek man who grew up in Turkey in the late nineteenth century convey a sense of terror to his son? In the era of genocide and trauma studies, surely these are not rarefied issues and questions. Since Lahr quotes Kazan in conversation with French film historian Michel Ciment, it seems likely that he would have read on in the interview. Kazan's reflection on his own family past in Turkey explains the impact of the Armenian massacres in his family's memory and his sense of the entwined lives of Armenians and Greeks in Turkey:

> The Anatolian Greeks are a completely terrorized people. My father's family comes from the interior of Asia Minor, from a city called Kayseri, and they never forgot they were part of a minority. They were surrounded with periodic slaughters—or riots: the Turks would suddenly have a crisis and massacre a lot of Armenians, or they'd run wild and kill a lot of Greeks. The Greeks stayed in their houses. The fronts of the houses were almost barricaded, the windows shut with wooden shutters. One of the first memories I have is of sleeping in my grandmother's bed and my grandmother telling me stories about the massacre of the Armenians, and how she and my grandfather hid Armenians in the cellar of their home.[6]

The film historian Foster Hirsch spends nearly three hours explicating the film in the DVD after-segment, and at least notes, even if in passing, that Kazan created at the outset "a complicated political context" in which Greeks and the Armenians were an oppressed minority in Turkey. But—it would have been appropriate for him to have explained to the viewer just a bit about what that complicated political context was. He makes no mention of the Hamidian Massacres, the event that is the guiding catalyst of the story. And it might have been of interest to the viewer of this film to know that the Hamidian Massacres made an impact in the United States in the 1890s to such an extent that the atrocities were widely reported in the press, and a nationwide relief and rescue movement ensued. Clara Barton took the first Red Cross mission ever out of the country when she led her teams to the Armenian sections of Turkey in 1896.[7] This was America's first international philanthropic rescue effort, and its impact on American history was significant. In the year which Kazan sets his story, *Harper's* magazine ran an illustrated cover story of Armenians being hunted down by killing bands.

There are some startling intersections between the film's narrative and the process of its making, and in his autobiography Kazan writes about the ordeal of filming the opening of *America, America* in Turkey in 1962. It was personal and historical irony that Kazan made his own journey back to the city of his birth, to a place and culture of which he had almost no personal memory, having left Istanbul in 1913 at the age of four, when it was still called Constantinople. Being in Istanbul in 1962 was not too distant from the Istanbul of September 1955, when the massacre and expulsion of most of the Greek community of the city occurred, in what became the final episode in Turkey's cleansing of its historic Greek population. Tens of thousands of Greeks were killed, and thousands of Greek businesses, private properties, and churches were destroyed or confiscated. Even though the military coup of 1960 had been supplanted by a constitution in 1961, Turkey was still an authoritarian society where Kemalist militarism was still congruent in many ways with late Ottoman nationalism, and state repression of intellectual freedom still left the jails full of writers, journalists, and ethnic minorities. Minor-

ity rights continued to be nonexistent, and with the Greek and
Armenian communities destroyed, more than ten million Kurds
were not only disallowed civil rights, but were not allowed to call
themselves Kurds and forced to use the term "mountain Turks."

From the start, Kazan was required to go before the Turkish censorship board in Ankara to have his script evaluated for
anything that might be unacceptable, or anti-Turkish. In anticipation, Kazan admits to having cut any scenes he thought
would be offensive to the government. His description of being
interrogated by five men, two of them in army uniforms, in a
government office, captures some of the Kafka-like bureaucracy
he encountered. Although the censors had read the script, "they
weren't certain what their opinions were," Kazan recalls, because
no one wanted to let a seditious movie through if it might offend
the higher bureaucrats. However, eager to bring half a million
U.S. dollars into their economy, the censors went back and forth
until, finally, the head of the censorship board told Kazan that if
he were to shoot in Turkey, he would have a government official
at his side each day to monitor each scene.

When Kazan tactfully assented, the director of the censorship board replied: "Our pasha hopes you are sincere. But as they
say in your country, talk is cheap. What we must expect of you
is a film masterpiece that will show our people not as they are
shamefully portrayed in American films but as they are in truth,
honest and hard-working, with great love for their soil and for
Allah." Kazan replied: "That is precisely my intention."[8]

Filming street scenes in Istanbul, Kazan recalls feeling a
kind of fear that wasn't so different from what his father had
conveyed to him about being Greek in Turkey. Having already
written Stavros's story and now in the place of his birth and his
character's life, he recalls: "I was still afraid of Turks and would
never get over it." One Turkish newspaper reported that Kazan
had come "to shame the Turkish people," and, as Kazan put
it, "The effect of this accusation was intensified by my fearful
imagination. Besides, it was close to the truth."[9] Having already
developed the trope of Turkey as "a land of shame" in his script,

Kazan's return to his birthplace seemed to be overlapping with the traumatic life of his protagonist in that very place, sixty-five years later.

When Kazan's cousin Stellio came to watch scenes being filmed in downtown Istanbul, he looked on from far away, kept walking, and never acknowledged his famous American cousin. As Kazan watched his cousin scuttle between buildings, afraid to be seen near the set or him, it brought him to a moment of recognition: "If George Kazan had not brought his wife and two sons to America in 1913, I could have been there now, dressed as my cousin was dressed, hustling everywhere as he hustled everywhere, 'invisible.' If it hadn't been for my father's courage—a quality I had not until that day associated with him—I'd now be what my cousin was."[10] It seemed that there, on set, on site, in the place of his birth and family's past, Kazan experienced a self-recognition and a sense of a larger historical self and its link to history.

Although Kazan managed to appease his censor so they could, at least, start shooting, one day on site shortly afterward, as he was directing a scene that involved bargaining in a bazaar, a secret-police officer came running onto the set, screaming to the censor that this scene must be disallowed because it would show the Turkish people as overemphatic bargainers. "Why eight hands waving like that? The world will think Turkey an insane asylum."[11] As the scene was being shot, the secret-police officer fired the censor and took his place. After this, Kazan conjectured that their hotel rooms were bugged, and he and his associate producer, Charlie Maguire, now believed that the whole film company was under Turkish surveillance. "They got cops on their cops here," Maguire told Kazan, and then confessed to him that they had only gotten this far because he had been paying daily, hefty bribes to censors and police.

The filming continued to unravel in a day-for-night way as events on and off the set dovetailed, and finally Kazan, like his protagonist Stavros, realized that he must get out of Turkey. In retrospect, he recalled that the experience of filming in Turkey was now turning out to be "a source of inspiration" for the film. Maguire convinced Kazan to shoot the rest of the film in Athens, and assured him that he had a plan to get the good footage out of the country. To dupe the customs agents and the secret police, Maguire put the exposed film into boxes marked "raw stock" and the unexposed film into boxes marked "used." The customs agents confiscated the wrong boxes, and Kazan recalls their celebration in Athens as they sat in a hotel restaurant shaking the canisters of good film in victory and imagining the Turkish agents handing over the blank film to their superiors.[12]

>>><<<

There is an edgy neorealist texture to this historically situated bildungsroman. In its representation of the complexities of life for Christians in Ottoman Turkey and its social-psychological realism, *America, America* owes something to Eisenstein's historical epics, and also to postwar neorealism; Fellini's *La Strada,* De Sica's *Bicycle Thieves,* and Kazan's own *On the Waterfront,* for example, are among films of the era that engaged the harsh real without sentimentality.

Few feature-length Hollywood films of midcentury dealt with human rights or ethnic cleansing (the Hamidian Massacres were a prologue to a modern age of genocide, the Armenian case of 1915 being the first)[13] in the telling of a boy's coming-of-age story with such aesthetic complexity and social and psychological depth as Kazan does here. Out of a haunted passion for his family story of leaving Turkey for America, Kazan created a memoiristic film that achieved mythic dimensions in its absorption of history and culture and politics, and this is clearly why he continued to call *America, America* his favorite film, the one that brought his career—as a writer *and* director—together.

Furthermore, in its representations of ethnic difference, religious ideology, and class and its depictions of power and gender in a traditional Middle Eastern culture, Kazan anticipated certain kinds of postmodern and contemporary questioning. *America, America*'s depiction of working-class life, especially among the hamals and prostitutes is rendered in a dark, grainy austerity, and a tenebrific light that gives a haunting depth to this subaltern culture. We encounter the urban underclass eating garbage, living in the streets, and being massacred by the police in the sewers during their labor meeting and the brothels where women barely survive as they are exploited by pimps and owners. These scenes are shot with inventive, long, and slow camera shots, so that the texture of place and detail of culture are rendered with depth and nuance. In scenes of domestic Greek village and city life, male-dominated rituals and control over women are depicted with a psychological texture that gives us insight to the traditional culture of the time and place. Women are subservient, sometimes trapped, sometimes contentedly ensconced in the patriarchal dynamics of the culture.

Kazan, Haskell Wexler, and Dede Allen created scenes of unusual texture in depicting the great urban crossroad of Constantinople (Istanbul) with its architecture of domes and minarets, ports, restaurants, rug stores, squalid streets, sewers, and brothels that give us a sense of a complex city at a complex time. Scenes move between the sublime and mysterious Anatolian highlands and the grimy interiors of raki houses and brothels; the affluent parlors of a wealthy Constantinople Greek family and an Armenian village church going up in flames; Manhattan's Flatiron Building and the Turkish cavalry kicking up dust in an Ottoman village. Such is the range of the film's mise-en-scène and its cinematic reach.

America, America is a film that seems to me to speak to our contemporary concerns with even greater intensity than it might have had for a general audience in 1963. In some symbolic way, it may be a film about America, but its breadth and sweep, its unusual blend of neorealist edge and expressionistic drama, create a strange and arresting mix of historical depth, social realism, and a probing psychological portrait of a young man's coming of age and epic journey across cultures and continents. In telling a deeply personal family story and the story of Stavros's decent into the harsh realities of adult experience, Kazan pulled off a remarkable exploration of the politics of religious and ethnic difference, the exploitation of state power and mass violence over minorities, the violence of class conflict, and gender complexity. Few films of any era have traveled along such cultural landscapes, have embodied personal, psychological, and historical trauma, collective family memory, and mythic structures that are transformed in an expressionistic lyrical idiom that never forsakes the real.

10

Siamanto's Bloody News

More than my house I need the truth.
But I need my house too.
« BERTOLT BRECHT »

My grandfather died more than a decade before I was born. But when conversation turned to him, there was sometimes mention of a book of poems with which he had something to do. It was in Armenian literature an important—what one might call a flammable—book, written by his friend Adom Yarjanian, whose pen name was Siamanto. Siamanto and my grandfather, Diran Balakian, were born in 1878 in Akn and Tokat, respectively, provincial cities of Turkey. As progressive, outward-looking Armenians, they went to Europe to complete their educations, my grandfather to medical school in Leipzig, Siamanto to Paris to study literature and philosophy.

After graduating from medical school in 1905, my grandfather returned to Constantinople and, shortly thereafter in the spring of 1909, went with a group of Armenian physicians and relief workers to Adana in southern Turkey—a part of historic Armenia in the medieval period known as Cilicia—to do relief work for the Armenian survivors of the massacres of that region. Somewhere between 20,000 and 30,000 Armenians were

killed, mostly in the month of April, as a result of ethnic back-
lash in a time of political turmoil in Turkey. A new government
had emerged from the Young Turk revolution of 1908 that had
toppled the Sultan Abdulhammit II, permanently terminating
the political authority of the sultanate. By 1909, the new regime
was waged in civil conflict with the Sultan's counterrevolution-
ary army, and the Armenians, in the Adana region in particular,
were being mass-killed and their businesses looted and burned
by the local population and counterrevolutionaries who were re-
acting with more than hostility to reforms for Christians that
had accompanied the Young Turk revolution. Before it was over,
the new Young Turk army that came to the region to quell the
violence also engaged in the mass killing of the Armenian population. In short, Armenians were being scapegoated by both the
new, secular, and purportedly liberal Young Turk government
and the embittered forces of the recently dethroned Sultan,
whom the Young Turks had driven from power.

In various ways, it was a sign that the new Young Turk era
reforms for minorities were not going to work, and it was also a
harbinger of the full-scale genocide of 1915 that would result in
the death of more than a million Armenians and the erasure of
almost all of Armenian life and culture in Turkey, where Armenians were among the indigenous peoples of Anatolia for more
than 2,000 years. In one sense, the Adana massacres of 1909 were
part of a "continuum of destruction" to use Irvin Staub's phrase,
which had begun with Sultan Abdulhammit's Armenian massacres in the 1890s, when more than 100,000 Armenians were
killed and thousands of others ruined and displaced.

In Adana in 1909, my grandfather worked as a physician aiding the survivors. He became a witness to atrocities and destruction the way a physician might be. He was single during these
years (not marrying my grandmother until 1913), and he wrote
letters home regularly to his family in Constantinople. The letters, which have not survived, were filled with details and narratives about the atrocities. Siamanto was a close friend of the
Balakian family and lived near my great-grandparents in the

Scutari section of Constantinople (today Istanbul). Not only did he read the letters my grandfather sent from Adana, but he used them as his source for a book of poems.

When my father wrote his father Diran Balakian's obituary for the *National Cyclopaeida of American Biography*, he noted this: "During 1909–11 he served with a group of Armenian doctors in Adana, Turkey, aiding stricken refugees of the Turkish massacres of those years. During that time he wrote a series of letters to his friend, the poet Siamanto, describing the conditions in Adana and the plight of the refugees, and these were published by the poet in 1911 [*sic*] under the name *Sanguineous [sic]News from My Friend.*" My father's statement about his father's letters home from Adana has one inaccuracy: Siamanto didn't publish my grandfather's letters verbatim. But I suppose in some way my father was acknowledging how deeply a joint venture this book of poems was—a physician and a poet collaborating to articulate some harsh realities. As for my father's translation of the title, I remember, after this history had ceased to be taboo in my family, my father and his sisters Anna and Nona, who were literary critics and scholars, discussing it. Should it be *Red News from My Friend, Sanguinous News from My Friend*, or perhaps *Bloody News from My Friend*? My father's translation—"Sanguinous"—seems to me too diffuse and even euphemistic. *Garmeer* in Armenian is "red," and in the context of these poems clearly means "bloody."

Siamanto was arrested on April 24, 1915, in Constantinople/Istanbul along with the famous group of about 250 Armenian cultural leaders; he, along with one segment of that group, was sent to Ayash near Ankara, where he and most of the others were killed by the Turkish gendarmes in the summer of 1915, somewhere outside of Ankara. He was a poet whose identity and writing were an important part of an Armenian cultural renaissance in the first decade of the twentieth century and part of what was the beginning of Armenian literary modernism. He was a central voice in articulating poetry's role in reclaiming history and myth in order to make a new language and a richer culture. In this sense, he is a poet whose cultural situation bears some resemblance to that of Yeats in Ireland, Neruda in Chile, or Whitman in the United States, especially during the Civil War. Although he wasn't a polemical writer, he believed that poetry could not be entirely separated from the social sphere and, in this case, that meant the pressing conditions of the Armenian people under Ottoman rule. He would have agreed with Whitman's insistence that "a bard is to be commensurate with a people." And Siamanto was a poet of bardic affinities. He was a public poet who declaimed his poems before audiences and crowds and was popular in the café culture of Constantinople in those years before 1915.

For the reader unfamiliar with Armenian literary history, it is worth noting the context from which Siamanto emerged at the turn of the twentieth century. In the second half of the nineteenth century, both Eastern Armenia (in the Russian Empire) and Western Armenia (in the Ottoman Empire) were in the midst of a cultural revival. From the second half of the eighteenth century on, both Eastern and Western Armenia had absorbed different dimensions of intellectual tradition from Europe and Russia. The European Enlightenment and Romantic movements had impacts on Armenian writers and thinkers. Voltaire, Racine, Rousseau, and Hugo, for example, embodied ideas about civil liberties and human egalitarianism, and Armenian writers appropriated these ideas to help them address Armenia's deplorable social and political conditions under Ottoman rule.

Although the impact of French culture on Armenian writers and thinkers seems to have been primary, Byron and Shelley, Swift, Milton, and Shakespeare also contributed their share to the Armenian cultural revival, as did the Italian Risorgimento by way of the Armenian monastery on the island of San Lazzaro in Venice. There, Mekhitarist monks—who had taken in Byron in 1816 for his year of studying classical Armenian—had been a bridge between Armenia and Italy since 1717. Dante, Manzoni, and Leopardi were translated into Armenian from the middle of the nineteenth century. To Armenians, the democratic revolutions in France, Germany, and Italy in the middle and later parts of the nineteenth century were also signposts of progress and the ideals for liberty.

While nineteenth-century European influences helped shape Siamanto, so did a revival of interest among Armenians in their art and culture. Like various European cultures, Armenia in the late nineteenth century was involved in its own Romantic movement, and Armenian writers and artists were rediscovering their pre- and early-Christian poetry, such as the epic of David of Sassoun and the inventive mystical poems of Gregory of Nareg, as well as the ballad tradition of Sayat Nova and village folk music, which the priest and composer Gomidas Vartabed was collecting, arranging, and composing. There was also new excitement about the extraordinary medieval manuscript painters such as Toros Roslin and Sarkis Pidzak and the pioneering architectural achievements of early Christian and medieval Armenian churches, exemplified most dramatically by the uncovering of the lost medieval Armenian city of Ani by the Russian archeologist Nikolas Marr in the 1890s.

In this milieu, Siamanto came of age with a kind of cosmopolitanism that was new for Armenian intellectuals. Like other modern Western Armenian writers of his generation—Daniel Varoujan, Vahan Tekeyan, Zabel Yessayan, and Krikor Zohrab, to name a few—Siamanto absorbed European traditions into Armenian traditions. Looking back from the twenty-first century, the loss is hard to comprehend: an entire generation of Western Armenian writers were extinguished by the Ottoman government just at a moment when they were emerging into a generation that was bringing Armenian literature into modernism and into an international light. Fortunately, a solid body of their works survive, among them numerous fine translations of poetry into English, many of them done by the poet Diana Der Hovanessian, which has given them another audience.

>>><<<

There is nothing like *Bloody News from My Friend* that I know of in twentieth-century poetry. It is a book that was forged from certain salient late-nineteenth century literary modes, but some-how along the way turned into something startling and new. The *Bloody News* poems undermine traditional norms of genre and poetics that defined late-nineteenth-century poetry in Arme-nian literature as well as those in the Anglo-American tradition. Although Siamanto assumes certain late-nineteenth-century Armenian conventions in creating dramatic monologues and narrative mimetic lines, the harsh violence that he sought to rep-resent drew him into a language of such a raw, blunt, and stark nature that it subverted anything that might evoke, hint of, or imply a genteel aesthetic, or a pursuit of inspirational nature, or the sublime that much of fin-de-siècle poetry was defined by in American and British poetry.

In making a rougher language and a vernacular voice, Sia-manto often dispensed with traditional notions of metaphor. His blunt realism strikes me as owing more to Whitman's Civil War poems than to *l'art pour l'art poetics* of Malarmé or the pre-Raphaelites that defined much of the of the fin-de-siècle. As the British World War I poets would, Siamanto found that the im-pact of mass violence veered him away from the more romantic aesthetic that had driven his earlier poems, in which he sought to reclaim a sublime Armenian past, to reinvent Armenian myth, and to capture transcendent forces.

Because the *Bloody News* poems wrestle with "raw evil," to use his phrase, Siamanto is obsessed with Turkish Islamic culture and its modes and capacities to demonize the other. What hap-pened to the Armenians of the Ottoman Empire in 1909, and then in 1915, also happened in different forms to the Greeks of western Turkey and the Pontus and the Assyrians of southeast Anatolia during this period of genocide and ethnic cleansing of Ottoman Christians from 1915 through the burning of Smyrna in 1922. Thus, the texture of these poems has broad implications about the dynamics of power and the demonizing of the other. In this sense, the *Bloody News* poems have an increasingly vis-ible place in the ongoing interest in the dynamics of poetry in relation to situations of mass violence. The popularity of po-

ems like "The Dance," "The Cross," and "Grief," since their first
appearance in Carolyn Forché's anthology *Against Forgetting:
Twentieth-Century Poetry of Witness*, and then in the English
translation of *Bloody News from My Friend* in 1996, strikes me
as a barometer of a certain broadening of poetics in our current
literary culture.

Although poems like "The Bath," "The Dagger," "The Atone-
ment," and "The Cross" may be shocking in their graphic depictions, they avoid the sentimental. Siamanto is interested in
depicting the ways the perpetrators conceived of "the Armenian"
as other—that stereotyped personage who had been denigrated
by the hegemonic culture as *gavur* (infidel). *Bloodthirsty* is a word
that Siamanto uses again and again, and I suspect it was a word
my grandfather used in his letters. What Armenians experienced
during the massacre and genocide period was inseparable from
what psychiatrist and historian Robert Jay Lifton has called
"death saturation,"[1] in which the bloody mess of killing and the
phenomenon of mass corpses comes to define the survivor's traumatic aftermath or, in the case of my grandfather, medical witnessing in those weeks and months after the massacre. Perhaps
the intensity of gore and bodily pain of the mass killing is hinted
at in U.S. Ambassador to Turkey (1913–1916) Henry Morgenthau's defining memoir about the Armenian genocide, *Ambassador Morgenthau's Story*, published in 1918:

> I have by no means told the most terrible details, for a complete
> narration of the sadistic orgies of which these Armenian men and
> women were the victims can never be printed in an American pub-
> lication. Whatever crimes the most perverted instincts of the hu-
> man mind can devise, and whatever refinements of persecution and
> injustice the most debased imagination can conceive, became the
> daily misfortunes of this devoted people. I am confident that the
> whole history of the human race contains no such horrible episode
> as this. The great massacres and persecutions of the past seem almost
> insignificant when compared with the sufferings of the Armenian
> race in 1915.[2]

It is that kind of "sadistic orgy" that Siamanto tries to depict in *Bloody New from My Friend*. "The Bath" "The Dance," and "The Cross," for example, raise ethical and philosophical questions about the relationship between religious ideologies and political power. Whether we are encountering Turkish Muslims torturing, killing, or raping Armenians, or the Nazis' mass incineration of European Jews in concentration camps in the 1940s, or Serbian Christians massacring Muslim Bosnians at Srebrenica in 1994, we are always forced to ask questions about ethnic and religious ideologies in relation to extreme nationalism.

In assessing aspects of literary representation, one finds these poems remarkably modern in their imagistic concreteness, their unromantic depictions of human suffering, their daring use of vernacular, and their ways of moving discursively with epistolary episode and eyewitness-like reportage. Ezra Pound and the modernist movement would extol some of these qualities in the ensuing decades in his new credos. In certain peculiar ways, Siamanto found some prevailing elements of modernism by virtue of his sensibility and his historical and cultural predicament. It seems to me that we are much better prepared to read these poems today than we might have been when they were written. Not only in the wake of modernism, but in light of a new historicism, which, in part, shaped the poetry of the second half of the twentieth century.

>>><<<

The *Bloody News* poems might be noted as poems of witness, a term that's been given visibility by Carolyn Forché's anthology of 1992 and by an evolving genocide studies discourse. But I'm more inclined to reflect on Siamanto's ability to ingest violence and setting the lyric poem the task of transforming and manipulating the event. By engaging conditions of extremity, torture, killing, and rape, Siamanto attempts to find a language capable of linguistic compression and lyric precision to allow the poems to create scenes, images, and dialogical voices. In most of the poems, Siamanto withholds a personal voice in order to create distance and detachment by setting up characters through the dramatic monologue and at times even a dialogue of voices. The poems have something of a playwright's sensibility in this sense. The point of view and framing techniques in most of these poems are the poet's way of conveying violence with some detachment that creates its own kind of irony.

As the title *Bloody News from My Friend* suggests, the poet has received from his friend the physician eyewitness accounts of what has happened to his Armenian countrymen and -women in, to use that phrase of the big city, "the interior." Because Diran Balakian, the physician, had sent letters from the killing fields that reached his friend, the poet, Siamanto, back home in Constantinople, the poet is able to establish some distance, and this distance is essential to the perspective of the full thirteen-poem cycle. Many of the poems begin in medias res, as if a conversation between the physician and the poet is an ongoing thing. In poems such as "The Dagger" and "The Cross," the voice of epistolary witness speaks clearly: "I don't want this letter to scare you," or "forgive me today my good friend of old dreams." The poems convey the authority of one who is seeing firsthand the dead, the wandering, and the displaced or gathering narratives from others who have.

"The Dance" is told by a German woman, an eyewitness who is aiding Armenian victims. As she nurses a dying woman, she watches from her window the torture of a dozen women as the gendarmes douse them with kerosene and burn them to death while they are forced to dance. In "The Mulberry Tree," an Armenian woman, a deportee, tells the story of an old woman who has gone mad after seeing her grandson killed. In "Strangled," "A Victory," and "The Son," an omniscient voice tells tales of heroism and horror. "Strangled," for example, deals with a mother who is forced to suffocate her infant so that she and a group of Armenians hiding in a dug-out cellar won't be found by Turkish soldiers.

Siamanto's depiction of sexual violence is embedded in many

of the poems in the cycle. And while sexual violence in the Adana massacres was prevalent, Siamanto's focus on violence toward women is an emanation of the precarious conditions of Christian women in the Ottoman Empire. Armenian women, like all minority women, were vulnerable in Ottoman society; the abduction, rape, and selling of women into harems was the result of the asymmetrical legal system under which minorities lived as *dhimmi* (non-Muslim citizens living in a Muslim state) in the millet system. During the genocide period, the Armenian men of a household were killed first, leaving the women vulnerable to rape and abduction, and forcible conversion to Islam. It's estimated that between 100,000 and 200,000 Armenians were disappeared in these ways.[3]

Other poems dramatize how religious ideology fueled the killing. "The Cross,"[4] for example, deals with a mother pleading for her son's life outside a church where she is met by a Turkish mob and some gendarmes. "Don't worry," they tell her, "he's in the vestibule praying for you . . . he'll be free today." They strip her, soak her dress in his blood, and push it in her face. "Doesn't it smell familiar?" they taunt her. Then they paint a cross in blood on the wall, and the poem closes:

In the church that Turk pointed to the cross.
"Kneel down and pray.
We'll do it to you like you did it to Christ.
Pray, mother, to your son.
Have you no faith in the resurrection?"

In "The Dagger," sexual violence and sadism are inseparable from Turkish envy of Armenian wealth, which often fueled resentment against Armenians, especially during this period. In this epistolary poem, the witness refers to Armenia's hope of "Ideal Brotherhood" going up in flames. Here, the Armenian family's wealth becomes the focus of denigration. The Turk dresses the Armenian woman in her own jewels before killing her: "Let me sprinkle your hair with these brooches and gem-studded hair pins . . . pick your own slippers—gold thread or pearl." With a dagger he tries to force the woman to kill her son: "Feast your eyes one last time on your wealth, infidel, / because I'm passing out to all my guests your jewels." The poem has a strange twist, but in the end the culture of death subsumes everything.

In "The Dance," the killers taunt a group of Armenian women, forcing them to circle dance:

> dance till you die, infidel beauties.
> With your flapping tits, dance!
> Smile for us. You're abandoned now,
> you're naked slaves,
> so dance like a bunch of fuckin' sluts.
> We're hot for your dead bodies.

The gendarmes then douse the women in kerosene and light a match as they watch the women collapse to their deaths. The ghoulish ritual here is neither exaggeration nor melodrama; this method of torture and killing was witnessed by survivors throughout the mass killing sprees. The burning to death of naked women is in complex ways inseparable from the patriarchal denigration and humiliation of Christian women that was embedded in Ottoman culture.

Elaine Scarry, in *The Body in Pain*, notes that "what is remembered in the body is well remembered,"[5] and this pathological sense is something that defines a psychological layer of meaning in these poems. Scarry's notion that torture approximates what she calls "the undoing of civilization,"[6] also suggests something about Siamanto's perspective on traumatic breakdown and the shutdown of self and human voice. Perhaps the title of Scarry's book is an apt trope for the *Bloody News* poems. Scarry goes on to note that torture is a totalizing infliction of bodily pain, such that the victim is rendered speechless, stripped of voice, and subjugated in the most complete sense to the power of the regime. Torture, she asserts, is not only the "unmaking of civilization" but the "mutilation of the domestic, the ground of all making."[7] The grandmother in "The Mulberry Tree" testifies to something like this when she grieves over the loss of her domestic life:

You should've seen my home, what a hearth of good things—
lambs, hens, a white cock.
Everything in my sheepfold burnt down.
In my granary I had a handful of wheat for autumn,
under my garret two bee-hives.
In one day the whole village was burned.
Every morning smoke puffed out my chimney.
What did they want from me? Tell me . . .

If torture unmakes human consciousness, breaks down the connection between self and other, self and world, and severs the voice, then the poem, Siamanto suggests, can offer some ethical counterforce in the aftermath. The poem's ability to create a voice for the voiceless pushes lyric language to a graphic intensity as well as to an acquiescence to absence, to voicelessness, to gestures of silence, which also push back in these poems in dialectical ways. The wretched in the *Bloody News* poems are often speechless. At the end of the "Mulberry Tree," the companion of the narrator, having seen the grandmother go crazy, begins to "cry like a child," and at the end of "The Dance," the German narrator renders a speechless gesture, "How can I dig out these eyes of mine?" The poem "Strangled" concludes with the woman who suffocated her infant, begging for her death, "Take my throat, my hands are too weak." The victims of torture are rendered in some kind of agony in which they make what Scarry calls "sounds anterior to learned language."[8] If the violence is silencing as it is in fact in the acts of killing and torture, the poem emerges as some kind of answer to total silence: a refusal to let the victims go voiceless into the dust.

Although many of the *Bloody News* poems rely on narrative lines, a poem like "Grief" reminds one of Siamanto's lyric inventiveness. The poem's opening, civic voice veers into some wilder leaps and surreal associations: "You stranger, soulmate, / who leaves behind the road of joy, / listen to me." The sense of shock and betrayal at the eruption of the massacres in Adana give way to a strange sense of the absurd and to some questioning of larger meaning. Siamanto's gift for wry bitterness and surreal humor in

the face of atrocity are nowhere better heard than in the middle
of the third stanza:

> walk down the roads without rage or hate
> and exclaim: what a bright day,
> what a sarcastic grave-digger . . .
> what a mob, what dances, what joy
> and what feasts everywhere. . . .
> Our red shrouds are victory flags.
> The bones of our pure brothers are flutes . . .
> with them others are making strange music.

In the closing, Siamanto isn't afraid of a big rhetorical gesture
with a touch of something philosophical: "if you are chased
down by raw Evil, / don't forget that you are born / to bring forth
the fruitful Good," or "The law of life stays the same . . . human
beings can't understand each other."

>>><<<

Working with my collaborator and friend, Nevart Yaghlian, who
provided me with literal translations and her literary and linguistic intelligence, I did my best to render these poems into an idiom that best corresponded with late-twentieth-century poetry
in English. I think a translator of poetry in particular is obligated
to bring the language of one poet of one historical time into the
other language of the historical time in which he or she is working. Because I felt that some of Siamanto's oratorical flourishes
did not have an effective equivalent in English, I did not try to
reproduce all of the sound play of his Armenian, and so at times
I needed to trim phrases or lines. I also felt it was necessary to
make contemporary some of the dialogue, which was also contemporary in its early-twentieth-century Armenian, so that the
language reads as idiomatically vernacular as possible in our own
American English. Most importantly, I have remained faithful
to the meaning, the spirit, the ideas, the images, and the voice
of the poems, and I have done my best to create the same sense
of response in our audience that Siamanto hoped to elicit in his.

Bloody News from My Friend was first published in Constantinople in 1909, and a year later it came out in Armenian with the Hairenik Press of Boston, where Siamanto was living at the time. In 1985, the Donikian Press in Beirut reissued *Bloody News from My Friend*. This is the first edition of *Bloody News from My Friend* to appear in English, although poems from the volume have appeared in various anthologies, including *Anthology of Armenian Poetry*, translated by the poet Diana Der Hovanessian (with M. Margossian), and "The Dance" and "Grief" appeared in *Against Forgetting: Twentieth-Century Poetry of Witness* in my and Nevart Yaghlian's translations.

Looking back at *Bloody News from My Friend* from the end of the twentieth century, one can sense something postmodern about the disruptive strategies in these poems. In refusing to be ornamental, generic, metaphysical, Siamanto insisted on seeing in a clear way something about the impact of mass violence on the self, the fabric of social organization, and, of course, the imagination in aftermath. To read a simple line from a poem in the collection called "The Son" is to encounter a prophetic emblem written at the beginning of the twentieth century: "for miles, the cinders of farms, strewn corpses, and in his living room his wife, naked and stabbed." Even before the British poets of World War I found themselves stuck in the trenches, Siamanto's poems had ingested a kind of experience that would alter our idea of poetry's reach and range.

Bob Dylan in Suburbia

We were running wind sprints at the nearby grammar school, training for football, early, for the fanatics who "wanted it bad," as coach said. It was late July, and in northern Jersey in dead summer, the humidity swells the windowsills, crabgrass wilts, any shirt sticks to you. The ground you run is dust, and you swallow it. After practice, we were dripping wet in the muggy air that was turning purple, walking in the hum of air conditioners on suburban streets, the water-pulsing sound of sprinklers on evening lawns. The dust was mud specks on our faces, and one of the older guys on the team asked me to come over to his house to pump iron. He was the best player on team, and I was pleased to be asked. As we walked the quiet streets to his house, I was humming a song I couldn't get out of my head, "Mr. Tambourine Man," by the Byrds.

"It's a Dylan song," my friend said.

"Yeah," I said.

"You know Dylan's version?"

"Sure," I said. Everyone knew it was a Dylan song. The DJs kept saying it was a Dylan song.

I followed my friend into a dimly lit basement, linoleum floor, paneled walls. The bench press with big black Joe Weider disks on the bar in the center of the room. My friend turned on the air conditioner, tightened the collars on the weights, and put the needle down on a record. After a couple seconds of gravelly needle sound on plastic, a voice came out.

It didn't blast out of the speaker like Grace Slick doing "Somebody to Love" or Levi Stubbs belting "Bernadette." It wasn't the operatic flourish of Roy Orbison in "Crying" or the power-soul voice of Martha Reeves in "Dancing in the Streets." Dylan had been identified with folk music by the DJs, but this was nothing like the clean-cut, slightly sentimental sound of the Highway Men or the Kingston Trio, or the crystalline melancholy of Joan Baez, or the sincere harmony of Peter, Paul, and Mary.

The voice came as a sinuous sound crawling into the air. It was quiet at first and gravelly, as if it were coming from the upper throat and nasal tunnels. There was something gritty and earthy in it, something nervous and edgy. This voice came out of the speaker and just hung there in that dense, humid air of a suburban basement. The voice hit me like broken glass under a tire, like metal scratching concrete. It wasn't sweet; it was needling, like hitting nerve and skin, slightly liturgical—something minor key, the way the ghost notes wavered as they rose and fell. There was something ancient and primal in the voice, something raw and naked and intuitive, weirdly new. In that voice I would come to hear an estuary of traditions—bluesy, post-Guthrie Dust Bowl, folk, country and rock, Jewish cantering and political edginess, social aberrance and poetic opacity. It was a transformative voice that carried with it some of the sediment of American culture. Some of those tonalities seemed familiar to me from the chanting and the drone modes I knew in the Armenian church on Sunday mornings and the cantering rabbi at the bar mitzvahs of my friends. The voice stung me as I stood there oblivious of my talented friend as he pumped the bar on the bench press with grunting vigor. Finally, he said to me: "Hey are you spotting for me or what?"

"Sure," I said, and took the bar out of his hands.

I listened to the rest of the album while doing my own bench presses, listened as if I were captured into another space, and went home with the sound in my head. The next day I went out and bought the album with "Mr. Tambourine Man," *Bringing It All Back Home*, and two days later I bought *Freewheelin' Bob Dylan*, *The Times They Are a-Changin'*, *Another Side of Bob Dylan*, and that first album, *Bob Dylan*. Before high school was over, there would be *Highway 61 Revisited*, *Blonde on Blonde*, *John Wesley Harding*, and *Nashville Skyline*, in the spring of 1969.

>>> <<<

1965, Tenafly, New Jersey. Mostly playing for the coach. Pumping iron, being on the team. Studying as hard as needed. Dating girls in the progression of courtships, going steady, and breaking up. But mostly playing for the coach. Halfback one season, point guard another, shortstop another. More important than the girls, the camaraderie of the guys, inseparable on and off the field. The hours on the phone were split between talking with Debby or Arlene or Michele, or with Ed, Michael, Bill, or Brian. Talking, talking about nothing; just talking about songs and things that happened in a day or a class or on the field. This was suburbia, affluent, kind, white, full of love, or half-love, hypocrisy, fear, and repression.

But news leaked through. The war was on TV. The war was someone's brother who came back in a box in the next town. The war was the submerged anxiety of the unspoken. We knew it was waiting for us. We had ideas about jungles and swamps and people who didn't look like us. We caught fleeting images in fuzzy color on the nightly news. *VC, Nam, napalm, Gulf of Tonkin, McNamara*—sound bites that floated through my head at night.

On the news we saw Dr. King in crowds, at podiums, in jail. We saw James Meredith trying to get in the front door of a university. We saw Negroes—men, women, and children—this was just before Black Power and Black Panthers. We watched Negroes in the South picketing, getting blasted by fire-hose water, getting mauled by dogs. We watched Muhammad Ali telling off America about the war and about racial equality. We watched his dance in the ring, his amazing hands. There were Negroes in the neighboring town of Englewood, and they came across the town line at night to play basketball with us. Under the lights of the clean, affluent Tenafly courts. It was a moment to rub up against each other. Nothing serious was ever said. We passed and ran the court for hours, jockeying for rebounds, pushing the ball, driving to the hoop. Sweating on each other. We would shake hands, say "nice game," and go back to our separate worlds.

In that strange mix of unknowing and sensing the world beyond our town, Dylan's voice came like strange music. Between reading *Romeo and Juliet*, the history of battles at the Somme, and diagramming plays for Saturday's game, Dylan's voice snaked out of the nylon white-mesh speaker of my new RCA red-and-white vinyl record player. (This was before stereos with speakers and amps and woofers). It wasn't just a voice with music, it was words; not just words, but language, something that was connected in some indefinable way to what I was reading in school. Shakespeare, Homer, Hawthorne, Whitman, Dickinson. The Dylan words had fresh energy, passion, strange combinations of sensations. The songs told stories as ballads do, or sometimes as poems do, or sometimes as some fusion of the two.

I was struck by the reality feeling I got from them. What I had seen on TV about the war and civil rights, or read in *Newsweek* or the *New York Times* had come to life in words, guitar, and harmonica, sung by this guy from northern Minnesota—improbable as it seemed, a Jewish guy from the iron-ore range whose real name was Robert Zimmerman, who had now become synonymous with Greenwich Village and who had transformed the words and stories through a harsh, playful, nasal register that had grit, guts, rawness in it. He seemed to have taken the cleaner voice of folk and sifted it through the dirt of country blues, the raspy pain of hard-times ballads, and the moral poignancy and outrage of the new decade with its new wars at home and far away.

I'm not sure whether I knew the word *apocalyptic* then. But ever since the Cuban Missile Crisis, in October 1962, ever since our *Weekly Readers* in fourth and fifth grade at Stillman School brought us images of Cuba and Russia, Laos and Vietnam as dangerous places of enemy force, I felt for the first time a sense of uncertainty about the order of things. I felt an undercurrent of anxiety that I couldn't always shake off in the glow of a Yankees game or an episode of *The Dick Clark Show* or *Leave It to Beaver*. A feeling came over me at night as I lay in bed imagining the new hydrogen bomb, the radiant mushroom cloud rising into the sky, an image that had become an emblem of American power by the time I was ten, but an image that also meant the end of things. Later, when I read what Norman Mailer wrote in his essay "The White Negro," I had another way of thinking about my dread:

> We will never be able to determine the psychic havoc of the concentration camps and the atom bomb upon the unconscious mind of almost everyone alive in these years. For the first time in all of history, we have been forced to live with the suppressed knowledge . . . that we might still be doomed to . . . a death by deus ex machina in a gas chamber or a radioactive city.[1]

That undercurrent of anxiety was part of the mood of *Freewheelin'*, and I played it over and over, staring at the album cover with its whimsical image of Dylan in his scruffy jeans and winter jacket, arm around his girlfriend, Suzie Rutolo, as they walked a Greenwich Village street. The album moved with a narrative flow in which Dylan mixed slightly melancholic love ballads like "Girl from the North Country" and "Don't Think Twice" with the quiet civil rights ballad, "Oxford Town," and a diatribe against the military-industrial complex, "Masters of War," a song that shook with the apocalyptic, and, finally, with "Blowin' in the Wind"—which had become an anthem of 1960s liberation; had been covered by Peter, Paul, and Mary; and was so overplayed that it was, for me, already a cliché.

I loved Dylan's humor, which seemed like a blend of vaudevillian slapstick and playful, witty satire. The parodic "I Shall Be Free" kept playing in my brain as I sat in math class or through the long Armenian church service on Sunday morning. Dylan's cement-mixing imagination lampooned sex, free love, celebrity, politics, advertising. With a Lenny Bruce–like verve, he poured acid on racism: "I flip the channel to number four / Out of the shower comes a football man / With a bottle of oil in his hand / It's that greasy kid stuff / What I want to know, Mr. Football Man, is / What do you do about Willy Mays, Martin Luther King, Olatunji." He had plucked the nerve of the color line in sports, but did he really know that Jim Brown had been denied the Heisman Trophy because he was black? When President Kennedy telephones to ask: "My friend, Bob, what do we need to make / the country grow?" Dylan answers, "My friend, John, Brigitte Bardot / Anita Ekberg / Sophia Loren." Did Dylan know about Kennedy's womanizing back in 1962? Who was this strange, scruffy guy from northern Minnesota, with antennae for the currents of our culture? Tom Lehrer was a good talking, folk-style political satirist of a 1950s intellectual type, but Dylan could write a song that flashed from a parody of a politician eating "bagels," "pizza," and "chitlins" to "chasing a woman up the hill / Right in the middle of an air raid drill," as he jumped "a fallout shelter, / a string bean, / a TV dinner." There was an Apollinaire-like craziness in his jumps and leaps.

"A Hard Rain's a-Gonna Fall" wound round and round my brain in the shower, in the football huddle, and in the morning when I was half asleep in homeroom as roll was called.

> Oh, what did you see, my blue-eyed son?
> Oh, what did you see, my darling young one?
> I saw a newborn baby with wild wolves all around it
> I saw a highway of diamonds with nobody on it
> I saw a black branch with blood that kept drippin'
> I saw a room full of men with their hammers a-bleedin'
> I saw a white ladder all covered with water

Those Hebraic, anaphoric catalogs and the tone of biblical prophecy put against an austere repetition of blues chords were beguiling, as were the images that were both contemporary and allegorical. A certain sense of symbolic language had come over me as I was reading *The Odyssey* in English class and Isaiah and Ecclesiastes in Sunday school, and the Dylan allegory in "A Hard Rain" popped with allusiveness that was fresh and connected to life in the early 1960s with its anxieties about nuclear war. The innocent boy and girl ("blue-eyed son," "darling young one") were making their Blakean journey into experience—violence, injustice, war. Dylan encoded the racism of the Jim Crow world in his allusions: "a black branch with blood that kept drippin'," "a white ladder all covered with water," "a white man who walked a black dog," "where hunger is ugly, where souls are forgotten, where black is the color, where none is the number."

It was hard to miss the apocalyptic warning as Dylan's voice wavered and droned: "I heard the sound of a thunder, it roared out a warnin' / Heard the roar of a wave that could drown the whole world." He crescendoed with prophetic, even messianic words: "I'll stand on the ocean until I start sinkin' [a riff on Jesus?] But I'll know my song well before I start singin'. And it's a hard, it's a hard, it's a hard, it's a hard / It's a hard rain's a-gonna fall." The voice intensified in its adenoidal whine as it dragged on "rain." It stuck in my ear like a dying bee.

The album was a more profound response to the trauma of living with nuclear war anxiety than anything I'd ever heard on an LP, and it was recorded during the period of the Cuban Missile Crisis and released in the spring of 1963. "Talkin' World War III Blues" hit a post-Holocaust and post-Hiroshima survival nerve and played its wildness off the meted-out, flat, talking blues-speech that Woody Guthrie had made popular. The song was framed as a dream told to a shrink. Dylan's irony was vaudevillian, and his self-styled blues harp made an edgy sound against the steady strumming: "I said, 'Hold it, Doc, a World War passed through my brain' / He said, 'Nurse, get your pad, this boy's insane.'"

With some surreal black humor, the protagonist (the Dylan character) is underground when the bomb drops, and in the aftermath he wanders an empty town, rings the "fallout shelter bell," drives a Cadillac down 42nd Street (this seems to be Manhattan), then turns on the "Conelrad" (the 1950s emergency broadcasting station that brought us civil defense emergency news, warnings that the bomb was coming, even though it was "only a test"). At a hot dog stand he says "Howdy friend / I guess there's just us two. / He screamed a bit and away he flew. / Thought I was a Communist." Feeling lonesome and blue in the new empty world, he "call(s) up the operator of time" (is this God? or just Bell Telephone?) / "Just to hear a voice of some kind."

When the shrink interrupts him to say that he, too, has been having the same dreams, Dylan takes the talking blues ballad to a new place; allegory becomes self-referential, and metaphor is now a fresh way of thinking about survival as well as a riff on an 1858 Abraham Lincoln speech. It was a brilliant cultural play for the young Dylan to pull off. The song's closing hit me bluntly with its cleverness and ethical vision: We can only survive if we inhabit each other's dream of survival.

Well, now time passed and now it seems
Everybody's having them dreams
Everybody sees themselves
Walkin' around with no one else
Half of the people can be part right all of the time
Some of the people can be all right part of the time
But all of the people can't be all right all of the time
I think Abraham Lincoln said that
"I'll let you be in my dreams if I can be in yours"
I said that

The whole album was inflected with Dylan's sense of end-time and "images of extinction," to use Robert Lifton's phrase. As the post-Hiroshima and post-Auschwitz world swirled in the early 1960s into thermonuclear war possibility, Dylan's outrage in a song like "Masters of War" was stinging. With his monophonic drone in a minor chord, the cantoring Dylan voice was hypnotic:

Like Judas of old
You lie and deceive
A world war can be won

You want me to believe
But I see through your eyes
And I see through your brain
Like I see through the water
That runs down my drain

You've thrown the worst fear
That can ever be hurled
Fear to bring children
Into the world
For threatening my baby
Unborn and unnamed
You ain't worth the blood
That runs in your veins.

It was the only song he had ever written, he confessed, in which he wished for the death of others—the war makers: "And I hope that you die / And your death'll come soon / I'll follow your casket / In the pale afternoon."

>>><<<

Just months after *Freewheelin'* in the spring of 1963, *The Times They Are a-Changin'* appeared and offered another kind of realism. There seemed to be two Dylans—one who could spin apocalyptic allegories and one who was still wedded to the rural blues of Woody Guthrie, Leadbelly, or Robert Johnson. Dylan made something new out of that tradition with his layered language playing off a quiet acoustic arrangement. Although the songs were less wild in their imaginative risks, they had a thrumming social realism, a spare meanness, a confrontation with racial violence, and an occasional philosophical tone.

Dylan's vision of poverty and racism took me out of Tenafly. This was not the poverty that we pretended not to see when we went into the city on weekends, as we drove through Spanish Harlem to get to my aunts' apartments on Riverside Drive near Columbia, or through the Bronx or Queens. But poverty in the great middle of America, a place we called the bread basket, the

Great Plains, a place out there that was just a vague land to us East Coasters.

The simple country picking that opens up "Ballad of Hollis Brown" creates an earthy blues mood for a story of a man trying to farm in the South Dakota prairie. "Your grass it is turning black / There's no water in your well / You spent your last lone dollar / On seven shotgun shells." In a dead economy of scalded land, Hollis Brown watches his family go mad with hunger and kills himself, his wife, and his children. It seemed to me that there was more darkness, more edge in this ballad than in Guthrie's Dust Bowl songs that had come out of the real Depression.

In his cantering, minor key, which owed something to Jewish vocal tradition and something to blues, Dylan's voice brought news of another America in "The Lonesome Death of Hattie Carroll," a ballad (based on a true story) about a Negro hotel barmaid, a humble fifty-one-year-old mother of ten children who was bludgeoned to death by a twenty-four-year-old rich, drunk, Maryland tobacco farmer. "William Zanzinger killed poor Hattie Carroll / With a cane that he twirled around his diamond ring finger / At a Baltimore hotel society gath'rin' / And the cops were called in and his weapon took from him / As they rode him in custody down to the station / And booked William Zanzinger for first-degree murder."

The way Dylan whined and dragged the name "Wil-lia-mm . . . Zan-zin-ger" was as exciting as it was unsettling—as if the meaning were so deep he had to wail it like a gospel singer hitting a note for the Lord. My obsession with phrases was part of me for as long as I could remember; words would get stuck in my head: toothpaste and cigarette ads, disc jockey rant, phrases from pop songs and college football cheers, weird things said around the house. All day and for days or months or more, some phrase that had some rhythmic energy, some odd force of syntax, music, and image would keep whipping or slowly rolling between my brain and ear. So the name *Zan-zin-ger* became a private mantra, one of those Dylan phrasings that hung around in my head all day—an encoded word that evoked racial injustice. As the song unfurled, Dylan's voice grew into high-pitched emotion on certain phrases, against which the strummed chords were a quiet acoustic. An occasional mouthing of the harmonica creating that sense of pathos and then outrage, when in the end, justice is not delivered and the murderer is given a six-month sentence.

Could a song on a record album engage not just history but historiography? Could such a song be called a song? What did it have to do with top-40 music, or any music? "With God on Our Side" remains for me the most singular history lesson ever put on black plastic. Woody Guthrie and Tom Lehrer's songs were political in their satire and calls for social justice, but this was something else. "With God on Our Side" grappled with the idea of American exceptionalism. Dylan was pedagogical and personal: "My name it means nothin' / My age it means less / The country I come from / Is called the Midwest."

The opening harmonica chords make a wheezy, atonal sound that evokes a heartland image of a guy sitting on a porch telling a story. The guitar so flat, the beat so loose—the voice, really speaking more than singing so that words and guitar are in dialogue, not in sync. I came to see that Dylan had created this looser, more expressive acoustic so that language with its richness could be the primary force. In eight stanzas, Dylan takes us through a history of American manifest destiny. "Oh the history books tell it / They tell it so well." He was critiquing our curriculum in which American history—from the Civil War on—is dished out as righteous and romantic: "The cavalries charged / The Indians died"; of World War I: "The reason for fighting / I never got straight," but "you don't count the dead / When God's on your side."

In the penultimate moment, the voice rises higher in its whine to exclaim that in the Cold War age, if we must fight the Russians, whom he's "learned to hate" "all through my whole life," or drop a nuclear weapon, "One push of the button / And a shot the world wide," we "never ask questions / When God's on your side." And then Dylan makes one of those leaps:

Through many dark hour
I've been thinkin' about this
That Jesus Christ
Was betrayed by a kiss
But I can't think for you
You'll have to decide
Whether Judas Iscariot
Had God on his side

Even this young, Dylan roamed the storehouse of Western myth and history, and got Jesus and Judas into a song about American exceptionalism that pushed the imagination to deal with irony and tragedy. I wished the song had ended there with that question hanging, a question that evoked Nietzsche and Camus, rather than the more heavy-handed, didactic way he closed it with the ironic idea that "If God's on our side / He'll stop the next war."

Another civil rights ballad, "Only a Pawn in Their Game" opened with a smack to the head: "A bullet from the back of a bush took Medgar Evers' blood" prompted me to ask my father one morning, as he sat at the kitchen table sipping coffee in his starched white shirt and perfectly knotted tie, who Medgar Evers was. "The head of the NAACP in Mississippi who was gunned down in his driveway by a Klansman," he replied, as he peered out from the *New York Times* with a quizzical look. At eleven, I had been riveted by the James Meredith case, but somehow I had missed the Medgar Evers assassination, and this song prodded me to pay more attention to what was going on out there beyond Tenafly. When riots broke out in Watts in Los Angeles, the images of smoke swallowing buildings, of fire and flashing light and bleeding people, made me feel that the war in Vietnam and the war at home were sliding into each other.

The Dylan songs made interesting complements to books I had been reading about race in America. In seventh grade, I picked up a pulpy-paged, dog-eared small paperback by John Howard Griffin called *Black Like Me*. It was the story of a white man who darkened his skin and traveled through the Deep South to experience what life was like for black people. I read it in a day, and it hit me so deeply that for weeks I felt transported to the rural South where black children lived on dirt floors in wooden shacks eating gruel a couple times a week—if they were lucky. I soon found James Baldwin's *Notes of a Native Son*, a stinging narrative with razor-like images about coming of age as a black man only miles from where I lived. His ability to walk the thin line of raw emotion and make a language that could hold that emotion in a transformed tension shook me up and gave me a sense of some of the places language could go. The image of the young Baldwin being refused service at a diner and thrown out into the street in Trenton, New Jersey, just a couple of hours away in my own New Jersey, gave me a deeper sense of the ubiquity of racism in our own so-called progressive North. I realized how little I knew about my country, about how some of America lived. In Dylan's ballad, it was too easy to blame the white trash for their bigotry; they were being manipulated by the Southern white power structure: "A South politician preaches to the poor white man / 'You got more than the blacks, don't complain. / You're better than them, you been born with white skin.'"

In that strange way that language and music can get inside one's head, these songs brought me news of the world outside Tenafly and outside the prep school I was now attending in Englewood, the part of Englewood that was perched on the hill, high above the Negro sections on the other side of town, where small clapboard houses were bunched together and porches were often falling down, and half-painted, half-rusted cars of the 1950s sat in too-small driveways, and local bars and groceries and gas stations looked like they had survived the Depression without renovations. There was a world apart from football and girls and parties at the chic, postwar split-level and ranch houses of my friends up on the east hill of Tenafly, where we drank and pumped iron and brought our dates. Sometimes I thought of going over to the 4th Ward of Englewood, to the streets behind the war monument at the end of Palisade Avenue, to walk around or even talk with Negroes who had lived there for decades, but

I never did. Those streets were two miles from Crabtree Lane, where we lived, but the 4th Ward might as well have been Harlem to our white world.

As I sank deeper and deeper into Dylan, I came to feel in ways that weren't fully articulate to me yet, but still alive in me as instincts and intuitions, that my suburbia seemed to be about trying to blot the world out. Even in my family, which had inherited the dark legacy of survivors of the genocide of the Armenians in Turkey in 1915, the prevailing ethos on that past was one of repression and silence. In those lower frequencies of my head I was left to imagine a place called Armenia lost inside a place called Turkey as a grainy sepia panorama of ruins. Because no one spoke about the Armenian past, that, too, became part of the conspiracy of silence that pretended life was good and happy in America. History was better left to the dustbin of memory. But Hattie Carroll, Hollis Brown, and Medgar Evers stayed with me, as characters in literature do—haunting and rinsing the imagination, pushing the image bank to new places and empathic frequencies, creating a sense of the other. More than the history textbooks we were reading, more than the news, the language of these songs created a visceral and vivid sense of a historical present.

When *Another Side of Bob Dylan* came out in 1964, with its black-and-white image of Dylan looking more introspective, with longer hair, a tad feminine, a New York city street in the background, it evoked a changing Dylan. The album was also wildly satiric, as in "I Shall Be Free No. 10" or "Motorpsycho Nightmare," both of which played with American Cold War Communist paranoia, and was a continuation of Dylan's preoccupation with what Richard Hofstadter would term that very year the "paranoid style in American politics." "Talking John Birch Society Blues" had become a cult song and was an incomparable satire on post-McCarthyist anti-Communist irrationality, and when I heard it first at 15 on the underground album *John Birch Society Blues*, which I bought from a street vendor on the corner of 113th Street and Broadway—it just hit the core of the ludicrousness of the new conservative-movement Barry Gold-water paranoid style:

> Well I was sittin' home alone an' started to sweat,
> Figured they wus in my T.V. set.
> Peeked behind the picture frame,
> Got a shock from my feet, hittin' right up in the brain.
> Them Reds caused it!
> I know they did . . . them hard-core ones.
>
> Now Eisenhower, he's a Russian spy,
> Lincoln, Jefferson and that Roosevelt guy,
> To my knowledge there's just one man
> That's really a true American: George Lincoln Rockwell.
> I know for a fact he hates Commies 'cus he picketed the movie
> Exodus.

"Motorpsycho Nightmare" and "I Shall Be Free No. 10" continued Dylan's preoccupation with the absurdity of Cold War Commie phobia. Dylan kept topping himself with comic mediations such as in "I Shall Be Free No. 10," where in the playful upbeat rhythm of his talking blues harp inflected riff, he put it this way:

> I'm liberal but to a degree
> I want everybody to be free
> but if you think I'll let Barry Goldwater
> Move in next door and marry my daughter
> You must think I'm crazy!
> I wouldn't do it for all the farms in Cuba.

Another Side was autobiographical in bald ways—"Ballad in Plain D" was about the breakup of a relationship (I assumed it was about Suze Rotolo) with a dose of self-lacerating honesty. And in the signature song, and one of Dylan's best ballads, "My Back Pages," the still-young song-bard (he was only twenty-three, after all) took a look at himself and the journey he had been on since arriving in New York in 1961, and critiqued his naiveté and his moral high-mindedness. The refrain—"Ah, but

I was so much older then / I'm younger than that now"—was sung with such minor-key nasal whining that he must have been davening—it seemed to forecast the end of a phase of his work. He had taken the voice, the ballad, the social vision, and the Jewish Midwest blues, it seemed, as far as he could.

Yet one piece, "Chimes of Freedom," looked forward to things to come. It was the most aesthetically visionary song Dylan had yet written and the synesthesia embedded in the song's trope "we gazed upon the chimes of freedom flashing" was Rimbaud-esque in its derangement of the senses. To "gaze" (sight perception) upon sound ("chimes") that was welded to a concept ("freedom") that opened into an image ("flashing") was something incomparable in the history of song lyrics. "The Chimes of Freedom" fused and merged, blended and spliced hallucinogenic seeing with the weird and arresting social realities of contemporary life:

> Far between sundown's finish an' midnight's broken toll
> We ducked inside the doorway, thunder crashing
> As majestic bells of bolts struck shadows in the sounds
> Seeming to be the chimes of freedom flashing
> Flashing for the warriors whose strength is not to fight
> Flashing for the refugees on the unarmed road of flight
> An' for each and every underdog soldier in the night
> An' we gazed upon the chimes of freedom flashing.

Perhaps Hart Crane and Ginsberg were behind some of this new kind of seeing, but whatever was driving Dylan forward, this new visionary sensibility was about to crack open some of the notions we had about language, song lyrics, and music.

>>><<<

When *Bringing It All Back Home* appeared in the spring of 1965, there was something different in Dylan's voice—something sharper, quicker, more urban. Electric guitars appeared in songs like "Maggie's Farm" and "Subterranean Homesick Blues." Dylan had broken a taboo in the folk world by going electric, had been booed at the Newport Folk Festival for selling out, and was going his own way. But the best songs on *Bringing It All Back Home* were still made of the voice and the acoustic guitar with haunted interludes of harmonica.

There was something darker, more ominous there—not the apocalyptic prophecy of *Freewheelin'*, but a more occluded vision, a voice with cynicism and a new edge. The album cover stared back at me every morning as I grudgingly slapped a tie and sport jacket on to meet the requirements of prep school. Dylan stared back at me with long curly hair that looked teased. No more rural dusty Midwest or Greenwich Village folk Bob. Now in a black jacket and a fancy shirt with a slice of lavender cufflink showing at the wrist, Dylan was holding a gray kitten, sitting in a room with a neoclassical fireplace in the backdrop. Evocative artifacts made the cover a collage: a "FALLOUT SHELTER" sign and an image of *Time* with LBJ's squinting face; Jean Harlow on another magazine; a splay of album covers by cultish singers (Lotte Lenya, Ric von Schmidt, Robert Johnson); a glamorous woman (Dylan's producer Albert Goldman's wife) in a chic red pants suit on a flame-stitch fabric divan. Dylan's brooding face was partly shaded. Dark. Encoded. Mysterious. Intellectual rococo-chic. The engagé of *The Times They Are a-Changin'* was replaced by this new urbanity and alienation. It hit me as drama and departure, somewhat trumped up for the marketplace, too, but still alive with the wild currents of the mid-1960s and its continuous change as the antiwar movement and civil rights activism swirled and blurred at times into pot and LSD and psychedelic concerts where bell bottoms were replacing jeans and boys were wearing beads around their necks.

The word *alienation* seemed to be around now: in class, or among the intellectual kids in the older grades, as Camus and Salinger embodied the new alienation of my prep school curriculum. In the conversation I overheard between my literary-critic aunts, Anna and Nona: "the postwar novel is defined by alienation"; "at least Proust fended off alienation"; "John Leonard is interested in the new alienation"; and so on around the dinner table at their apartments on the Upper West Side on Sundays.

I remember the cold, damp wind off the Hudson in March tunneling down the streets off Riverside Drive. Certain bars in New York would serve anyone who walked in, and I had been hanging out for a few months now at a place called The Third Phase on 113th Street off Broadway near the Columbia dorms. The Phase, as it was called, was sawdust and peanut shells on the floor, like an old speakeasy you got to by descending a long flight of stairs into a hole below the sidewalk. John Coltrane and Miles Davis coming from the speakers in the ceiling, lights low, old graffiti-carved tables, foamy beer in pitchers, free peanuts, a menu of burgers and fries.

In the middle of a conversation with one of the older guys who had driven us from Jersey, Dylan came up. I overheard Al talking about Dylan, and I butted in: "What the fuck do you know about Dylan?" Al flicked some peanut shells at me, and I threw a handful back at him, and he reached across the table to grab my shirt and I caught his wrist and twisted it, and before it went further, two of the older guys took me by the collar, and one of them said: "Let's not forget who's underage here." I backed off, and Al said, "What the hell do you know about Dylan?" Feeling the buzz of a few beers, I started in a low voice: "Darkness at the break of noon / Shadows even the silver spoon / The handmade blade, the child's balloon / Eclipses both the sun and moon / To understand you know too soon / There is no sense in trying." I reeled off all twenty stanzas (muffing a word here and there) of "It's Alright, Ma." "Not bad, Balakian," Al flipped back, and we spent the rest of the evening tossing around ideas about that song, the song that defined the album for me.

What hit me about "It's Alright, Ma" was the sustained lyric performance. Each stanza disjunctive with the next; not the ballad idea of continuity anymore, but lyric leaps that were supposed to be held together by a refrain: "It's alright, Ma"—with a differing phrase after each refrain: "if I can't please him," "I can make it," "it's life and life only." But when I put the lines up against the poetry I was reading in class—T. S. Eliot, Hart Crane, E. E. Cummings, Emily Dickinson, Walt Whitman—Dylan's lines were a letdown. The obsessive end rhymes were banal, cli-chéd if not in meaning then in sound.

A month earlier, I had told a friend that I was losing faith in Dylan as a poet. But still I kept playing the song over and over, and I came to see that Dylan's words couldn't always survive the page alone, because they were made for this medium that Dylan had invented: his voice, his harmonica, his guitar, his arrange-ments that were strangely simple but complex, now expanded to include electric guitars, keyboard, organ, piano, horns, drums, and other percussion instruments. The words expanded in the Dylan medium just as they could shrink on the page.

"It's Alright, Ma" was lyric invention pushing toward opacity and still wanting to be social commentary, albeit with an exis-tential twist of alienation. Dylan's voice was more insistent here than I had ever heard it, and there was more variation in rhythm now, the staccato strumming playing off Dylan's chant-like voice, genius with phrases, sustaining the song.

> While preachers preach of evil fates
> Teachers teach that knowledge waits
> Can lead to hundred-dollar plates
> Goodness hides behind its gates
> But even the president of the United States
> Sometimes must have to stand naked

The song had a balance between inventive language, narrative voice, and social vision; when Dylan got that balance, he was at his best. And in its ambition, "It's Alright, Ma"—with its sinu-ous, accusatory, and sometimes sullen voice—was brilliantly suc-cessful, much more so than anything else on the album.

While "Mr. Tambourine Man" had bursts of inventive images, an ecstatic druggy language, it became a hackneyed emblem of Dylanmania, and phrases like "the smoke rings of my mind," and "the foggy ruins of time" caved to cliché. And "Gates of Eden," with its thrumming chords, harp inflections, and passionate wailing, created an ominous mood, but when I pulled the words apart, they were clotted, overstuffed, pretentious: "With a time-rusted compass blade / Aladdin and his lamp / Sits with Utopian hermit monks / Sidesaddle on the Golden Calf." Still, nobody out there—and there were some weighty songwriters at work, like John Lennon, Paul McCartney, Laura Nyro, Paul Simon, and Leonard Cohen—was pushing language like this, striving for opacity and depth, myth and history, and making a new kind of music and language-sound.

When "Like a Rolling Stone" was released as a single in late July 1965, it came as a wild opening in the sky, a sound so fresh and real, I later thought of what it must have been like to pick up Allen Ginsberg's *Howl* in 1956. I was on the phone with my friends, for whom Dylan also was becoming a mythic figure, talking about the sound, the Dylan voice that wailed, dragged, and whined; the language that had electric energy with its combination of mythic characters that now worked better than "Gates of Eden"; and a narrative that told a story about alienation, modern life, and misplaced values. A lyric tirade against a privileged woman and society's trappings.

In fact, Dylan was singing now—not talking, chanting, or cantering. The music had more surprise and variation, and the mix of instruments was startling: piano, organ, bass, drum, and acoustic guitar, with bluesy swipes on the harp. With that opening slap of a drum and the mingling of electric guitar, piano, bass, and Al Kooper's gospel-sounding organ—Dylan brought folk, blues, country, gospel, and rock into a new fusion. People were calling it folk rock, but it was something else—as if everything Dylan had ever done was now mixed and blended into a new hybrid. And the refrain ("How does it feel / How does it feel / To be without a home / Like a complete unknown / Like a rolling stone?") opened up a new dimension in Dylan's voice: a new distorting and dragging of phrases, yielding encoded anger, passion, mixed with outrage and parody. When he got to the last word of the first stanza, "About having to be scrounging for your next meal-aaahl," he dragged, flattened, and rolled the word *meal* into a wad of emotion that set up the rest of the song. In this ballad of class anger, Dylan's cast of metaphoric characters created a vision of the carnivalesque in which Dr. Seuss seemed to be colliding with Hart Crane. "You used to ride on the chrome horse with your diplomat / Who carried on his shoulder a Siamese cat. You used to be so amused / A Napoleon in rags and the language that he used."

I played the song over and over until the black vinyl of that 45, with its red Columbia label, was like sandpaper. As it became a background noise in our house, a diffuse wail coming through the walls of my room, my father, who found Dylan's voice an irritating oddity, was asking me to turn it down, or to give the song a break: "What's wrong with that Bob Dylan? Why can't he sing?" "He can," I shot back. "It's a new kind of voice." Trying to show he was not just the square, proper, suburban physician he knew I thought he was, my father chimed in: "If he could really sing like some of the black singers he's trying to imitate, it would be okay." I was furious with what I thought of as his half-informed putdown of Dylan. "I didn't know you knew anything about blues," I said with sarcasm. "Okay," my father said, "let's give George a call and ask him what he thinks about Dylan and real blues." George Avakian, the legendary jazz producer at Columbia Records, was our good family friend. Whenever a dispute about popular music came up, my father invoked George as if to remind me that there were cool guys of his generation who knew more about music than I did.

When we called George, he answered us in a canny way—slicing the difference between father and son by noting that Dylan had once seemed to have aspirations to be a real blues singer, but he clearly wasn't. He was, George said haltingly, "something else." The hesitation in George's voice over "something else" led me to sense that George may have shared my father's misgivings about Dylan's voice. Only years later did George tell me that when he first heard Dylan audition at Town Hall for a group of record producers, he couldn't make out Dylan's words because they sounded so garbled. He was also put off by Dylan's costume of a railroad engineer cap and a red bandanna, which to George, who had produced Louis Armstrong, Miles Davis, Mahalia Jackson, and others, must have seemed a bit silly.

Dylan's new sound wasn't psychedelic in a pop, trendy way. In the epic song of *Highway 61 Revisited*, "Desolation Row," Dylan kept pushing the idea of language and song. With two acoustic guitars, an evocative kind of Mariachi picking, and a bass, the sound was ominous and dark; for me, it quickly became *The Waste Land* of rock music—a vision from alienation, if not from death row then from its spiritual analogue. It was as relentless as it was long—ten segments packed with a wild crew of characters out of pop culture, myth, fairytale, legend, and literature. As if Dylan were rubbing Andy Warhol and T. S. Eliot together. Was there ever a song of any kind that brought together Bette Davis, Romeo, Cinderella, Cain and Abel, the Hunchback of Notre Dame, the Good Samaritan, Ophelia, Noah, Einstein, Robin Hood, the Phantom of the Opera, Casanova, Nero, Ezra Pound, and T. S. Eliot? Add to that Dylan's homemade characters: the blind commissioner, Dr. Filth, a jealous monk, the superhuman crew, insurance men, calypso singers, fishermen, and mermaids. It was one thing to have taken T. S. Eliot up on his idea of the "mythic method" for writing modern literature, but was Dylan being a "mythy" wit or just "method" happy? I didn't ask that question at the time.

The pastiche of allegorical scenes that made up "Desolation Row" was carnivalesque with a wildness that was grotesque, comic, playful. Perhaps the song's success was in Dylan's effort to do what Pound and Eliot had done with poetry in the first decades of the twentieth century—assemble, collage-like, the cultural resources of the past to make it new.

> They're selling post cards of the hanging
> They're painting the passports brown
> The beauty parlor is filled with sailors
> The circus is in town
> Here comes the blind commissioner
> They've got him in a trance
> One hand is tied to the tight-rope walker

The other is in his pants
And the riot squad they're restless
They need somewhere to go
As Lady and I look out tonight
From Desolation Row

Either you are in the zone of desolation row or you're not, and if you're not, our Dylan protagonist says, you're not in touch with the deeper truths. "Don't send me no more letters, no / Not unless you mail them / From Desolation Row." You could have a field day doing literary analysis of this concatenation, or you could dismiss it as an overstuffed ruse, but I couldn't let go of its tone, its cultural richness, its play and parody, and its appeal to a kind of existential meaning. At fifteen, I found it more compelling than Holden Caulfield.

>>><<<

Outside of the circumscribed world of the locker room, things were getting weirder and stranger. One of my friends, a star of our junior high years, had quit football and was now wearing bell-bottoms and high boots, smoking pot, and having me over to listen to Hendrix's "Purple Haze" and Cream's *Disraeli Gears*, which were inflected by the new LSD craze. I was shocked by his leaving the cult of football, but I admired his rebellious sense of freedom, his scoffing at the expectation that he would be a star athlete and lead our team to victories and glories. Sitting in his basement refusing a joint, I watched the reefer glow and crinkle into ashes as the air filled with the sweet smell of weed, as the meandering electric whine and vibration of Hendrix's guitar seemed to tangle in curlicues of smoke.

As the psychedelic wave moved across the George Washington Bridge from the East Village, it threw some new challenges my way. By senior year, I would be the captain of the football, basketball, and baseball teams, and, because this was a small prep school, I don't wish to give the impression that I was a Brian Taylor or a Jack Tatum. I played hard, loved the landscapes of all three sports, kept the coaches' credos. Kept my hair relatively short, kept pumping iron, refused alcohol during football season (winter and spring were another matter), and stayed away from drugs. But as soon as I had a driver's license by the end of my junior year, I would take my father's blue Buick, on nights when he allowed me to have it, over the bridge with my girlfriend to find a parking space off Avenue B or C in the East Village, from where we'd walk through the pot-filled air past the Peace-Eye bookstore, which was the hangout of the Fugs. Bars and coffee shops and clubs gave off the fumes of cocktails and beer and occasional strobe lights, and the painted-over facades of buildings that had graffiti all over them. The whole place was alive with men and women in their twenties and thirties. Beards, long hair, bell-bottoms, leather jackets, men and women with beads and rings and earrings. The hippy scene was electric, and I felt its hum as I walked west on 10th or 8th Street feeling both distance and allure. I began going to the Fillmore East as often as I could to see Blood, Sweat, and Tears or the Chambers Brothers, Iron Butterfly, or whatever I could get tickets to. The Fillmore had just opened in early 1968 in an old Yiddish theater on 2nd Avenue in a section that was once called the Jewish Rialto. I loved the fragrance of incense and pot mingling as I walked in with Lori on a Friday night. As we watched the Joshua Light Show pour its liquid colors, morph like lava, swirl and blow blue-green-yellow-red across the ceiling of the theater, she turned to me and said: "What would coach say if he saw you now?"

In that moment for me in 1968—in which straight, jock, short hair, Levi cords, and pumped biceps collided with bell-bottoms, thick belts, work shirts, long hair, beads, pot, acid, the woozy electric sound of Clapton or the needling metal of Hendrix— *Blonde on Blonde* was my island of inner counterculture, I could float on that sound as the Vietnam War morphed out of control, and fire hoses blasted through the burned-out buildings of Newark after the riots, as I pumped iron and stayed with beer a little while longer.

I was feeling in a strange mental haze as I drove home from

baseball practice on a Saturday in April. I had dinner with my brother and sisters and parents in the usual Saturday night fashion, but instead of going out in the usual Saturday night fashion, I told my parents I was tired and was heading up to my room. I slept for twenty-four hours, and the next day my father said, "Let's go down to the office for a blood test." When the test came back the next day, my father informed me that I had mononucleosis. The word *mono-nucle-osis* came out of my father's mouth like some kind of cartoon balloon, and as I heard it pop in the air and then dissolve, I sat speechless on the side of the bed. "How the hell could I get mono after the second game of the season?" I heard myself say, and my father shrugged with his physician's demeanor and replied, "We can't control these things."

"What time is it?" I asked my mother when she came in to see how I was doing. "Dinnertime," she said. "I'm not hungry," I said. "Just sleep," she said. "Put on the record player," I said. She put the needle down on the black plastic, and the soft drumming and harmonica seemed to weep forth: "With your mercury mouth in the missionary times / And your eyes like smoke and your prayers like rhymes." The voice was slow and seemed valium-inflected as it dragged certain words: "Where the sad-eyed prophet says that no man comes." I was spinning in and out of fever and sleep as the song wrapped around an image of a ball going off my bat and over the fence three days earlier, and the smell of the dust of the batter's box, and the sound of the ball thudding the leather of the glove swirling in my brain. Friday night at Deborah's rolling around on the couch in her parents' den. Lori's Heaven Scent and the sound of Sinatra upstairs drifting among adult voices and cigarette smoke. The gray-and-white cover of the Kitteredge *King Lear* on my nightstand. Goneril and Regan screwing over Cordelia. The scent of allspice floating on the chicken soup my mother brings on a Persian turquoise enamel tray: *the kings of Tyrus Spanish manners Arabian drums Cannery Row.*

"Sad-Eyed Lady of the Lowlands" was the epic of *Blonde on Blonde.* A meditation, a love-prayer, an invention of the beloved that turned into something else. Everyone was saying the sad-eyed lady was Jackie O. Years later, Dylan said he wrote it for his soon-to-be wife, Sara Lowndes. What epithalamion ever traveled such surreal acrobatics? Dylan's white goddess, cloaked in mystery and floating between an edgy street life and romantic exotica: "your matchbook songs and your gypsy hymns," "your childhood flames on your midnight rug / And your Spanish manners and your mother's drugs," "the child of a hoodlum wrapped up in your arms." In the end, it is another of Dylan's wired journeys that turns out to be more about language than the beloved, more about metaphoric density than anything ever packaged on black plastic.

As stunning as *Highway 61 Revisited* was, who could have been prepared for *Blonde on Blonde*? Dylan took the new electric mix he had created in *Highway 61* and pushed it again into something new. The album had a wholeness that brought together form and content. The music kept growing; more variation, more shape, more adventurous and complex than anything he had ever done. The petal steel-slides mixing with piano, a gospel-gothic organ, drums, bass, acoustic and electric guitars, a trumpet, and trombone at times. It was a sound that oscillated between manic highs and druggy lows; the blending of Dylan's vestigial blues with a tone that was hallucinogenic and carnivalesque, and its mix of great musicians that included Robbie Robertson, Al Kooper, Charlie McCoy, Pig Robbins, Joe South, Wayne Butler, Kenneth Buttrey, and Sandy Konikoff.

The recording sessions, most of which took place in Nashville, were so fertile, Dylan's writing on such a roll, that it turned into a double album. All fourteen songs dealt with relationships with women, courtships, break-ups, and with a soul searching that led me to feel that Dylan was exploring that quarrel with himself, as Yeats put it, that could be the source of poetry. Unlike the earlier love ballads or allegorical love songs, there was a wilder letting loose here, an invention of landscapes of the interior that were psychological and visionary, and a relentless, combustible language. It all seemed like a personal rock opera about emotional entanglements with many, perhaps too many, women in a tumultuous time of his own cresting celebrity and confusion on the eve of his secret marriage to Sara Lowndes. Out of that he turned his turmoil into a new sound.

The opening wheeze of Dylan's harp in "Visions of Johanna" makes a melancholy slide into Al Kooper's eerie organ notes and occasional twangs of electric guitar, and the dark room is moving on a floating cushion of phrases like gravel under tires, of melting curtains, of bookshelves dissolving into the window and the trees falling like water falling, and *the voice* was the whiskey air of the back seat with Joan of the blue eyes who opened herself to my jukebox of longing, to the melting pianos, skittery organs, the manic saber wires strung along the brain. In the Café Wha? of smoke and cymbals, faces appeared and disappeared, chairs moved through windows and the picked strings of anytown america in the country night where gas was pumped under a simple light and something floated into the birds that flew out of the hanging lanterns and winding Persian vines in my head.

On that cushion of sound, on *that voice* that was a passageway down and out into a place where history refused to disappear, for all the drugged-out air waves of the East Village, Medgar Evers and James Baldwin became red lights on the high towers along the Pike, and *the voice* spliced them into the open boat of chaos on the streets of Newark as the smoke and broken glass poured from the TV into the sound of discordant passion and grief, and LBJ disappeared into the dust of the coach barking in the autumn air and the flannel pockets of my blazer as the words *veritas fortissima graven on our shield* rose from the voices of boys at morning chapel as the day began.

The absence of the woman, the mysterious Johanna, drives Dylan's stanza-ending evocations as the voice drags on the syllables: "these visions of Johanna have now taken my place." Rimbaud's "derangement of the senses" was a pretext for the deeper subject of the song—the poet's consciousness, lost in self-exploration.

> See the primitive wallflower freeze
> When the jelly-faced women all sneeze

Hear the one with the mustache say, "Jeeze
I can't find my knees"
Oh, jewels and binoculars hang from the head of the mule
But these visions of Johanna, they make it all seem so cruel

Dylan was hitting incomparable sensory blendings—an intensified sensibility crawling along the nervous system of the arrangements and the voice, with hyperaccentuation and longer voice glides on mysterious words. Night after night I went to sleep sliding from "Sooner or Later One of Us Must Know," with its blues harp drags and its back room out-of-tune piano and ghostly organ, to the jumpy amphetamine surrealistic "Absolutely Sweet Marie"; and "I Want You," with its jamming piano, rattling electric chords, harp screeches, and leaping images was as fine as anything Dylan had ever done. The voice drag of "I want you" bringing the notion of desire to the neurons.

"Stuck Inside of Mobile with the Memphis Blues Again" kept spinning in my ear all day and night, the compulsive conglomerate of phrasing stuck in my head, and often at inopportune times I'd break into speech in the middle of class or dinner or the locker room, and friends and family would do a double take, and I'd shrug my shoulders as if to acknowledge that there was nothing wrong with singing to yourself. Sometimes my friend Michael and I would burst into song with our self-styled comic gesticulations as we performed that hyperloaded refrain—"Oh, Mama, can this really be the end / To be stuck inside of Mobile / With the Memphis blues again"—as if to affirm our ineffable love of this song with its carnivalesque keyboards and organs, tapping cymbal bell, acoustic and electric guitars working off each other, making an electric blues.

Dylan's cartoon-like, Berryman ironies get to something about entrapment, death, violence; an acid view of the state of the union: "But the post office has been stolen / And the mailbox is locked," "Now the senator came down here / Showing ev'ryone his gun / Handing out free tickets / To the wedding of his son." "Now the preacher looked so baffled / When I asked him why he dressed / With twenty pounds of headlines / Stapled to his chest."The song climaxes with one of Dylan's most memorable aphorisms: "An' here I sit so patiently / Waiting to find out what price / You have to pay to get out of / Going through all these things twice." This wild pop culture surrealism was starting to define how I was feeling about the state of America even as I dutifully showed up each day for the coach and poured my heart out.

>>><<<

When news of Dylan's motorcycle accident hit in the summer of 1966, my friends and I were swallowed by the myth and mystery that ensued. Dylan was alive—that seemed sure—but there were rumors that he was paralyzed, disfigured, had gone into retreat, was living in the backwoods with hillbillies. He was reported to be somewhere in upstate New York—that land that rose north of the Jersey border where, from the perspective of our suburban town, there was a vast unknown wilderness spreading for miles like Siberia. Dylan was up there and was now accruing a James Dean–like status, and for a while that seemed like a long time, there was silence, and then we felt great relief when a strange-looking gray album appeared in December 1967.

A flat, dun, quiet album cover with a mysterious black-and-white photo of Dylan in some backwoods. Was he returning to his Iron Range, north country roots? There he was standing next to what looked like a couple of Native Americans (only later did we discover they were two South Asian musicians) and a man who looked like a local white guy who had been out hunting. Dylan looked quieter now, with a thin beard along his jaw, a western hat, a dark coat opened to a dark shirt, a boyish smile on his face. It was a long way from the teased hair and the satin jacket of *Highway 61* and the decadent pose of *Bringing It All Back Home*. It was jolting to see that Dylan was back to country—harmonica and acoustic guitar, an occasional bass and drum. The voice was as clear as it had ever been; the high whine of the early ballads and the hyper, druggy, dragging voice of the recent work had given way to something calmer, more grounded. After the recent albums, the language of these new ballads was austere. Narrative and allegorical, the songs reached into salient American myths with an appeal to the lore of the West.

As I listened to the title song, "John Wesley Harding," on a rainy December Sunday night, I called my girlfriend late on the yellow wall phone in our kitchen to rant with joy about the new Dylan sound and how the title song reminded me of the movie *Shane*—of the good gunman played by Alan Ladd as he navigates the morality of violence in the nineteenth-century West, that mythical American West that would keep fueling Dylan's imagination for albums and CDs to come. Wesley Harding was the good gunman, a Shane or a Wyatt Earp, who roamed the West ("with his lady by his side") taking a stand against the bad guys, and never making a foolish move; there simply "was no man around / who could track or chain him down." Dylan was back to America—the multilayered USA—combing it again as he had in his north country ballads and civil rights songs of 1962 and 1963, and I began to get the sense of his desire to take on the breadth of something of a broader American experience. Part of him, at least, wanted to map American culture in ways that Whitman and Ginsberg had. His ballads reached toward the strange, vast complexity of the country with its conglomerate of landscapes and regions and its dozens of ethnic cultures that gave America its great hybridity and seeming endless human resources and imaginations.

But Dylan was a realist with his eye on the ironies of democracy and the suffering of the marginal and the outsiders. On *John Wesley Harding*, the other side of expansive American freedom was poignantly clear in songs like "Dear Landlord" and "I Pity the Poor Immigrant." Dylan dealt with the illusions of the American dream, the immigrant who has come to pursue the hope of wealth and finds himself locked in poverty and "with his fingers cheats / And who lies with ev'ry breath." "I Am a Lonesome Hobo" and "Drifter's Escape" deal with hard-luck cases, men who are cast out, on trial for crimes, escaping, on the lonesome American country road. These ballads weren't as dense and layered as the songs about Hollis Brown or Hattie Carroll, but they engage the possibility of the American open road, where the outsider—the drifter or hobo—can still find a place to "light out" as Huck Finn once said, or to find ruin and betrayal.

As I listened to these songs over and over through Christmas week of 1967, I thought about Dylan for the first time as a Jew. All I knew was that he was born Robert Allen Zimmerman in Duluth, a multiethnic Rust Belt city of the Great Lakes, before he moved to Hibbing at the age of six, when his father contracted polio. Hibbing was a melting pot on the range, where Swedes, Finns, Poles, Slovaks, Germans, Norwegians, and Jews settled in the early part of the twentieth century. They came to mine and soon created the largest open iron ore pit in the world. Whatever Dylan disguised with his new name and his pan-pop culture radical chic identity, he always had some ineffable Jewish sensibility and some Iron Range grit. Years later in his autobiography, *Chronicles*, he noted that his maternal grandmother with whom he was close—a woman who had only one leg, was a seamstress, and lived in Duluth—was from the town of Kagizman, "a town," he wrote, "in Turkey near the Armenian border." The family's original name was Kirghiz, and his grandfather, too, had come from the same area, where they were "shoemakers and leather workers." He confessed that his grandmother's journey from Turkey across the Black Sea to Odessa and then to America was alluring to him, and how as a boy he identified with the mystery and outsiderhood of her past.[2] Reading this in 2004, I found myself staring at the page unwilling to suspend my disbelief.

Kagizman—a place I knew well from my work on Armenia; it was an Armenian village, a very old Armenian village in the heart of historic Armenia not far from Armenia's famous medieval city—Ani—today a walled city of ruins in the highlands of Turkey at the ravine on the Akhurian River, just a few feet from the Armenian border and a few hours by car from Mount Ararat, which is still Armenia's national symbol even though it's inside Turkey today. Given my own life and work, this small bit of family history that Dylan mentioned in passing but noted in precise detail hit me in the strange way that odd historical coincidences do when they intersect on one's own private map of life. I knew Dylan well enough from years of interviews and biographies to know he was a fibber and a mythmaker and liked to spin layers of exotica around himself. Was this bit of family history true? Dylan's mother's family—Jews from Armenia? Jews from a town that had not only been an ancient part of Armenia, but a place that endured destruction and massacre during the Armenian genocide. I wanted to ask Dylan face-to-face if it were so, and I regretted more than ever that I had been unable to attend the two dinners with him to which I had been invited several years earlier by my friend Jacques Levy, who had written *Desire* with Dylan and had also directed the *Rolling Thunder Revue*.

However the immigrant experience played out in Dylan's mind, in these new ballads he was probing his sense of American outsider identity, and his historical sensibility had returned. There was, for the first time, a religious vibe creeping into the songs. Dylan was playing with biblical allegory, but not of the prophetic kind of the apocalyptic *Freewheelin'*. There was some presence of mystery and of the supernatural, as in "I Dreamed I Saw St. Augustine," a mystical song evoking the early church father whose famous autobiography tells the story of his conversion from a life of sin to the true light. Was this a premonition of Dylan's forthcoming conversion to Judaism and then Christianity? Listening to "The Ballad of Frankie Lee and Judas Priest," in which cryptic gestures engage good and evil, salvation and redemption, I thought of the Nathaniel Hawthorne stories I was reading at school, and it seemed that Dylan had made a kind of morality play out of the story of two gamblers. I had allegorical fun with the name Judas Priest, and when Judas lends Frankie money, he tells his friend that he can be found (to be paid back) "down the road" in "Eternity." When eternity turns out to be a brothel where Frankie ends up with Judas and then dies in his arms, I thought Dylan was doing some new kind of gothic that was mixed in with his new Western mythiness.

For me, the most brilliant song of the album was "All Along the Watchtower." In twelve clean, muscular lines, no wasted image or syllable, the acoustic was driven by a pulsing drum beat, a classic smear of opening blues harp, and the insistent strumming of a simple chord reminiscent of Dylan's earlier ballads. It was good to hear his earlier ballad voice again with its passionate whine, and it struck me as one of those rare songs in which the images and characters move seamlessly into allegory.

"There must be some way out of here," said the joker to the thief
"There's too much confusion, I can't get no relief
Businessmen, they drink my wine, plowmen dig my earth
None of them along the line know what any of it is worth"

I argued with my friends about meaning, or rather pushed my idea of meaning on them. As one of my comrades rifled back at me one day in the midst of one of my exegetical sessions, "Goddamn it, Peter, can't you listen to a song without analyzing it?" The thief, I insisted, is like the Zen master with a simple truth to tell the joker. If "there are many here among us who feel that life is but a joke," the thief knows to stay on the track of your journey. While it closes with some of Dylan's stock storybook flourishes, "princes" keeping watch in the tower, "while all the women came and went, barefoot servants, too," he leaves the song with ominous evocations: "Two riders were approaching, the wind began to howl." It would be a while before Dylan hit the whole thing like that again.

When *Nashville Skyline* came out in the spring of 1969, I tried to go along with my friends who were celebrating it. It had come out after much speculation about Dylan after his brush with death with the motorcycle and the effect of the domestic pull of his new life with his wife and children. The smiling face with its scruffy beard and leather hat was framed by a blue sky. Dylan was back to country, but not the Dust Bowl grit of the tragic northern plains with Hollis Brown and dead iron-ore pits, or haunting ballads of immigrants, hobos, gamblers and other drifters of *John Wesley Harding*. It was billed as Nashville, which to me was the capital of a good deal of cornball music. How could Rimbaud be sharing a studio with Loretta Lynn?

The voice was gone, replaced now by a smoother sound. He did a remake of "Girl from the North Country" with Johnny Cash. "Is he kidding me?" I mumbled amidst my friends as we were drinking beer in Bill's TV room and waiting for Dylan to come on Johnny Cash's variety show one Saturday night in May. What had happened to the voice of edge, irony, excoriating satire, carnivalesque wit? The new country ballads were soft and romantic; "Lay, Lady, Lay," "Tonight I'll Be Staying Here with You" and the others had some twang and melody that made me feel that Dylan's soul had found some respite from the surreal swirls of "Memphis Blues" and the modern wasteland of "Desolation Row." So why shouldn't I be happy for him?

Self Portrait soon followed, and then *New Morning* before Dylan was really off into his next decade. I love some of the songs on those albums, but I don't revisit them often. There was always an interesting sensibility at work, good leaps of metaphor, a soulful engagement with a woman, communing with nature, spiritual quest, an autobiographical ballad. But *the voice* had changed. And while Dylan would show that he was always good enough to hit an edgy song on almost every album he would make over the next forty years, he wouldn't return to that thing that led him to make something new for modern music.

Between 1962 and 1967, in a five-year period, between the ages of twenty-one and twenty-six, Dylan mined a wild array of cultural resources, pulling everything he could out of his imagination—mixing, mashing, cutting, and splicing, making wild collages like musical versions of Rauschenberg's great combines. At times a magpie, a clever or transparent thief, a ventriloquist in various guises, he poured blues into rock, country into blues, R & B into country, electric into acoustic, the harmonica into distorted studio sounds, into keyboards, twanging pedal guitars, organs, drums and cymbals, trumpets and trombones, and came up with ballads, prose poems, mythically entangled opaque images; it was as if Hart Crane were reborn as a rock musician who had slid out of northern Minnesota into a Columbia Records studio by way of Greenwich Village. Even the Christmas carol was grist for his epic-ballad passion, and when he came out with his rendition of Christmas carols in 2009, *Christmas in the Heart*, I realized how obsessed he was with the whole American songbook—how he wanted to swallow as much of it as possible for as long as he could.

In the end, his linguistic turgidness and his cultural and historical expansiveness owe something to an American literary tradition that includes Whitman, Hart Crane, Faulkner, and Ginsberg, and out of that wellspring he invented what I call literary rock—that fusion of music and language, embedded in a unique acoustic that embodied something of what it means, still, to be living in our age.

12

Writing Horizontal: Notes Toward the Poem as Space

Writers recall moments when things happened that changed their sense of how they were writing—moments, or an arc of them, in which they see new ways to make a form that was fresh and energizing for them and still allow them to be in their sensibility and temperament and vision. For me, this particular moment wasn't a flash experience, a revelation, or an epiphany. It was a protracted series of events that happened when I was living in London in the fall of 1988 with my wife and two children. I mark this time by many things, but first by the birth of our son James, who was born at the Great Portland Street Hospital just off Marylebone Road near Regents Park. That September we walked in and out of the maternity ward amid the paparazzi who were roosted there for the birth of Princess Beatrice. We were living in a posh flat because of Colgate University, for whom I was directing the English department's study group. Living on Cheyne Walk, on the Chelsea Embankment across from the Albert Bridge, gave me an interesting view of history and a beautifully comic sense of displacement.

We were neighbors to a tall, pink, Queen Anne townhouse with its reportedly heated indoor swimming pool, owned by

Bianca Jagger, who was recently divorced from Mick. Other nearby neighbors included the National Trust houses of Thomas Carlyle, William Turner, Henry James, and the commemorated spot on Cheyne Walk where Henry VIII's manor house once stood. The alleyways, mews, and back streets with their Georgian brown brick, their transoms and fanlights, their neoclassical doors and entrance moldings, made daily walks something of a historical jaunt, especially for an American living, for the first time, in this stretch of London. The Albert Bridge lit up the gray Thames all day with its pink and white and pale blue colors. Our local pub, The King's Head and Eight Bells, was a quiet place with its domestic feel of parlor chairs and tables so unlike the louder, more garish American bar. Here, in the quiet beer-scented air, fresh ales were pumped all day, and our four-year-old daughter Sophia developed a keen taste for stilton, ham off the bone, and fresh tomatoes on crusty bread. We lounged there for dinner a few days a week and later walked along the Embankment and the night-black river.

Teaching contemporary British poetry that fall, I was more engaged with how much the contemporary lyric poem in England was still residing much closer to formal conventions than most American poetry, and how British poets often valued a drier voice that played in wit, in ways that the American poets generally didn't. I was aware of how little Whitman's long line—his freer verse and open-endedness—appealed to British poets. There were exceptions, of course, like Basil Bunting, Ted Hughes, and David Jones. But, for the most part, the wilder long line and the more open field kinetics of William Carlos Williams and Charles Olson had been less appropriated by the British mainstream.

I remember having lunch at the Grey Hound pub off Kensington High Street with Andrew Motion, who was coming to my class that day to read his work. He was a young rising star then who would go on to become Poet Laureate. It was a week or so before the celebration of T. S. Eliot's birthday centennial, and London was gearing up for the event that would be accompanied by the publication of a volume of Eliot's letters. In anticipation of the releases of the letters and the birthday, the London *Times*, which was a more intellectual newspaper then, was running a six-part series on Eliot's life. As an American poet reading the mainstream, popular newspaper of London, I was astonished to see every day that week a several-page spread about Eliot's life. The pieces included dramatic photographs, facsimiles of manuscripts, drawings, catchy headlines like "A Poet in the Editor's Chair" and "The Price of a Masterpiece," and so on. All week I passed out copies of the *Times'* spread on Eliot to my students, who were at first bewildered and then increasingly impressed and excited to see that a mainstream newspaper was covering a poet with such depth, flair, and sense importance. Everyone in the class agreed that this would never happen for Whitman or Dickinson, or Faulkner or Hemingway in the United States.

The night before Eliot's birthday I took my students—all twenty of them, many in dresses and sport jackets (some even wore ties)—to St. Stephen's Church on Gloucester Road, where Eliot had been a lifetime parishioner. It was a clear, early fall evening, and when we walked into the packed church, there was even a kind of Christmas feeling about it. The celebration involved readings of Eliot's poems and plays by actors and congregants, and music by the Ockendon string quartet. Eliot's widow Valerie was present, as were bishops and other distinguished clergy and cultural and political celebrities. It was pageantry and mystery mixed with canonical, authorial literariness, a dying idea it seemed then in the wake of the poststructuralist wars over authorship, language, and literary value. And all this for—a poet—which seemed even a rarer cultural performance for the late 1980s Reagan-Thatcher neoliberalism, with its celebration of money and its giddy materialism.

Talking with Motion over one of those pub lunches of warm ale, shepherd's pie, and Branston pickle, I was taken off guard by his small tirade against all this "Eliot nonsense" that was filling up the city. "Peter," Andrew said, "England will never accept T. S. Eliot into its poetic tradition." "Eliot," he went on, as his calm tone rose a bit, "has nothing to do with us." Andrew made it clear to me that the modern English poetic tradition began with Houseman and Hardy and went on to Edward Thomas and down to Philip Larkin. I grinned and noted that the Eliots were, after all, New Englanders uprooted to St. Louis before Tom Eliot was shipped back to New England, before he shipped out to Oxford and London, where he converted to Anglo-everything. Andrew quipped, "Well, he should be shipped back to America."

Walking King's Road each day to Sloan Square and then tubing it to Kensington, I worked on new poems and read a stash of new books by British and other UK poets. I loved working on poems in the daily rush of urban life, especially on the tube, where, amid the white noise and crowd blur, I could settle into my own zone of phrases and lines. And I could also settle into those thin Faber, or Oxford, or Carcanet, or Bloodaxe paperbacks of poems. The spare, nimble lines of Motion, Tom Paulin, Craig Raine, Carol Rumens, Christopher Reid, and poem titles like "A Martian Sends a Postcard Home," "Fivemile Town," "Pea Soup," "The Dancing Hippo," or "Outside Oswiecim." There was a different kind of irony and wry humor that made an interesting face-off with the more lush lyricism or intensified persona voices of the American grain. Sylvia Plath, Anne Sexton, Charles Wright, Galway Kinnell, Adrienne Rich, or even John Ashbery and James Merrill were not in this drier register.

That fall, I got interested again in the point and counterpoint of British and American language-music. I thought of how John Lennon might have heard the voice of Little Richard, or how Michael Jackson might have taken in Mick Jagger, Joe Cocker Ray Charles, or Dusty Springfield, Martha Reeves. Those crisscrossing registers, the music of English across cultures and vernaculars, idioms, and lyric compressions were part of the genius of the language. In the exceptional expanse of the English language, there seemed always new kinds of fusions of sound and rhythm that the full-bodied art of poetry often initiated and introduced into the general language, in the way that poetry creates hybrids within hybrids, lines competing and comingling in their aspirations for some cold eye casting, or sublime seeing, or self-lacerating or self-loving confession.

I was enjoying the lines and the tone of these British poems. It afforded me a fresh moment to think about how tone creates perception, how tone and its relationship to the line creates a perspective, how the line with its arrangement of image and voice opens up possibilities for ingesting experience. I had no strong commitment to the virtue of the long line over the four- and five-beat line, or the skinny, two- and three-beat line. Each musical register offered something potentially rich if the poet could take advantage of it and its musical potential.

In the midst of my own enjoyment of this moment of comparative poetics, I was also feeling a sense of global life more acutely, and while this had something to do with being out of context, as Henry James once put it, the state of things on the planet had begun to feel more chaotic in the past decade. Here in London, I felt bombarded by the very good BBC and TV 3 coverage of the international scene. All through the 1980s, it was hard not to feel more and more bombarded by reports of continual mass violence in faraway places, and by violent paroxysms of the new Wall Street culture and its deregulated assault on the poor and the middle class and the ensuing poverty that often resulted from its abuses. Images on the screen poured over me in ways that disrupted the privileged domestic space in which I lived. Perhaps there was something new about this, perhaps this was as old as the TV Age, which was not that old, but old enough for my life to have been defined by it. But now the TV camera's focus on the world was more acute and in-depth than it had ever been. It was hard to get images out of one's head: Iranian students storming the U.S. embassy in Teheran; the space shuttle *Challenger* disintegrating in tunnels of white smoke in a midnight-blue sky; crowds swarming the Berlin Wall that had come down in seeming spontaneity; Chinese soldiers in Tiananmen Square firing on students; the dead bodies in the mud from the toxic gas leak at Bhopal; the images of wasting men dying of AIDS. I was finding the experience I understood to be shaping the planet increasingly bizarre not dreamlike but nightmarish, pushing the imagination to engage harsh realities that evoked the fantastical, magical, unreal. Such large events had strange ways of bridging time and space in jolting and immediate ways. And during the fall of 1988 in London, I encountered some of these time/space jolts in new ways.

That December we decided not to head home for the Christmas holiday, but rather stay in our pale pink flat with its ivory-white moldings and its blend of Regency furniture and English country chintz. We could get chicken tikka masala, three kinds of taramousalata, eggplant (better known as aubergine in London) rollatini from Sainsbury's, and continue our explorations of single-malt Scotch at the local Oddbins. Our three-month-old son was happy in his pram, and our daughter was enjoying the cosmopolitan life at the King's Head and along the Thames, where her day-care school was. It seemed like a moment to relax and go slow rather than rush back to New York.

On Wednesday December 21, I walked down King's Road in the slightly warm winter gray dark London air to Oakley Street, and then to the Embankment around 7:00 PM on the shortest day of the year. I walked into the flat just as my wife Helen turned on the TV to see images of something exploding in the night sky. It was just light flashing in black air, but the text and broadcast was clear: it was Pan Am 103, over Lockerbie, Scotland. I felt some panic rise in my chest because I knew that some of our students might be on that plane. In a couple minutes, the phone rang, and it was Martha from the Off Campus Study Office at Colgate telling me that one of my students was on the plane. "I'm watching it," I said. "Are you sure S. was on the plane?" "Yes," she said, as were numerous students from Syracuse University, including another one of ours who was with their program." I was staring at my three-month-old son in his pram, his wild brown hair cowlicking up, his eyes alert and looking around the room. December 21 would have been a natural day for us to have flown back to New York, and this would have been a good time of day to have taken Pan Am 103 with the time difference working well for landing at Kennedy. I stood with the phone propped in my neck, watching the flashing light in the sky over Scotland and writing down instructions from Martha back at Colgate about what to do when my student's parents arrived. How many parents and families would be coming to London to deal with the death of their children who had been blown up in the night sky by a bomb set off by Libyan terrorists? I kept looking at the replay of the exploding plane. I glanced at my son in his pram. I could see my daughter in the next room combing the hair of her toy pony. I was trying to hold these images together, or not together. I was stuck with them. I was beginning to see the world caught/positioned/stuck/divided between such discrepancies and ironies. Holding them together in any kind of relationship was challenging. I felt scissored in a perceptual gap. I felt lucky, thus far at least, to be an onlooker, a bystander who, through prisms and screens, apertures and cracks, takes notes, looks on, tries to grab a filament of the event or materials of the event. Poets hope that sight will yield insight in the register of language rhythm and image viscosity. And that insight will matter to readers, to a wider world.

Two weeks earlier I had turned on the TV in the early morning to see the aftermath of an earthquake in the western section of Armenia, then a Soviet republic. A small landlocked country, the surviving fragment of historic Armenia after the genocide of the Armenians in Turkey in 1915. Seeming always to be holding on by a thread, it was now lodged between Turkey, Iran, Georgia, and Azerbaijan in a matrix of political tensions and internal social problems, many of which evolved from decades of Soviet rule. On December 7, I stayed in most of the day staring at the TV screen, gazing at the remains of Gyumri (formerly Alexandropol and Lennikan), a sizeable city near the Turkish border and at other Armenian towns and villages that had been smashed and avalanched. Tens of thousands were dead; one city, Spitak, was so obliterated it seemed to cease to exist. On the TV screen I could see apartments sliced open, and dressers and lamps, pots and pans, toys and stoves, bookcases, chandeliers smashed, piled in the streets.

The quake happened just before lunchtime, so thousands of

children were in classrooms, and small bodies can survive in small places before they succumb to crush syndrome. Crush syndrome, I learned, was something that happened when the slabs of concrete were lifted off a crushed body and the toxins from the crushed limb or area were released in a rush and overwhelmed the kidneys. If adequate dialysis machines were not on hand people would die of kidney failure on the spot. Already the reports said that the smell of decomposing flesh was making the street fires acrid.

Because I had recently finished a book on the American poet Theodore Roethke, I was spending some time that week interviewing Beatrice Lushington, Roethke's widow who had lived in England with her second husband for decades since Roethke's death in the early 1960s. Over lunch and tea off Kensington High Street, we talked about Roethke, their lives together, and the poetry scene in the 1950s. She spoke with a certain endearing and quiet candor about Roethke's drinking, his manic episodes, and his great musical love poems of the 1950s. "Those poems were written to me," she said. "I know," I said. "He had discovered Yeats's line and me at the same time." "I know," I said. While part of me was feeling the pleasure of literary nostalgia listening to Mrs. Lushington recount some complicated episodes of her life with Roethke, I was having a hard time focusing on it all. When we finished the last interview in the late afternoon, I took the tube to Heathrow airport where I joined one of the relief projects and loaded clothes and canned food into planes that were flying relief daily to Armenia. I was trying to keep my grief and anger about the Armenian earthquake to myself. Most days that week I took the tube out to Heathrow to load up planes, and the musty stink of used clothes stayed on me all day. When I returned to the city, I found myself going to the Armenian church in South Kensington, where I sat in the quiet dark thinking.

I didn't want to fall in to the old Armenian syndrome, or the old Jewish syndrome, or was it an old blues syndrome that African Americans had creatively made into art. The mud-bottom moaning, the why-why-why-us syndrome, the isn't there any end of suffering and misfortune syndrome, etc., etc., etc. Walking back to Cheyne Walk in the dark, I recited poems as a kind of therapy, as a kind of companionship: Emily Dickinson's "Before I Got My Eye Put Out," a dart about vulnerability and seeing; Larkin's "This Be the Verse," a poem that made me feel better about the miserable world; Michael Harper's "Dear John, Dear Coltrane," a poem about feeling black; Bob Dylan's "I Shall Be Free," a talking blues poem about the absurdity of the real.

>>><<<

It seemed to me more and more as I walked around London in the fall of 1988 that the old TV screen was also being supplanted and augmented by the new screens of personal computers and Internet reality, which I was just beginning to use. Screenic culture was making the new into something digitally combustible and seemingly visually inexhaustible; virtual forms and meta-meanings were becoming new zones of seeing and thinking. Digital life was creating new prods on the brain's circuitry. This added to a sense of being overwhelmed by political explosions and mass violence in a cultural moment that was defining itself in some new ways.

For various reasons that had something to do with this sense of the world and some inner needs of my own, I wanted to find my own ways for the poem to have a broader reach, to be a wider net, to have a more spacious arena to absorb stuff, things, ideas, voices, bric-a-brac, a bit like a Rauschenberg combine. The idea of what I was privately calling "writing horizontal" was nothing more than an instinct, a personal orientation, a way of feeling and pushing the poem for more space and layers and flexibility.

Whitman and Eliot have always struck me as two primary horizontal poets because they made new forms out of an aesthetic-kinetic force that was able to ingest a social/cultural/historical terrain that pushed and changed the poem. Whitman had opened up the poem's lens to absorb social scenes in motion, panoramic landscapes as well as the self's inner crises. His free verse (once considered irreverent by Victorian conventionalists) had gliding rhythms and a candid spoken voice that could incorporate erotic love, fecund nature, the pain of amputees in Civil War hospitals, crowds in streets, transcendent visions, commuters crossing the river, transcendent feeling, solitary depressed longings. Whitman was that noiseless patient spider of his own poem that "marked how to explore the vacant vast surrounding" and, in doing so, "launched forth filament, filament, filament, out of itself." Whitman's filaments were also "unreeling" lines as he calls the spider's process—his ars poetical way of seeing. For Whitman, the soul is synonymous with the poet who seeks to connect the spheres: "And you O my soul where you stand / Surrounded, detached, in measureless oceans of space / Ceaselessly musing, venturing, throwing, seeking the spheres to connect them." "Measureless oceans of space": that was a trope for the new poem of this new age too. Whitman could keep self and other, self and a verifiable world out there, in some interesting kinesis, some dialectic that allowed a part of self—often for Whitman a partially visible self—to mingle intimate feeling with a wider world.

Eliot's disruptive vision of the poem in "The Waste Land," was a collage-like assemblage, an expansive box in which the poet could collect and pour a "mish-mash potpourri," as Eliot called it, to bring disconcerting entities together, to make a form out of disparate materials: texts, voices, discourses that challenge genre boundaries, that let the poem grow into weird spaces and then spaces within spaces. *The Waste Land*, with its cinematic cuts and shifts, its quick, startling movements from a Hebraic text to a scene in the Bavarian mountains, to lines from a Wagner opera, to a woman's boudoir, or to a working-class woman talking in a pub, must have seemed like silent film to readers in the 1920s. In Eliot's ventriloquism and efforts to eschew the personal voice, a visible personal self was far from, if not oppositional to, Whitman's intimate confessional self. Yet both poets found ways of allowing the poem to be a flexible chamber for the unexpected, the large indigestible experience of culture and self in their many layers.

The world of the late twentieth century struck me—and still strikes me in the early twenty-first—as a fast moving landscape with its multifarious, colliding planes of shifting realities, and jolts to the senses and to our cognitive wires. These kinds of jolting image landscapes—Pan Am 103 exploding in the night sky over Scotland, or a section of Armenia disappearing in a few minutes into rubble and corpses—reproduced on the screen in complexly repeated and protracted ways made the real and the virtual intersecting vectors in the brain; and this changed how the handheld camera in my head was working. Furthermore, the smooth filaments of Whitman's noiseless, patient spider seemed less accessible, and Eliot's assurance about the power of Western canonical texts were challenged in new ways. The late twentieth century demanded more ingesting of discordant vectors and fraying wires.

Writing horizontal was for me not an aesthetic program, but rather a way of opening up space both linguistically and in the mind. The horizontal poem, I felt, could still hold on to the verticality of the conceit's self-reflexiveness, so that the germ at the beginning of the poem could unfurl in ways that could be connected to itself, the way the poems of Donne, Marvell, and Herbert so often did. Verticality could keep the horizontal poem rooted in itself, giving the poetic field a disciplined center. But horizontalness allowed for nuanced feeling and perception that could skitter along mental wires and optical alleyways. It was liberating to play more with splicing and shifting in ways that advanced a larger consciousness of the poem, a spaciousness that meant more opportunities for movement—the music of rhythm could glide into the image in unsettling ways.

Coming back from London that winter, I wanted to capture something about my own personal encounter with living in rural America, as a privileged university professor who receives messages about disasters happening in other parts of the planet. This was a very early sense of my moving horizontal.

FROM "GEESE FLYING OVER HAMILTON, NEW YORK":

That's how I woke
to a window of chalk sky

like indifference, like the sheet wrapped
around two people,

and the radio sounded like fuzz
on a boom mike,

the rhetoric needling in about the dead in Croatia

then the light came and the branch
of a sycamore on the wall
        was the menorah
on the arch of Titus

I was thinking like

the cows by the paddock in a peel of sun

when they cut a wide arrow—
their feathers oily with tundra,
the gabbling like field-holler.

I looked out to the Fisher-Price toys
blue and yellow in fog,

silver light, gauche on the spruces,

and the words Pol Pot
the geese chromatic, then gone.

Phnom Penh static like snow the day may bring,
like a monsoon sweeping over a menorah

like the falling barn seeming to rise in white air.

>>><<<

In the late 1990s, I found myself in Amsterdam on a book tour
for my memoir *Black Dog of Fate*, at a time when my eight-year-
old son was receiving leukemia treatments back home in central
New York. I sat all day on a bright-blue-skied afternoon in an
elegant parlor at the Ambassade Hotel on the Herengracht ca-

nal, where journalists came and went to talk with writers on tour. I found myself staring at the canal, the sky over the lowlands, the Anne Frank House down the street, and fielding questions from an array of interesting journalists who held a mirror up to American culture. The fallout of the President Clinton–Monica Lewinsky episode was still around, as one journalist made clear. I got interested in the intersecting forces of that moment and wanted to make a weave that might capture the various threads of possible insights.

FROM "LOWLANDS":

"North Sea's just over there,"
the Flemish waitress said. You can see
everywhere but you can't see anything,

then the headlights make the fog a little gold
the way the maples turn in my yard
back in the upstate valley

where my son dives in a leaf pile
on his way to school with his friends,
and I keep turning his ritual over in my mind

two pills of chemo at night,
6 MP it's called, so familiar now like a ham and cheese sandwich.
Tomorrow when I drive north to Bruges, he'll get his shot

of methotrexate—nutriphils, platelets, the invisible
hooks between cells. On my book tour in Amsterdam
an Indonesian journalist asked me how

genital contact could bring a President down.
Histerica passio dragged our quarry down.
"Isn't that Yeats'," she asked. We giggled but just kept

the tape going. Through the window the canals shined
like they were varnished,
and I could see the lines beginning to form in front

of the Anne Frank House already at 8:30.
The charm of the brown brick
like something out of Vermeer—an absurdity,

as if it were a gloss
on the idea of Jews hiding out in the suffocating dark.
A girl your daughter's age menstruating there.

≫≫≺≺≺

Walking through the bombed-out Bosnian National Library in the summer of 2007, I was observing some residue of the aftermath of the violence of the war and genocide of the mid-1990s that had cracked open Sarajevo, that historically rich and multicultural city with its overlays of intersecting empires—both Ottoman and Austro-Hungarian. The ruined library—a grand Central European building with Moorish features that was an emblem of the cultural richness of the city and of the violent history that was still fresh in the gouged-out stone and broken glass—was being restored and rebuilt. The collision of the renovation in that moment of urban recovery in Sarajevo, with the recent past of the Serbian assault on the smashed library, was haunting. I wanted to create as much space as I could for a poem to explore that moment, that place, its history, and my own way of seeing it through various intersecting and fractured lenses that were part of my personal sense of history.

"SARAJEVO"

I.
The needle of the minaret disappeared in fog
and we were walking between Hapsburg courtyards
and the detonated façade of the National Library,

the wooden scaffolding rising up the Moorish pediments,
the stripped cement and under-brick, and then
the sun came and the Coke stand burned red.

Out of nowhere a guard opened the black metal door—
his boyish face and soft goatee startled us, and you slid inside
before he could shrug as if he were breaking the rules.

The blue poured through the metal grid
on the glass dome and we were walking
where a carillon fell into thumbed pages,

where students worked in the dry air
of glue and vellum, under the octagons
from which the light converged invariant and mosaic.

2.

Under the shanked-up arches I took a shot
of a patch of fresco and the paint flared—
a yellow star on a pink rosette:

Jewish/Muslim/Christian—and if it wasn't
one of Duccio's halos, it was drawn
a couple blocks away from where the gracious

open car of the archduke and his wife Sophie
traveled into the shadow of the image,
and then rail-lines were cut

and the city was a shrinking river running down
the hillside where the shelling began from Mount
Trebevič, late night August 25, '92.

3.

I followed you up a half-sliced staircase
into the memory of microfilm and quaint
catalog trays on a second floor landing propped by a plank,

and then you disappeared with your camera,
into the dark apse-space where the steam pipes
melted under molten glass and spread to the manuscripts.

4.

Back in the cool seminar rooms of the Hollywood Hotel,
at the edge of the city our conference went on

in the green din of post-Soviet comfort where
every third channel was porn and the arguments

about ethnic cleansing were spliced by
the disco-falsetto of the Bee Gees

and through the giant windows we watched
the women sun-bathing in the weeds

next to a bulldozer and a pile of rusted cans
as plastic swans of garbage flowed

in the sulfurous river where Princip
the archduke's assassin tried to drown himself.

5.
At Birkenau there were just white birch trees for a mile
before we reached the caved-in crematoria—so lush
the skeletons of chimneys and incinerated piles of brick
    surprised us.

Your family disappearing south of Krakow into the soft Polish
    countryside
by train with their kitchen spoons and sewing kits would have
been confused by the green shade, and even though Euclid

said any two points can be joined by a straight line,
what does that make the line from Budapest to Birkenau,

and where does that leave us under this dome
as order comes down in thin spindles of light into the
    dust-filled air
where a man stands on a ladder re-drawing a window?

6.
Had we fallen down some volute from the touristy hills
where we drank beer and looked out at the city

at the machines digging up the mud of Marshall Tito street
where no one was eating cabbage off sheet metal,

and the smell of roasting lamb was gorgeous
as it rose from the pavilions with their newly sealed windows.

7.
Down the boulevard past the tavernas
with their burnt offerings of meat,
the Haggadah of Sarajevo was breathing,

and you copied out the marginalia;

the copper and gold almost liquid,
the letters like bullet wounds on the calf-skin pages

from which the ink flew into the margins
of deliverance or extinction—

where Aaron's spear opened a chapter
the way the enjambed bullets hit the façade

after the lights went out and historical memory
was shaved to a hill of locusts on the flight out of Egypt,

8.
as the silks were blowing into the yellow wind
against the Ottoman pavilions of the Baśćarśija

and then it came down on us like roof-soot:
the burning pages of black snow

the phantasmal voices of index cards
the extinct dictionaries, the tongues washed away

in the puny brown river—between margins and colophons,
the residue of Quaranic texts that left just a dusting

on the scattered silverware under the bridge,
the invisible wires of verbs in the acid-pocked sky

the burning glue and rag that rose
into the black hole over the library

over the vanquished trees where every letter
was a country lost between latitudes and an internet café.

9.
Past teenagers making out
on benches in the Jewish graveyard
just under the hill where the snipers opened fire

we shot our heretical need
to see the horror of the past
through a wide angled lens

and the shutter speed snipped
the light that unrolled the violets
sprawling down the hill

where more Serbian kids chugged Cokes
and pumped all night with their Kalashnikovs
from the Sarajevo-Pale Road to the high ground.

10.

We heard the rhetoric of goats
as they hacked weeds and ate piles of cellophane

wrapped nougats at the feet of the women
selling scarves and candy

along the riverbank where the sky
snowed pulverized paper and phosphorous shells,

where they had breathed the ash-packed bindings—
and letters broke into wings in the black zinc dish of the sky,

where commas and dashes hooked the encrypted clouds
or reappeared outside the hyperlinks and cellular routers

returning to earth somewhere beyond the medusa
tongues of flags of foreign countries.

11.

Past the houses of no windows,
where the sound of Arabic was less than guttural,

where the refusal to hear the Other's testimony
was the distortion of a broken CD on a megaphone in a town
    square,

where the brandy bottles and spent shells
littered the picked-clean kiosk and the trace was washed away.

When we came down from the hills of Porticari
through swaths of fog and ruined houses

you said: *we found no Other, just the extension of self in the scratch*
    marks
on the photos of the disappeared.

12.

The sculpted slabs of tombstones
were sinking in the mud, there
where the Book of Splendor opened

between the smack of bullets
and the caved-in mikvah
where the embroidered shawls

and the gold-embossed prayer-books
sank into ruts and the violets went red
like our eyes in the photo

beneath the light that untied the Hasidic knots
in which the soul had Houdinied out
into the wild air after the expulsion from Spain.

13.
You asked: *If there is no one to listen to the story, what's left?*
The blown out ceiling with its tinge of Duccio-color?

where we walked in and looked up
at the strange blue coming down through the triangles and
    octagons,

onto the plaster-dusted marble floor.

De-facing the Other is a response to the transparency of the event—
look at the photos of the missing;

Books disappear like people, no, tombs, the pages stink and then
    they're soot,
and then the air is clean again.

14.
The river was clogged with the dialectic of garbage
as we watched books disappear on the rock-barges

that faded in the hammered gold light
that sank to bronze before its aubergine

blotted out the hills, and we let the letters
go, the focus frozen on imagining the intractable.

The restaurant was grilling chops and sausage,
the cabbage sweet, yoghurt smashed with garlic,
Croatian wine dry and cold, the streets still buzzing.

Acknowledgments

Gratitude to the following: Sven Birkerts, Jennifer Brice, Mary Ann Calo, Luca Caminati, Cathy Caruth, Colgate Writer's Conference, Michael Coyle, Doris V. Cross, Donna-Lee Frieze, Robert Garland, Michael Holobosky, Mary Beth Kelly, Anne Leone, Denise Stillwaggon Leone, Matt Leone, Betty Jean Lifton, Robert Jay Lifton, Askold Melnyczuk, Angela Miller, John Naughton, Jane L.Pinchin, Eric Simonoff, Kara Rusch, The Donald M. and Constance H. Rebar Chair Colgate University, Tom Sleigh, Bruce Smith, Joyce and Joe Stein and the Philibosian Family Foundation, Laura Tanner, Stewart Wallace, the Wellfleet Meetings, Jack Wheatcroft, Yaddo, Jim and Janet Balakian for Water Mill retreat; to my editor, Randy Petilos; and to Helen for many drafts.

>>><<<

Chapter 1 first appeared in slightly different form as "Poetry in Hell: Primo Levi and Dante at Auschwitz" in *American Poetry Review* (January 2008). Chapter 2, "The Poem as History," was given in parts as public lectures at the International Association of Genocide Scholars Auschwitz Seminar, Auschwitz, Poland (July 2007), the Colgate Writers Conference, Colgate University (June 2009), and the Wellfleet Meetings on Psychology and History (October 2010). Chapter 3 first appeared in an earlier form in *AGNI* 39 (1993). Chapter 4 appeared in an earlier form as the introduction to *Theodore Roethke's Far Fields* (Baton Rouge: Louisiana State University Press, 1989). Chapter 6 first appeared as "Yeghishe Charents: The Rise and Fall of a Revolutionary Poet" in *American Poetry Review* (January/February 1989). Chapter 7 was given, in part, as a lecture at the Colgate Writer's Conference at Colgate University (June 2010). Chapter 8 first appeared in *Art in America* (February 1996). Chapter 9 was first delivered at a lecture at the conference "Armenian and Greek Culture" held at Aristotle University, Thessaloniki, Greece (October 1994). And chapter 10 first appeared in an earlier form as the introduction to *Bloody News from My Friend: Poems by Siamanto*, trans. Peter Balakian and Nevart Yaghlian (Detroit: Wayne State University Press, 1996).

Notes

CHAPTER ONE

1. I am using Stuart Woolf's translation of *Survival in Auschwitz* (New York: Orion, 1959) and thus using Woolf's translation of *The Divine Comedy*. While I find Woolf's translation not as concise and elegant as others, such as those by Robert Pinsky or Robert M. Durling, I have stayed with Woolf's version because it is embedded in the narrative and thus intrinsic to the voice of the story.

2. Andrea Ciccarelli, "Dante and Italian Culture from the Risorgimento to World War I," *Dante Studies* 119 (2001), 142–43.

3. Albert Camus, *The Myth of Sisyphus*, trans. Justin O'Brien (New York: Alfred A. Knopf, 1955), 20.

4. *The Drowned and the Saved*, trans. Raymond Rosenthal (New York: Simon & Schuster, 1988), 131.

5. Ibid., 131.

CHAPTER TWO

1. Walter Benjamin, *Illuminations: Essays and Reflections*, ed. with introduction by Hannah Arendt (New York: Harcourt Brace Jovanovich, 1968), 255–56.

2. Czeslaw Milosz, *The Witness of Poetry* (Cambridge, MA: Harvard University Press, 1983), 35.

3. Ernest Hemingway, *A Farewell to Arms* (New York: Scribner, 1927), 185.

CHAPTER THREE

1. Carolyn Forché, *Against Forgetting: Twentieth Century Poetry of Witness* (New York: W. W. Norton, 1993), 41.

2. David Perkins, *A History of Modern Poetry: From the 1890s to Pound, Eliot, and Yeats* (Cambridge, MA: Harvard University Press, 1976), 102.

3. Elaine Scarry, *The Body in Pain: The Making and Unmaking of the World* (Oxford: Oxford University Press, 1985), 54.

4. Lawrence L. Langer, *Holocaust Testimonies: The Ruins of Memory* (New Haven, CT: Yale University Press, 1991), 77.

5. Cathy Caruth, *Trauma: Explorations in Memory* (Baltimore: Johns Hopkins University Press, 1995), 4–5.

6. Ibid., 5.

7. See Marianne Hirsch, *The Generation of Post-Memory: Writing and Visual Culture After the Holocaust* (New York: Columbia University Press, 2012).

CHAPTER FOUR

1. See Hyatt H. Waggoner, *American Poets: From the Puritans to the Present* (Baton Rouge: Louisiana State University Press, 1984), chap. 21, and James E. B. Breslin, *From Modern to Contemporary: American Poetry, 1945–1965* (Chicago: University of Chicago Press, 1984), chaps. 1–3.

2. Norman Mailer, *Advertisements for Myself* (Cambridge, MA: Harvard University Press, 1992), 338.

3. Cathy Caruth, *Trauma: Explorations in Memory* (Baltimore: Johns Hopkins University Press), 4–5.

4. James E. Miller, *The American Quest for a Supreme Fiction* (Chicago: University of Chicago Press, 1979), 5.

5. Allan Seager, *The Glass House: The Life of Theodore Roethke* (New York: McGraw-Hill, 1968), 145.

6. Ibid., 144.

7. Theodore Roethke, *On the Poet and His Craft: Selected Prose of Theodore Roethke*, ed. Ralph J. Mills Jr. (Seattle: University of Washington Press, 1965), 8–9.

8. Ibid., 39.

9. *Selected Letters of Theodore Roethke*, ed. Ralph J. Mills Jr. (Seattle: University of Washington Press, 1968), 142, 130. Hereafter cited with page numbers in the text.

10. Ibid., 40.

11. Ibid., 42.

12. *Selected Essays of Delmore Schwartz*, ed. Donald A. Dike and David H. Zucker (Chicago: University of Chicago Press, 1970), 187.

13. *Selected Letters of Theodore Roethke*, ed. with introduction by Ralph J. Mills (Seattle: University of Washington Press, 1968), 122.

14. Roethke, *On the Poet and His Craft*, 41.

15. Norman O. Brown, *Love's Body* (New York: Harper & Row, 1966), 39.

16. Kenneth Burke, "The Vegetal Radicalism on Theodore Roethke," *Sewanee Review* 67 (Winter 1950).

17. Roethke, *On the Poet and His Craft*, 39.

CHAPTER FIVE

1. John Untereker, *Voyager: A Life of Hart Crane* (New York: Liveright Publishing, 1969), 593.

2. Ibid., 674.

3. Ibid., 688.

4. Ibid., 662.

5. Ibid., 664.

6. Ibid., 691.

7. Ibid., 690–93.

8. Paul Mariani, *The Broken Tower: The Life of Hart Crane* (New York: W. W. Norton, 1999), 388–89.

9. Ibid., 696.

10. Ibid., 714.

11. Ibid., 395; Untereker, *Voyager*, 716.

12. Untereker, *Voyager*, 716–19.

13. Ibid., 729–31.

14. Ibid., 734.

15. Ibid., 736.

16. "Letter to Harriet Monroe," in *The Complete Poems and Selected Letters and Prose*, ed. Brom Weber (New York: Liveright Publishing, 1966), 234–47. Hereafter cited with page numbers in the text.

17. Untereker, *Voyager*, 739.

18. Ibid., 740.

19. *The Complete Poems and Selected Letters and Prose*, 745–56.

20. Untereker, *Voyager*, 753.

21. See *The Broken Tower*, chap. 16; *Voyager*, chap. 43.

CHAPTER SIX

1. *Yeghishe Charents: Poet of the Revolution*, ed. Marc Nishanian (Costa Mesa, CA: Mazda Press, 2003), 150.

2. All excerpts from Charents's poems are from *Eghishe Charents, Land of Fire: Selected Poems*, ed. and trans. Diana Der Hovanessian and Marzbed Margossian (Ann Arbor: Ardis Press, 1986).

3. Cathy Caruth, *Trauma: Explorations in Memory* (Baltimore: Johns Hopkins University Press, 1995), 4–5.

4. Christopher Walker, *Armenia: The Survival of a Nation* (New York: St. Martin's Press, 1980), 256.

5. *Across Two Worlds: Selected Prose of Eghishé Charents*, ed. and trans. Diana Der Hovanessian and Marzbed Margossian (New York: Ashod Press, 1985), 55–56.

6. Ibid., 9.

7. Nadezhda Mandelshtam, *Hope Abandoned* (New York: Athenaeum, 1974), 538.

8. Nadezhda Mandelshtam, *Hope Against Hope* (New York: Athenaeum, 1970), 190.

9. Marc Slonim, *Soviet Russian Literature* (Oxford: Oxford University Press, 1973), 236.

10. Hovanessian and Margossian, *Across Two Worlds*, xv.

CHAPTER SEVEN

1. Brandon Taylor, *Collage and the Making of Modern Art* (New York: Thames & Hudson, 2004), 8.

2. See Thomas R. Brockelman, *The Frame and the Mirror* (Evanston, IL: Northwestern University Press, 2001), chap. 1.

3. Shoshana Felman and Dori Laub, *Testimony: Crisis of Witnessing in Literature, History, and Psychoanalysis* (New Haven, CT: Yale University Press, 1992), pp.4–6.

4. Ibid.

5. Sam Hunter, *Selections from the Ileana and Michael Sonnabend Collection: Works from the 1950s and 1960s*, exhibition catalog (Princeton, NJ: Art Museum, Princeton University, 1985), 21.

6. Matthew Leone, *Shapes of Openness: Bakhtin, Lawrence, Laughter* (Cambridge: Cambridge Scholars Publishing, 2010), 8.

7. See Joshua Shannon, *The Disappearance of Objects: New York and the Rise of the Postmodern City* (New Haven, CT: Yale University Press, 2009).

CHAPTER EIGHT

1. Susan Sontag to Peter Balakian (February 1 1996).

2. Matthew Spender, *From a High Place: A Life of Arshile Gorky* (New York: Alfred A. Knopf, 1999), 375.

3. Arshile Gorky, *Goats on the Roof: A Life in Letters and Documents*, ed. Matthew Spender (London: Ridinghouse, 2010), 16.

4. Spender's claim that "Armenian immigrants" (a term that accrues derogatory meaning in his context; who are these people he alludes to?) are using the Mooradian letters to generate an Armenian narrative, after the letters have been disclosed as invalid, is, as far as I know, untrue. In the two major books that appeared (after the letters were discounted) written by scholars of Armenian descent—Nouritza Matossian's biography *Black Angel* (London: Chatto and Windus, 1998) and Kim S. Theriault's *Rethinking Arshile Gorky* (University Park: Penn State University Press, 2009)—the Mooradian letters are not used. Furthermore, Matossian addresses the counterfeit nature of the letters in her book. As for my own use of the letters in my 1996 essay, I gladly jettisoned them as soon as their flawed nature was revealed. Whatever the reasons for Spender's hostility to Armenians, one cannot but note that such unsubstantiated assertions limit the credibility of his analysis.

5. Hayden Herrera, *Arshile Gorky: His Life and His Work* (New York: Farrar, Straus and Giroux, 2003), 16–17.

6. Clarence D. Ussher, *An American Physician in Turkey* (Boston: Houghton Mifflin, 1915), 236–38.

7. Matossian, *Black Angel*, 68.

8. Herrera, *Arshile Gorky*, 68–69.

9. Karlen Mooradian, *The Many Worlds of Arshile Gorky* (Chicago: Gilgamesh Press, 1980), 26.

10. Spender, *From a High Place*, 4.

11. Matossian, *Black Angel*, 5–6.

12. Ethel Kremer Schwabacher, *Arshile Gorky* (New York: Macmillan, 1957), 66.

13. Herrera, *Arshile Gorky*, 471.

14. *Anthology of Armenian Poetry*, ed. and trans. Diana Der Hovanessian and Marzbed Margossian (New York: Columbia University Press, 1978), 148–50.

15. Spender, *From a High Place*, 375.

CHAPTER NINE

1. Elia Kazan, *Kazan on Directing*, ed. Robert Cornfield (New York: Alfred A. Knopf, 2009), 222.

2. Ibid., 218.

3. All excerpts from the film are from *America, America* with after commentary by Foster Hirsch (1963; Warner Brothers Entertainment, 2011).

4. Michel Ciment, *Kazan on Kazan* (London: Secker and Warburg for the British Film Institute, 1973), 9–11.

5. John Lahr, "Method Man: Elia Kazan's Singular Career," *The New Yorker* (December 13, 2010).

6. Ciment, *Kazan on Kazan*, 9–10.

7. Peter Balakian, *The Burning Tigris: The Armenian Genocide and America's Response* (New York: HarperCollins, 2003), chaps. 1–10.

8. Elia Kazan, *Elia Kazan: A Life* (New York: Alfred A. Knopf, 1988), 635–36.

9. Ibid., 642.

10. Ibid., 643.

11. Ibid, 644.

12. Ibid., 644–47.

13. See Peter Balakian, "The Armenian Genocide and the Modern Age," *The Sydney Papers* (Autumn 2008), 145–161. Balakian notes that although the mass killing of the Hereros in South West Africa in 1903 was the first genocide of the twentieth century, the mass killing of the Armenians was the first genocide done in a modern form. The Ottoman Turkish state in 1915 used its government bureaucracy, military, parliamentary legislation, nationalist ideology, and modern technology for the purpose of eliminating an unarmed, minority ethnic group in a concentrated period of time; this technique of mass killing was new and inextricable from twentieth-century modernity. From 1915–1916, about 1.2 Armenians were killed.

CHAPTER TEN

1. Robert Jay Lifton, *Death in Life: Survivors of Hiroshima* (Chapel Hill, University of North Carolina Press, 1991), chaps. 9–12.

2. Henry Morgenthau, *Ambassador Morgenthau's Story* (New York: Doubleday & Doran, 1918), 321–22. Reprinted with an introduction by Robert Jay Lifton and Roger Smith and epilogue by Henry Morgenthau III (Detroit: Wayne State University Press, 2003), 221.

3. Ara Sarafian, "The Absorption of Armenian Women and Children into Muslim Households as a Component of the Armenian Genocide," in *In God's Name: Genocide and Religion in the Twentieth Century*, ed. Omer Bartov and Phyllis Mack (New York: Berghan Books, 2001), 210–11.

4. All excerpts are from *Siamanto, Bloody News from My Friend*, trans. Peter Balakian and Nevart Yaghlian (Detroit: Wayne State University Press, 1996).

5. Elaine Scarry, *The Body in Pain* (Oxford: Oxford University Press, 1985), 110.

6. Ibid., 38.

7. Ibid., 45.

8. Ibid., 54.

CHAPTER ELEVEN

1. Norman Mailer, *Advertisements for Myself* (Cambridge, MA: Harvard University Press, 1992), 338.

2. Bob Dylan, *Chronicles*, vol. 1 (New York: Simon & Schuster, 2004), 92–93.

CHAPTER TWELVE

Excerpts from "Geese Flying Over Hamilton, New York" and "Lowlands" are from Peter Balakian, *June-tree; New and Selected Poems, 1974–2000*, (New York: Harper Collins, 2001). Excerpt from "Sarajevo" from Peter Balakian, *Ziggurat* (Chicago: University of Chicago Press, 2010).